Ab...

SCOTTISH MURDERS

SCOTTISH MURDERS

MARTIN BAGGOLEY

For Harry and Jean.

First published 2013

The History Press
The Mill, Brimscombe Port
Stroud, Gloucestershire, GL5 2QG
www.thehistorypress.co.uk

© Martin Baggoley, 2013

The right of Martin Baggoley to be identified as the Author
of this work has been asserted in accordance with the
Copyright, Designs and Patents Act 1988.

British Library Cataloguing in Publication Data.
A catalogue record for this book is available from the British Library.

ISBN 978 0 7524 5008 7

Typesetting and origination by The History Press
Printed in Great Britain

CONTENTS

ACKNOWLEDGEMENTS

I would like to thank the staff at the National Library of Scotland and the Newspaper Library at Colindale for the help given in writing this book.

CASE ONE   1814

DEATH OF A SEAMAN

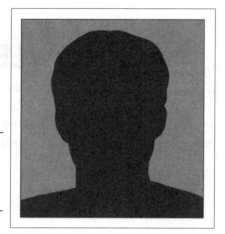

Suspect: Thomas White
Age: 25
Crime: Murder

In the early months of 1814, as the Napoleonic Wars were approaching their end, the Admiralty notified the Fleet that the Royal Navy was to be reduced in size. It was proposed that those seamen who had served the longest would be the first to be discharged and allowed to go home. However, once the order became known, many ratings decided not to wait for their official discharge papers, which led to a sudden and dramatic increase in the number of desertions. The authorities ordered that deserters must be halted and officers were therefore directed to use the strongest measures necessary to prevent men from leaving their ships in this manner. One ship for instance, the frigate *Unicorn*, had lost fifteen crewmembers, who deserted after being paid their wages at Stromness ten days before she arrived in Leith on 14 June 1814.

On 15 June, one of the *Unicorn's* boats, which carried two midshipmen, Robert Wright and John Levit, accompanied by six ratings, was sent to the yard with rigging in need of repair. One of the ratings was William Jones, who, despite being a good sailor, could be awkward and cause problems for the ship's officers. As soon as the boat docked, Jones sought permission to leave the yard but his request was refused. Later, he repeated his request, only to be turned down once again. In response, he turned to Midshipman Levit and said, 'You know you cannot keep me,' which was interpreted as a threat to desert.

Later that afternoon, the frigate's captain ordered another boat to be sent to the yard and among its crew were midshipmen Andrew Carroll and Thomas White. On its arrival, Levit advised his fellow junior officers of the possible problems posed by Jones. Midshipman White approached Sergeant Murrell of the West Norfolk Militia, who was acting as sentry at the dockyard gates, to instruct him that none of the ratings off the *Unicorn* should be allowed to leave unless accompanied by an officer.

Jones made a third request to be allowed to leave the yard, but this was once more refused by Levit. Jones replied, 'Here goes,' and ran through the main gate and out of the dockyard. Levit gave chase, caught the fleeing seaman and ordered that he should be confined in the dockyard guardhouse. Following this incident, the midshipmen visited the nearby Britannia Inn, where they dined and drank a great deal of ale. When they returned to their boats at seven o'clock that evening, they were told that four men had deserted.

White immediately called out for Jones, who replied, 'Here, Sir.' He had been released from the guardhouse but did not abscond with the others. However, he too had been drinking and was lying on his side close to the edge of the quay. When ordered to lower himself into the boat, he refused and told White that he was waiting for a barmaid from the Britannia to bring him some bottles of ale to take back for his shipmates on the *Unicorn*. This act of insubordination enraged White, who responded by drawing out his cutlass.

Addressing Jones, the midshipman demanded, 'Won't you go on board Sir, when I desire you?' Jones ignored him and joined in singing with those sailors who were already in the boat preparing to row back to the frigate. Angry at this further display of disobedience by the seaman, White struck him twice across the head with the flat of the blade. Jones rose to his feet but before he could say or do anything, the midshipman stabbed him once in the stomach. The wounded man staggered and fell to the ground and, as he did so, White stamped on his head. Jones fell off the quayside and as the tide was out he landed on some exposed rocks. Several members of the boat's crew picked him up and laid him out in the small vessel, but he died later.

Twenty-five-year-old White was not court-martialled but stood trial at the High Court of Judiciary on 12 July 1814, at which he pleaded not guilty to murder, claiming Jones's death was an accident. In court, powerful and hugely incriminating testimony was given by a number of respectable civilian witnesses, all of whom were local tradesmen who were in the vicinity at the time of the alleged murder. These included Leith bakers James Allen, David Thompson and John Bayne, carpenter Archibald Morrison and stocking-maker John Duff.

James Allen told the court that he shouted to White that he was a murderer and should hang for what he had done. White turned towards him, making threatening gestures with his cutlass and screaming that he

'The wounded man staggered and fell to the ground'

would kill anyone who attempted to restrain him. He continued to shout that he had only been performing his duty as Jones was about to desert.

White, who had been drinking for much of the afternoon, seemed to be confused and unsure what he should do next. He boarded the boat and made for the bowsprit, where the boatswain attempted to take the cutlass from him. White was able to struggle free but was threatened with a mallet by a crewmember. He jumped out of the boat and was eventually held down by the boatswain and a local innkeeper, Fowler Ferguson, who was able to prise the bloody cutlass from his hand.

White was escorted to the town's council chamber to await questioning while attempts were made to treat the wounded man. However, Jones was beyond help and died a short time later. A post-mortem revealed that death was due to one deep stab wound to his stomach and it was clear that the weapon must have been plunged into the victim with great force.

The first defence witness was Rear Admiral William Johnstone Hope, who described the pressure placed on the shoulders of junior officers given with the task of preventing desertions by men under their command. Another officer, Lieutenant Kedger of the *Unicorn*, recalled an incident three years earlier off the coast of Spain, when Jones was punished for striking a Master of Arms, thus making the jury aware of the fact that the dead man's disciplinary record was far from exemplary. The admiral and lieutenant spoke highly of the prisoner, who was said to have been an excellent young officer destined for a brilliant career with the Royal Navy.

The Crown had presented White as someone who acted with malice in a wholly inappropriate manner and who had used excessive and unnecessary violence against the deceased. However, midshipmen Carroll and Levit emphasised the disobedience of Jones on the day in question and his attempt to desert, which the defence believed put White's actions in a different light. Credence to this was given by a Mrs Christie, the wife of the captain's steward on board the *Appelles*, a sloop of war also berthed at Leith at the time. She witnessed the incident and told the jury that in fifteen years, she had never seen such blatant disobedience and despicable behaviour by a sailor.

Two ratings who served on the *Unicorn* named Baskin and Tough, both captains of the main top and therefore senior and experienced seamen in charge of a group of sailors, also appeared for the defence. They spoke highly of White, describing him as a just and humane officer who treated his men well. They insisted that he bore no ill-will towards the dead man and confirmed that three days before the alleged murder, White had spoken on behalf of Jones and prevented him from being flogged for being drunk on duty.

The jury returned with a verdict of guilty of culpable homicide and White was sentenced to be transported for fourteen years.

CASE TWO   1818

RAISING THE DEAD

Suspect:	Matthew Clydesdale
Age:	25
Crime:	Murder

On the afternoon of Wednesday, 26 August 1818, a foot race took place before a large number of spectators at Clarkston, near Airdrie. The competitors were two local handloom weavers, William More and twenty-five-year-old Matthew Clydesdale, a married man with two children. Clydesdale was the victor and afterwards, the two runners visited John Smith's tavern, close to the Clarkston toll bar, where they were joined by William's brother John and a friend, John Rankin.

The four men drank heavily for several hours and although drunk, they were in good spirits, especially Clydesdale, who was keen to celebrate his victory. However, when they were asked to leave at two o'clock in the morning, his mood turned ugly after his demands for more alcohol were refused by the landlord. It was only with great difficulty that his companions persuaded him to leave and when challenged to a race by William, he appeared to regain his good mood. Eventually, the men reached Laigh Drumgelloch, close to Clydesdale's home. They parted company but within a matter of minutes, William heard a cry of 'Murder!' coming from the direction in which Clydesdale had walked. Fearing his friend may have been the victim of a robbery by footpads, William ran in the direction of the shout, to offer assistance if it was necessary for him to do so.

A little earlier, eighty-year-old Alexander Love and his fourteen-year-old grandson, Alex, were preparing to leave home for the start of the early morning shift at Blackridge Pit, where both worked as colliers.

They set off, each carrying his pick, and after walking a short distance they encountered Clydesdale, who was recognised by Alex as the young-ster had attended the foot race earlier in the day. Alexander realised the man was very drunk and was in a belligerent mood. As they passed him, Clydesdale glared menacingly at Alexander and demanded, 'What do you want?' Wishing to avoid any trouble, the elderly collier replied, 'Nothing, I am on my way to work.' Without any warning, Clydesdale pushed Alexander to the ground and, grabbing his pick, began to strike him with it. He ordered Alex to kneel but the youngster refused and it was he who shouted 'Murder!' as he began running back towards home to seek help.

William discovered Alexander lying on the ground, moaning loudly. At first he thought he must have fallen and injured himself, as he could see nobody else. However, when he knelt by his side to tend to him, William realised he had been the victim of an assault as blood was flowing from his mouth and he noticed a number of head injuries. Hoping to attract more help, William shouted, 'Here is a murdered man!' After a few moments the silence was broken by the sound of someone, who had clearly been hiding in nearby bushes, running away in the

'Here is a murdered man!'

direction of Clydesdale' house. William did not realise that they were the footsteps of Clydesdale.

Meanwhile, Alex had reached home and alerted his parents, William and Catherine, together with his grandmother, who cried out, 'My man is killed!' Despite nursing a sick child in her arms, Catherine ran with her husband to the spot where Alexander lay and found William More cra-dling the elderly man's head in his arms. The two men carried Alexander home, where his distraught wife and grandson were waiting. Surgeon Mr Niven was called to the cottage and discovered that the injured man had suffered several deep wounds to the head and body. Each of these was a distinctive square shape, one quarter of an inch in diameter, and to the surgeon there could be no doubt that Alexander's own pick had been the weapon used to inflict the injuries.

Clydesdale fell under suspicion almost immediately and the police visited his home a few hours later. He was not there but his lodger told the officers that their suspect arrived home in the early hours, claiming he had been attacked by two tinkers who attempted to rob him. He managed to escape, but not before suffering an injury to his knee. It was presumed that Alexander was able to strike his assailant at least once during the struggle. The lodger also informed the police that Clydesdale was in such a rage that he smashed the family cat against the floor with such ferocity that it was killed and he threw its body onto the fire.

Clydesdale's description was circulated throughout the district and he was arrested soon afterwards. Alexander died on the following Sunday morning and it was for his murder that Clydesdale stood trial in early October, at which he entered a not guilty plea. In his opening address to the jury, the Crown barrister emphasised that it was in many respects a motiveless crime from which the perpetrator gained no profit. It was also clear that revenge was not the reason for the murder, which was committed simply because the killer was drunk and had lost all self-control. However, this in no way excused the crime, which should not be reduced in seriousness, for he was guilty of wilful murder.

In Clydesdale's defence, it was argued that there was sufficient doubt to enable the jury to declare him innocent and an important point in his favour was that before he died, Alexander was unable to state categorically that Clydesdale was the man who attacked him. The only witness was young Alex, who, it was argued, may have been confused in his own mind having seen him earlier in the day at the foot race. Furthermore, Alex told the police originally that the attacker was wearing white breeches, whereas all the other witnesses swore that Clydesdale wore breeches of a different colour that night. This, it was claimed, cast doubt on the reliability of the youngster's evidence and thus the jury could not convict the prisoner of murder.

The defence concluded by saying that all of the evidence pointed to Alexander being the victim of a planned robbery, committed by unknown footpads who had been lying in wait for the two colliers, who, due to their great age and youth, would have been incapable of offering any meaningful resistance. However, the jury was not persuaded by the defence's arguments and convicted Clydesdale of murder. He was sentenced to death and it was ordered that he should be fed only bread and water as he awaited his execution, following which his body was to be handed over to Dr Jeffray, Professor of Anatomy at Glasgow University, for dissection.

Three other criminals were sentenced to death at the sitting: Mary Kennedy for uttering a forged bank note, and housebreakers James Boyd and Simon Ross. The four convicted prisoners were put in a single cell together and made a determined but unsuccessful attempt to escape, which led to them being put in irons. Kennedy and Boyd were later reprieved, which left Clydesdale and Ross for execution on Wednesday 4 November at three o'clock in the afternoon.

On the Monday before his hanging, the governor of the gaol permitted Clydesdale to drink a bottle of ale. The bottle was not taken off him and during the night, the condemned man smashed it and with a fragment of glass inflicted severe wounds to his arms and throat in a determined suicide attempt. He was found close to death by a warder when his cell door was opened in the morning and he was only saved by rapid medical treatment by the gaol's doctor. This meant that he was fit enough to keep his appointment with the hangman the following day.

The last murderer to be hanged in Glasgow had been James Gilchrist in 1808, thus there was a great deal of excitement at the prospect of Clydesdale's execution and a large crowd awaited his appearance outside the walls of the gaol. At two o'clock, his arms were pinioned and he spent some time in prayer with the chaplain. Also in the pinioning room was Simon Ross and his father, who had been allowed to see his son for a final emotional meeting. The two men were then led on to the drop and were soon dead. After being left suspended at the end of the ropes for an hour, their bodies were cut down. Ross's corpse was buried, but Clydesdale's was taken in a cart to the university, where it was to be dissected. On its journey, the cart was accompanied by a large number of people who hissed and booed it all the way to its destination. As it was being lifted out of the cart there was a loud cheer, for there was no sympathy for this brutal killer of an elderly man who had been incapable of defending himself.

What was not widely known was that Dr Jeffray had invited Andrew Ure, Professor of Natural Philosophy at the Anderson's Institute, to perform a series of experiments on the corpse prior to its dissection, which involved using a galvanic battery to pass electricity through it. Professor Ure was following in the footsteps of Louis Galvani, who in the late eighteenth century had conducted similar tests on frogs, and also of Giovanni Aldini, who had later performed tests on the bodies of executed criminals at London's Newgate Gaol.

At the time, it was believed by many scientists that life could be restored in some circumstances using this method and in particular it could possibly assist in the resuscitation of supposed victims of drowning. There was widespread interest and many of Professor Ure's academic colleagues and members of the general public were crowded into the chamber to watch. What occurred next has become the stuff of legend and the following contemporary account, which was published in *The Examiner*, provides an accurate account of the four experiments performed on the body and their impact on those present:

On the 4th November last, various galvanic experiments were made on the body of Clydesdale by Dr Ure of Glasgow, with a voltaic battery of 270 pairs of 4 inch plates. The results were truly appalling. On moving the rod from the hip to the heel, the knee being previously bent, the leg was thrown out with such violence as nearly to overturn one of the assistants, who in vain attempted to prevent its extension! In the second experiment, the rod was applied to the phrenic nerve in the neck, when laborious breathing instantly commenced; the chest heaved and fell; the belly was protruded and collapsed, with the relaxing and retiring diaphragm; and it is thought that but from the complete evacuation of the blood, pulsation might have occurred! In the third experiment, the supra-orbital nerve was touched, when every muscle in the murderer's face was thrown into fearful action. The scene was hideous – several of the spectators left the room and one gentleman actually fainted from terror or sickness. In the fourth experiment, the transmitting of electrical power from the spinal marrow to the ulnar nerve of the elbow, the fingers were instantly put in motion and the agitation of the arm was so great that the corpse seemed to point to the different spectators, some of whom thought it had come to life! Dr Ure appears to be of the opinion that had not incisions been made in the blood vessel of the neck and the spinal marrow been lacerated, the criminal might have returned to life!

Following these dramatic events, the dissection performed by Dr Jeffray before what remained of the audience was no doubt something of an anti-climax.

CASE THREE   1820

THE DEADLY GAOL BREAK

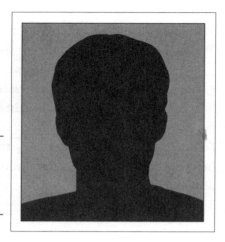

Suspect:	David Haggart
Age:	20
Crime:	Murder

In April 1821, following a conviction for picking pockets in Ireland, the prisoner, who had given his name as David Bryan, was sentenced to be transported and was taken to Dublin's Kilmainham Gaol to await a ship that would take him to New South Wales. However, Reverend Backer, a magistrate who visited the gaol regularly, believed that the prisoner fitted the description of a wanted man given in a recent edition of *Hue and Cry*, but who bore another name. This was twenty-year-old David Haggart, a fugitive from Scottish justice, who was declared an outlaw on 5 February 1821 and who was accused of murdering Thomas Morrin, a turnkey at the gaol in Dumfries, during his escape from the prison on 10 October 1820.

Haggart, although comparatively youthful and despite being born into a respectable family, was a notorious criminal. He was raised in the countryside surrounding Edinburgh, where his father was employed as a gamekeeper and dog trainer. As a child, Haggart often accompanied his father on shooting and coursing parties and when he was ten years old he abandoned his studies to work with him full time. However, he fell in with bad company and left home to live off his earnings as a thief and pickpocket, together with the prize money and proceeds of gambling he won from a fighting cock he owned.

In July 1813, when drunk, he enlisted in the Norfolk Militia, but despised army life and left after one year. He returned home and, intending to live by honest endeavour, began a six-year apprenticeship with millwrights and engineers Cockburn and Baird. However, he left after just two years and it was now, in his late teens, that he embarked on his life as a professional criminal in earnest. He visited fairs and race meetings in the south of Scotland and the northern counties of England, making a living from the proceeds of highway robbery, burglary and other serious crimes.

In January 1818 at Durham, under the name of Morrison, he was sentenced to death for an offence of burglary, but made his first successful escape from gaol, thus avoiding the noose. He was one of a group of prisoners who seized a turnkey, took his keys, bound and gagged the man, and afterwards scaled the wall. A few weeks later, on the 1st of March, he

'highway robbery, burglary and other serious crimes'

was recaptured at Leith, but after three weeks he got hold of a file, sawed through his leg irons, removed a large stone from the local gaol's outer wall, and once again made good his escape. He was arrested for another burglary and was due to stand trial at Dumfries. It was whilst awaiting his appearance in court for that offence that the escape took place which led to the death of Thomas Morrin.

Now a free man, he travelled to Belfast, where he was betrayed for a large reward by a former cellmate who recognised him. Haggart was detained by the police but was able to escape from the courtroom he appeared in, after which he travelled throughout Ireland, living as he always did, by crime. It was at a fair in Castle William that he committed what would be his last offence. He picked the pocket of a pig-drover, but was seized by his victim and two of his friends. He was held in Downpatrick Gaol and although he was not able to escape, he and a number of other prisoners were able to barricade themselves in their block, preventing staff from regaining control for two days, during which, the male and female prisoners joined together in drunken debauchery.

On learning of Reverend Blacker's suspicions, the Dumfries authorities ordered local police officer John Richardson to make the journey to Dublin. The officer knew Haggart well and on his arrival was able to confirm his true identity. Within a matter of days, Haggart was returned to Scotland and stood trial for murder on Monday, 11 June 1821. Thomas Hunter, Keeper of Dumfries Gaol, was the first to give evidence and he began by describing what was known as the 'Cage', which was located on the second floor of the building. Despite its name, the Cage was popular with prisoners, as it was well ventilated, contained a privy and the fresh air was in stark contrast to the dank atmosphere which permeated much of the institution. At noon on the day of the escape, there were three prisoners inside the Cage. These were Haggart and John Dunbar, both of whom were due to stand trial, together with John Simpson, who was serving a short sentence for vagrancy and who was due to be released the next day. The Keeper gave the men their meals and left them at 1.40 p.m., so was not present when the crime took place.

The next witness was John Simpson, as it was acknowledged by the Crown that he played no part in planning or executing the escape. He testified that Haggart had managed to conceal a large stone in a canvas bag, which he brought into the Cage, clearly intending to use it as a weapon. An adjacent cell contained a condemned prisoner by the name of Edward McRory, who had been convicted of assault and robbery and who was due to hang eight days later. Thomas Morrin was taking a bowl of soup to McRory, and Dunbar asked him to unlock the Cage as he wished to return to his own cell. Immediately Thomas did so, Haggart picked up the bag containing the stone and struck the unsuspecting turnkey several vicious blows to the head. Haggart removed the keys from the badly stunned man's belt and rushed through the gaol towards the main gate, followed by Dunbar.

Mary Gracie was Thomas Morrin's servant and was in the gaol's kitchen. She told the court that she heard Dunbar ask to be allowed to return to his cell, the sound of the attack, and Simpson shouting, 'Murder! Murder! Haggart is out and has killed Thomas.' On stepping out of the kitchen, she was confronted by the fleeing prisoners. She saw that Haggart's hands were covered with blood and he was holding the keys to the main gate. She screamed 'Murder!' and attempted to block their escape route but Haggart threatened her and she was forced to retreat into the kitchen and let them pass. She saw them open the main gate and flee. Dunbar was captured a short distance from the gaol but Haggart was able to flee the town.

Imprisoned for debt, Alexander Rae and John Jardine were the first to reach Thomas, who was alive and standing unaided. Nevertheless, Simpson appeared to realise how serious his injuries were and was in a very distressed state. He told the two prisoners, 'Thomas has got his death and Haggart and Dunbar are off.' In their testimonies, the two debtors confirmed that the turnkey seemed able to think clearly and told them, 'Haggart did it.' Within a few minutes Margaret Huddleston, who lived close to the prison and realised there was some kind of problem, ran to help. She also told the court that Thomas told her, 'It was that Haggart.'

Surgeon Archibald Blacklock attended to the turnkey's five head wounds. The most serious of these injuries was two inches long and had exposed the bone above his left eye. Although sensible and able to speak in the immediate aftermath of the attack, his condition soon deteriorated and he became delirious. Thomas died at ten o'clock that night and a post-mortem revealed he had suffered several skull fractures.

When he addressed the jury on behalf of the Crown at the conclusion of the evidence, the Solicitor General reminded its members of the number of witnesses who had heard the deceased state that Haggart was solely responsible for his injuries. Furthermore, there was the eyewitness account given by John Simpson. The evidence was such that a conviction for manslaughter or any other less serious charge was not acceptable and the only possible verdict was guilty of murder.

In his summary of the evidence, the defence barrister urged the jury to ignore the testimony of Simpson, the only eyewitness. His word, he claimed, could not be relied on as he had been a prisoner at the time and was thus a man of low character, and nobody should be sent to the gallows on the evidence of such a man alone. Furthermore, he argued it could not be said categorically by the witnesses, who were not medically qualified, that the dead man had been in full possession of his senses when he made the incriminating comments against Haggart. The lawyer continued by suggesting it was highly suspicious that the Crown had not called Dunbar to give evidence, despite his being present at the time and having planned the escape with the accused. He would therefore have been a hugely important witness but had been transported before the trial opened. This prevented the barrister from conducting a cross-examination, as it was Haggart's assertion that Dunbar was in fact the murderer.

The jury was not convinced and, without leaving their seats, convicted Haggart of murder. He was sentenced to death and the judge warned him not to expect leniency as it was essential that those working in gaols should have the full protection of the law. Following his execution, his body was to be given to Dr Alexander Munro, Professor of Anatomy at Edinburgh University, for dissection and as he awaited his execution he was to be fed on bread and water only. There was to be neither a reprieve nor another escape.

His mother was dead and having bid an emotional farewell to his father on the Monday before the execution, Haggart spent much of his time reading the Bible. He spent a final and restless night in the lock-up having been taken there from Calton Gaol. On the morning of the execution, he shook hands with the magistrates and other officials who had assembled to witness the hanging. On the scaffold, he impressed the large crowd with his composure and his speech, in which he urged them to avoid 'The heinous crime of disobedience to one's parents, inattention to the Holy Scriptures, of being idle and disorderly and especially Sabbath-breaking,' all of which he blamed for his criminal lifestyle and his shameful end. He knelt down to pray for a few moments before signalling that he was ready to meet his end. Seconds later he was dead.

CASE FOUR 1823

THE MADAM AND THE PHRENOLOGIST

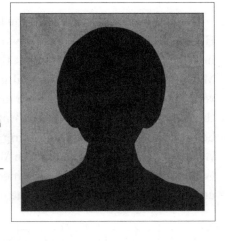

Suspect: Mary McKinnon
Age: Unknown
Crime: Murder

On the evening of Saturday, 8 February 1823, solicitor's clerk William Howat and surveyor Henry Kerr, who shared rooms in Broughton Street, Edinburgh, invited their friends Walter Grieve, Alexander Welsh and Mr Johnson to dine with them. After enjoying their meal, they were joined by another friend, Mr Wilkinson, and shared a bottle of whisky. When that was empty, they decided to go out on the town for some amusement. They were in a boisterous mood and were refused admission to Anderton's Inn, their first port of call. A few moments later the young men knocked on the door of the Black Bull, supposedly a public house but in fact a brothel managed by Mary McKinnon.

The party was admitted and ushered into a room containing a bed and sofa, where they were soon joined by three young women, Elizabeth McDonald, Elizabeth Gray and Mary Curlie. The men ordered whisky, which they shared with the prostitutes, but decided to leave the premises after finishing their drinks, intending to continue enjoying themselves elsewhere. The women urged them to stay and of course to purchase more alcohol, promising the friends a good time in return. What began as good-natured banter quickly deteriorated into a fierce argument when the men continued to insist upon leaving the establishment. The men would later claim that the women blocked the door to prevent them from walking out, whereas the women said that the men became threatening and abusive.

Henry Kerr made his way to the kitchen, looking for another way out. He was followed by William Howart, who opted to stand quietly by the fire and keep out of the argument that was raging around him. Elizabeth McDonald rushed at Henry and grabbed him by the shirt with such venom that it was torn. She then forced him to the floor, screaming that the men must pay their bill. He protested that they had already done so, before rising to his feet and forcing his way past her. He met Grieve and Wilkinson in the hall but Elizabeth McDonald had followed him and struck Wilkinson on his head. He screamed, 'You bitch! Why do you strike me?' and he had to be restrained by the other men when he tried to grab hold

'You bitch! Why do you strike me?'

of her. By this time, Mary Curlie decided to find Mary McKinnon, who had gone out earlier in the evening. When she learnt what was happening, the madam hurried back to the Black Bull with her companions Jane Lundie and Samuel Hodge, a local grocer.

A few minutes later, a policeman was alerted by the fracas and entered the house. In the kitchen, the officer discovered Howart bleeding from a knife wound to his chest. James Stuart, an apprentice surgeon was on hand to offer treatment before the injured man was carried to the Royal Infirmary. Unfortunately, there was nothing that surgeon Robert Allen could do for him and Howat realised he was dying. He asked to make a deathbed deposition, which was taken two days after the stabbing by sheriff's officer George Tait. Mary McKinnon, who was by then under arrest, was standing at his bedside. Howart described his attempts to avoid becoming embroiled in the dispute by remaining in the kitchen. He pointed out Mary McKinnon and swore that she had run into the kitchen and stabbed him in the chest without any warning and for no apparent reason.

At her trial, the accused woman protested her innocence and attempted to place the blame onto the dead man's friend, Wilkinson. However, once all the evidence had been heard, especially the victim's deathbed deposition, it became clear that her version of events could not be true. A number of the prostitutes told the court that all of the men became violent and they were compelled to take strong measures to protect themselves. McKinnon's barrister suggested to the jury that if they were not satisfied someone else had been responsible for the stabbing, they might decide that his client had stabbed the victim in self-defence or to protect one or more of the other women. In these circumstances, they could convict her of culpable homicide rather than the more serious charge of murder.

The defence propositions were rejected by the jury and McKinnon was found guilty of murder. The prisoner fainted in the dock as the judge sentenced her to death and directed that afterwards her body be dissected. Once she had been revived, she was led from the dock screaming that she was innocent and begging for mercy.

She continued to claim that she was innocent of the crime from the condemned cell, insisting that she had seen one of the other women stab Howat. However, she was not believed and there was no reprieve. At a few minutes before eight o'clock on the morning of Wednesday 16 April, she dressed herself in a black silk gown, silk scarf, bonnet and veil. Although she vomited when the official party arrived to escort her to the scaffold, she quickly regained her composure

A crowd of 20,000 awaited her appearance at the head of Libberton's Wynd. She sat in a chair provided for her for a few minutes while she prayed and the executioner completed his preparations. After rising to her feet, her bonnet was removed and a muslin cap pulled down over her face. She stepped on to the drop and immediately gave a sign that she was ready. Seconds later she was dead.

Local solicitor and enthusiastic phrenologist George Combe was permitted to examine McKinnon's head and to make a cast before her corpse was dissected in front of a large number of spectators, who had gathered to witness the rare sight of a murderess being anatomised.

In the first quarter of the nineteenth century, phrenology was increasing in importance as it was believed that aspects of an individual's personality could be gauged by taking measurements of his or her skull. Certain areas of the brain were thought to have specific functions and the shape and size of those areas were mirrored on the relevant parts of the skull. It was argued that by taking measurements of these, the strength or weakness of those influences on an individual's character and behaviour would be revealed.

George Combe was an early proponent and he was particularly interested in examining the skulls of criminals, especially those who had been executed, as he believed it would be possible to use this information to predict criminal traits in individuals at an early age and take appropriate steps to minimise the damage they caused to society. In 1820, he co-founded the Phrenology Society of Edinburgh and was given access to the skulls of offenders, both dead and alive.

On Thursday 15 May, George Combe read a paper to a well-attended lecture on McKinnon's personality, based on the measurements he had taken following her execution. He described her as being typical of the type of killer who would not commit a premeditated crime and was more likely to kill on a sudden impulse. He described the back of her head as being a 'round cannon-bullet form', which indicated that combativeness and destructiveness were major features of her character. Secretiveness, cunning and love of approbation featured large but conscientiousness, reflection and benevolence were present to a much lesser degree according to his measurements. Combe suggested, for instance, that the need for approbation was evident in the care she had shown in choosing what to wear during her final hours rather than pay attention to the Bible and her prayers.

THE ABBEY MURDERS

Suspect: Robert Emond
Age: Unknown
Crime: Murder

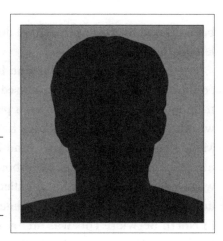

The hamlet of Abbey was a close-knit community near to Haddington and on the afternoon of Wednesday, 28 October 1829, worried neighbours gathered outside the cottage in which Catherine Franks lived with her daughter, Magdalene. They had not been seen since making their regular call on Marion Inglis four days earlier to purchase milk. Their neighbours became concerned on hearing the hungry squeals of Catherine's pig, which was housed in a sty in the garden. Finally, John Sorrie and Alexander Dudgeon decided to climb over the fence to investigate.

They found Catherine, whose throat had been slashed, on her back in the pigsty. Concerned for Magdalene, they rushed to her bedroom, where they found her body. Her killer had subjected the youngster to a terrible beating. Dr Thomas Hoden examined the bodies and confirmed that the throat wound was the cause of the mother's death, while there were eight distinct injuries to her daughter's head, and she died

'The floor was covered in blood'

as a result of several skull fractures. From the state of decomposition, the doctor calculated they both died late on Sunday night or in the early hours of Monday morning. Magdalene's bedroom had been ransacked, suggesting that robbery was the motive for the murders. The floor was covered in blood and a knife was found at the side of the bed. The police also noticed distinctive shoe prints in the blood, which appeared to have been caused by iron heels with a double rim and which must have been left by the killer.

The mother and daughter had been popular members of the small community and their deaths caused a great deal of distress to their many friends. Catherine survived on a pension from the Earl of Wemyss, for whom her late husband James had worked as butler for many years. Magdalene was an attractive, kind-hearted and intelligent girl who was always willing to help her neighbours. Catherine's other daughter, who was eleven years old and also called Catherine, lived with her maternal aunt, who was also named Magdalene, and her husband, Robert Emond, in North Berwick. This was an arrangement the sisters reached to ease the financial burden faced by Catherine in raising the girls.

As a matter of course, Inspector John Lloyd asked Emond, who was the victims' nearest male relative, to visit the cottage to formally identify the bodies. The inspector warned him of the gruesome nature of the murder scene, but was surprised at just how reluctant Emond was to view the bodies. This led the inspector to wonder if this was a reaction brought about by a guilty conscience. The police officer's suspicions were given added weight when he questioned Marion Inglis. She informed him that on the previous Sunday, when she last spoke to Catherine, she had accused her brother-in-law of stealing from her and of taking money from his wife. Inspector Lloyd decided to pay Emond, his wife and the younger Catherine another visit. The inspector learnt that on the previous Sunday, Emond and his wife argued following her refusal to give him some money with which to fund a proposed business venture. He beat her and attempted to throw her down a well in their garden. He was only prevented from doing so by a neighbour, who was alerted by the desperate woman's screams and had rushed to her assistance. The neighbour told the inspector that as the couple argued, his wife screamed that she and her sister Catherine were aware he had been stealing money from both of them.

Emond's wife later confirmed the argument did indeed take place and that afterwards, despite his apparent remorse, she insisted they slept in separate rooms that night and she was not therefore in a position to comment on his movements. Nevertheless, young Catherine told the inspector that she went to the room in which her uncle was said to be sleeping, in the early hours of Monday morning, to discover the bed had not been slept in and he was nowhere to be seen. However, she did see him return home several hours later in a dishevelled state.

This information meant that Emond was now the inspector's leading suspect and a search of his home was made on the Wednesday afternoon, which led to a number of incriminating items coming to light. These were a vest and pair of trousers, which were damp and stained with blood, together with a shirt which Emond had attempted to clean but which still bore the impression of a bloody handprint, suggesting it had been grabbed by an individual bleeding heavily from a wound. Also discovered was a pair of shoes, which Emond's niece had noticed he was wearing when he returned home on Monday morning and which she later saw him cleaning. He was shown all of these items and when told he was to be charged with the two murders, he sighed, 'Oh God be merciful to me.'

The arrested man was born in Selkirk in 1795, where he was raised by poor but respectable parents. His mother and father ensured that he had a good education but he was a violent youngster, known to the other village children as 'the fiend'. At fifteen he enlisted in the army, in which he served creditably and mainly in Ireland. Following his honourable discharge, he returned to Selkirk and opened a day school, but this venture was not a success.

He abandoned his idea of teaching as a profession and became a pedlar in worsted goods. It was then that he met his future wife, Magdalene Munro, known to everyone as 'Highland Mary'. She was raised on the Duke of Gordon's estate and as an adult turned to dealing in silk, lace and other fine materials. She built up a successful business and was reported to be worth several hundred pounds by the time she met Emond. Those who knew her were shocked when she agreed to marry him, as he was known to be thoroughly unpleasant and violent. Following their marriage, the couple settled in North Berwick, where he opened a grocer's shop and his wife carried on with her own business. She was therefore of independent means and earned a great deal more than her husband, which was most unusual at that time. It was an unhappy marriage and she very soon began to suspect him of stealing her money.

Despite the growing evidence against him, Emond continued to claim he was innocent of the crimes and from his cell in Calton Gaol he wrote to his wife, insisting he was not responsible for the murders. In the letter he offers an explanation as to how the bloodstains came to be present on his clothes, but expressed the hope that the police would not be able to find the coat he was said to have been wearing on the Monday morning. He wrote:

My dear wife,

I am now confined in the Calton Jail charged with the murder of your sister and daughter, of which I declare to you I am perfectly innocent, though I have done as much as deserves the gallows. My dear Magdalene, I am sorry and even wish to take my own life when I think upon what I have done to you. I can't get rest night or day. I confess that I am a great sinner and nothing hurts me more than to think that I am under suspicion of the crime of murder. I assure you that I am perfectly innocent of the crime laid to my charge and I hope God Almighty who sees into all things will be my advocate on the day of the trial. I am aware the people are inveterate against me, because the proof, in their opinion, is so much against me. I again, my dearest Magdalene, declare I am innocent, although at this time my mind is so much affected that I hardly know what I say. I have been examined before the Sheriff of Edinburgh several times but I think they can't prove nothing against me. The public are aware I understand of the iron heels of my shoes corresponding with some marks in Mrs Frank's house and with a bloody shirt found in my house, which you can prove was occasioned by the blooding of my nose, or you know better by the blood that flowed from your head the Sunday preceding that most horrid murder. I understand that the authorities in Edinburgh are anxious to discover my old coat, but I hope they never shall. My dearest wife, my name has been branded in Edinburgh by illiterate stationers and I suppose that even in North Berwick is held in as much dread as the notorious murderers Burke and Hare. I must allow suspicions are against me but that is nothing. I again implore you to banish from your mind the idea [that I am] a murderer of your sister and niece.

My love to all your friends, for friends I have none. Would that God take me to himself.

Robert Emond

At his trial on 8 February 1830, the accused man entered a plea of not guilty. The Crown argued that Emond had attempted to make it appear that robbery was the motive for the murders. However, it was argued that this was simply an attempt to disguise the fact that he had murdered his sister-in-law for persuading his wife not to loan him any money. His niece was murdered to prevent her implicating him in the crime.

The coat he mentioned in the letter to his wife was not found but there was much physical evidence linking him to the murders. There was the blood-stained clothing, although he continued to claim that the blood had flowed from his own injured nose or his wife's injuries sustained during their violent argument; or perhaps it was the blood of a chicken he had killed. However, he had no answer for the shoe impressions found at the crime scene, which were shown to a local boot maker who compared them with those of the accused. He confirmed it was a most unusual design and they matched the heels on Emond's boots perfectly.

Robert Tait, who shared a cell with Emond as he awaited his trial, testified that he asked Emond if he did indeed commit the murders. He replied, 'Oh yes, but do not speak of it, the very thought of it goes to my heart like a knife.' Emond's barrister told the jury this evidence was unreliable as the witness was lying in the hope of receiving a pardon or much reduced sentence.

The jury retired for an hour before convicting Emond of the murders. He was executed on 17 March at the top of Libberton's Wynd and afterwards, as was the custom, his body was dissected.

CASE SIX   1829

GIVING THE DOCTOR

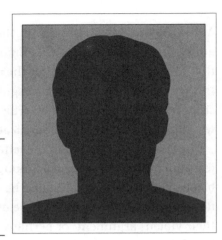

Suspects: John & Catherine
               Stuart
Ages: Unkown & 22
Crime: Murder

On the morning of 15 December 1829, Robert Lamont, a merchant
from Kilninian on the Isle of Ulva, boarded the steamer *Castle Toward* at
Lochgilphead. He was travelling to Glasgow on business with his close
friend and second cousin John Lamont. Partway through the voyage,
the two men decided to go below for some refreshments and it was here
that they fell into conversation with a group of fellow travellers, all of
whom had joined the boat at Tarbert.

Among the group were John Stuart and his wife Catherine, who, on
boarding, told the crew that they had no money but promised they would
be able to pay their fares on arrival at Glasgow, where they were being
met by friends. They carried no baggage but explained that all of their
property was on another vessel heading for Ireland. They provided docu-
ments which satisfied the captain they would be able to pay on reaching
Glasgow and he agreed to allow them on board. Also in the party was
Catherine McPhail, a hawker who had met the Stuarts for the first time at
Tarbert as they waited for the boat.

After enjoying a few drinks, John Lamont left the group to go on deck for
some fresh air and left Robert enjoying the company of the others. When
he returned some time later, John found that Robert was now paying for
all his companions' drinks. He heard Robert ask a waiter for a bottle of
porter and when advised there was none, Mrs Stuart volunteered to go
for a bottle of ale, the money for which Robert handed to her. She was
absent for several minutes and on her return to the table, she poured

the ale from the bottle, which was already open. She offered the glass to Mrs McPhail who put it to her lips, but she grimaced after taking a sip, saying it tasted awful and refused to drink any more of it. John Stuart offered to drink what remained and stretched out his hand to take the glass from Mrs McPhail. However, before he could take hold of it, his wife remonstrated with him, saying he had already had too much to drink. She grabbed hold of the glass, the contents of which spilled out, thereby preventing him from drinking any of it.

John was not in the mood for drinking and again returned to the deck. As he left, he noticed Mrs Stuart handing another glass of ale to Robert. As the boat approached Glasgow, John went below to join Robert but was horrified to find him alone and barely conscious. He was seated in his chair with his head between his knees and unable to speak. John immediately suspected that he had been drugged and robbed.

John informed the captain of his suspicions and accused the Stuarts of plying Robert's drinks with a drug to render him unconscious and of stealing £28 from his pocketbook, which lay discarded nearby, together with a

'alone and barely conscious'

purse, in which Robert kept his coins. The captain ordered that the couple be arrested and searched, but nothing incriminating was found on Mrs Stuart. However, her husband had £20 in notes in his pockets. He acknowledged his claim to have had no money when boarding the boat but insisted he lied to avoid paying for the journey. He claimed that he earned the money honestly working for his brother. Stuart was also found to be in possession of an empty bottle, which was giving off a strong smell of laudanum.

As the captain continued to question the Stuarts, Catherine McPhail became unwell and she accused the couple of attempting to drug her also, intending to rob her, as they knew from their conversation the previous evening that she was carrying £16. John Lamont also became ill and vomited a number of times. As he was a regular passenger on boats on the Kyles of Bute, he realised it was not seasickness. Both informed the captain they had drunk some of the ale purchased by Mrs Stuart, although clearly not enough that they lost consciousness.

While he and his wife were being questioned by the captain, John Stuart attempted to give the impression that he was drunk. However, all of those present believed he was pretending, probably because he was trying to convince everyone that he had drunk a large quantity of the suspect ale without falling ill or losing consciousness. He fooled nobody and the Stuarts were held on the boat to await the arrival of the police.

Following their arrests, the Assistant Town Clerk, William Leggatt, was given the task of investigating the charges against the Stuarts and decided upon a novel method of determining whether or not the couple had administered laudanum to their alleged victims. He bought a bottle of the drug, a quantity of which he poured into a glass of ale and asked John Lamont and Mrs McPhail to drink a little. They both agreed to participate in the experiment and confirmed the taste was similar to that of the drink they were given on the boat by the Stuarts.

A stomach pump was used on Robert but unfortunately he died at five o'clock the next morning. A post-mortem was performed by Dr McCorkindale, assisted by Doctors Fleming and Ure, and they agreed there was nothing to suggest that he died of natural causes. The stomach was cut open and there was an overpowering smell of laudanum, the taking of an excessive dose of which was given as the cause of death. The Stuarts, who were arrested initially for robbery, now faced the additional charge of murder.

Further evidence against the couple emerged following police interviews with Robert's widow Euphemia and daughter Catherine. One of the bank notes found in John Stuart's possession bore a distinctive red mark, which Euphemia identified as one she gave to her husband and which she saw him put in his pocketbook before he left home on the fateful morning. Furthermore, when John Stuart was searched initially by the boat's captain, a member of the crew noticed him take a purse from his pocket, which he dropped to the floor, intending that it should not be found on him. Catherine confirmed it was one she had sewn for her father and she knew that he never left home without it, nor would he have voluntarily handed it to anyone else.

The authorities knew nothing of the Stuarts other than the information they volunteered about themselves. John said he was born in Ireland

and was of no settled address. He claimed to be a blacksmith by trade and that in the recent past he had been travelling throughout Scotland and England looking for work. He repeated his claim that the cash found on him was paid to him by his brother in Newcastle but he could provide no address at which he could be contacted to corroborate his account. His wife said she was twenty-two years of age and had married her husband six years earlier in Gretna. She agreed with the account given by her husband and, like him, denied having laced any drinks with laudanum or of robbing their stupefied fellow passenger.

Their trial took place on Tuesday 15 July and the Stuarts were charged jointly with robbery and murder. The Crown called those who had witnessed the events on the *Castle Toward* and important testimony was provided regarding alleged conversations with Stuart by two fellow prisoners while he was awaiting trial. Malcolm Logan and Archibald Anderson testified that Stuart told them that he and his wife boarded the steamer with the specific intention of sedating and robbing any of the passengers they knew to be carrying cash or items of value. They offered drinks laced with laudanum to a number of people but only Robert Lamont had succumbed and passed out. His wife carried the drug in the bottle found on him, after he had poured the contents down the boat's water closet. However, he did not have sufficient time to dispose of the bottle prior to being detained and searched by the captain. He described their *modus operandi* as 'giving the doctor'.

The defence highlighted the criminal history of both of these witnesses, suggesting their accounts should be ignored. Logan was accused of lying out of malice as he and Stuart had argued violently in gaol. Logan denied this in the strongest of terms and insisted he had never said he would 'see him hang'. Credence was given to the evidence of the two prisoners by Gruer McGruer, a prison turnkey, who spoke with Stuart on a number of occasions. He told Gruer that he was foolish to have told his fellow prisoners what he and his wife had done and asked if he thought they would be called to give evidence at the trial and, if so, did he think they would be believed.

The defence also attempted to persuade the jury that Robert Lamont may have taken the laudanum himself. Two Glasgow druggists, Dr Scruton and Dr Milner, were called into the witness box, from which both stated that the drug was popular with many as a stimulant and as a means of becoming intoxicated very cheaply. Some individuals took between three and four ounces each day and the lowest weight that could be purchased was one eighth of an ounce at a cost of a penny. It was suggested that Robert became unconscious by his own hand and, having realised this, the Stuarts took advantage of the situation and robbed him. Given that there was sufficient room for doubt, the jury should find the couple guilty of robbery only.

The jury deliberated for a few minutes before returning guilty verdicts on both the accused of robbery and murder. As he sentenced them to death, the judge, Lord Gilles, acknowledged the leading role played by Catherine but added they acted in concert and therefore were equally responsible. He described it as, 'A crime of a most novel, most dangerous, most subtle and daring nature'. He warned them there would be no hope of a reprieve for either of them.

A large crowd gathered in Edinburgh to witness the unusual sight of a married couple being hanged together. The Stuarts mounted the scaffold at eight o'clock on the morning of Wednesday 19 August and shook hands with each other before simultaneously falling through the drop.

CASE SEVEN   1830

THE GILMERTON OUTRAGE

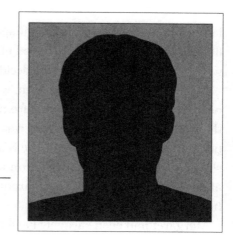

Suspects: David Dobie &
                    John Thomson
Ages: 26 & 21
Crime: Murder

In the early hours of Tuesday, 13 July 1830, at the conclusion of their sixteen-hour long trial in Edinburgh, from which the public had been excluded for much of the time due to the sensitive nature of the evidence, David Dobie and John Thomson were sentenced to death. The jury had found them guilty of the rape and murder of Margaret Paterson and also of robbing her. On hearing the judge order that their bodies should be dissected after their executions, Dobie shouted, 'My Lord, it's a grand thing ye canna dissect the soul!'

Theirs had been a particularly heinous crime committed three months earlier on the night of Saturday 17 April. Dobie and Thomson were carters, who on the night in question visited Colin Pentland's tavern at Cellar Bank, where they met Margaret, who had stopped for a drink on her way to Dalkeith, where she lived. She asked the men to take her home and they agreed to carry her on their cart as far as Gilmerton. They sat by the fire as Margaret enjoyed a pipe of tobacco and bought the men whisky in lieu of payment. The three of them appeared to be in good spirits and remained on the premises for two hours.

Some time later, Thomson's cart arrived in Gilmerton without him, the horse having made its own way home. Villager Walter Dingwall was concerned initially for his neighbour's safety after finding a woman's shawl and bloodstains in the bottom of the cart. He roused several other villagers and they set off in search of Thomson, meeting him minutes later as he walked towards the village. He explained that he had given a lift to a young woman he dropped off a few minutes earlier and as they were saying goodnight, his horse decided to start for home without him.

Meanwhile, Alexander Denham, who was also searching for Thomson, heard a woman's groans coming from a field at Gutterdike. He peered over the wall and saw Margaret, who was clearly very badly injured. She was taken initially to the home of the Bamberry family in Gilmerton, where she was treated by Doctors Benton and Morrison. However, it was only after she was removed to her parents' home that the full extent of her horrific injuries became known.

Margaret had been savagely beaten and bore the marks of many kicks to her head and body, but she had also suffered appalling internal injuries. It was discovered that a large jagged stone, a quantity of hay, coal

'appalling internal injuries'

dust and several small pieces of coal had been forced into her vagina and the bone of her corset had been inserted into her rectum. She died of her injuries at three o'clock on the afternoon of the following Thursday. A post-mortem revealed that so much force was used to inflict the injuries that her gall bladder had been ruptured. She had also been robbed of a gold earring, two pawn tickets, three shillings and sixpence in silver, a handkerchief, a green shawl, a quantity of bread and meat, and a small tobacco tin. Despite her injuries she was able to provide a lucid account of what happened and named Dobie and Thomson as those responsible.

Margaret was an attractive, respectable and hardworking thirty-five-year-old woman. She had worked in domestic service in Edinburgh for a number of years, but twelve months before her murder she returned to live with her elderly parents in Amos Close, Dalkeith. Her father, William, had been employed as a gardener for thirty-two years on the estate of the Duke of Buccleugh and had recently retired with a weekly pension of six shillings. Since coming home, Margaret made a living by touring the surrounding countryside selling lace and was well known and popular throughout the area.

As for her alleged killers, Dobie was a twenty-six-year-old married man with three children, the youngest of which was just one month old. Dobie's father was unable to work due to injuries sustained in a serious accident which left him unable to use his arm, and, as a result, Dobie left school at an early age to start earning a wage to support his family. He began by helping his older brother who was a carter, before purchasing his own cart and working for himself. He specialised in selling coal in small quantities to the poor of the district who were unable to purchase it in larger amounts. Dobie's friend of many years, Thomson, was a twenty-one-year-old single man who lived with his widowed mother, and he too made a living by selling coal to the poor.

Following their arrests, it was established that Dobie arrived home at least one hour before his friend. He admitted being present when the assault on Margaret began, but insisted he left the scene before she was raped and her massive internal injuries were inflicted. He offered to turn King's evidence and testify against Thomson, however, the police learnt that on the Tuesday after the attack, Dobie had joked with a blacksmith at Greenend about the assault on Margaret. This was before she died and when he did not realise just how serious a predicament he was in. It led the police to believe that he knew what happened and if he did not participate in inflicting the more serious injuries, he was probably present and was thus equally guilty. His offer to give evidence for the Crown in the hope of saving his own neck was refused.

Furthermore, three days after the crime, Dobie gave Margaret's tobacco tin to a friend. When questioned about this, Dobie insisted that Thomson handed it to him some time after the crime. However, his co-accused denied having done so, which led the Crown to believe Dobie stole it at the time of the assault, which implicated him in the crime. Nor did it assist Dobie's case when it was discovered he attempted to suborn a witness. From his cell, before the trial began, he wrote to a female cousin asking her to swear she saw Thomson give him the tobacco tin. If she did so it would provide him with an explanation as to how he came to possess such an incriminating piece of evidence and distance him from the most serious aspects of the crime. However, the letter was intercepted by staff at the gaol and it was handed to the Sheriff. He questioned the young woman, who admitted that she had not seen Thomson hand the tin to her cousin.

At their trial, both men were found to have been equally guilty. The judge's observations no doubt reflected the feelings of many regarding the depraved nature of their behaviour, when he told the two convicted men:

No words which I can use are capable of describing the unparalleled brutality, cruelty and wickedness of the foul transaction which has been disclosed this day. I shall not enter into details farther than to remark that the exhibition you have made is calculated to make every man blush. Such wickedness and brutal abomination could not have been believed to have been committed had it not been sworn to in evidence. Following the principle of law by which the proceedings have been conducted with closed doors till this stage of the proceedings, I shall refrain from saying anything of the crimes of which you stand convicted on the clearest evidence ever produced before a jury. But it is my duty to warn you to prepare for the inevitable fate which awaits you in this world and I warn you in the most earnest manner to prepare to appear before the judgement seat of the Almighty to answer for all the deeds done in the body. Rest assured that if ever there was a case in which the law will take its full course it is yours.

Not surprisingly, there were no attempts made to save the condemned men. Immediately after the trial they shared a cell in Calton Gaol, but as their executions drew closer they began to argue and threaten each other, which led to them having to be separated. Thomson received his last visit from relatives on the Friday before the hanging, and Dobie's wife and children had an emotional final meeting with him on the day before his execution. He had already written to her six days earlier and in the letter, acknowledged his guilt:

My Dear Wife,
I write these lines to you hoping you may receive some consolation from them. This is the only comfort that I can now bestow, to let you know the state of my mind; although my guilt does stare me in the face, I trust God will be merciful to me, a humble penitent. Although my hands are stained with the blood of that young woman I trust

the blood of Christ will wash for me my guilt. Dear wife, I am quite resigned to my fate. I forgive all my enemies and trust they will also forgive me. I die in peace with all men. You will not have the pleasure of laying my body in the dust. I beg you, as a last wish that you do not grieve on this account as these dry bones will perhaps live in future glory, where men cannot scatter them.

Dear wife, show this letter to the aged father of Margaret Paterson, whose hoary head we have brought with sorrow to the grave. We sincerely ask his forgiveness, which is but poor consolation to him for the loss of his daughter whom he held so dear, which by our wicked and subtle hearts has left him to bewail the loss of a child and you a faithless husband. Give my sincere respects to all my friends and comrades, and the grace of God I leave to you for ever. Farewell. Farewell.
D. Dobie

Thomson and Dobie's executions were due to take place on the morning of Wednesday 18 August and the night before, they were taken to the lock-up, in which they spent a few restless hours. They were visited at six o'clock in the morning by the Reverend Dr Lee, with whom they prayed and drank tea as they waited to be pinioned and led out on to the scaffold at the head of Libberton's Wynd. In their final minutes the men became reconciled and shook hands. It was agreed that Dobie would give the signal to the executioner that they were ready and, after ensuring Thomson was prepared, he did so.

They fell through the drop and the vast crowd watched as both men struggled for several minutes before finally becoming still, their agonies over. After being cut down their bodies were taken away in carts to be dissected.

CASE EIGHT   1830

TOUCHED BY EVIL

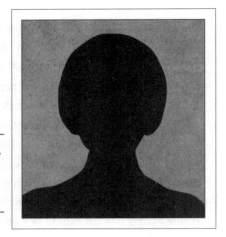

Suspect: Catherine Humphrey
Age: 52
Crime: Murder

Jean Craig was convicted of stealing articles of women's clothing from a bleach field at Huntly and was hanged in Aberdeen on 23 July 1784. Standing in the large crowd who had gathered to witness the execution was five-year-old Catherine Davidson, who stayed behind to watch the body being cut down after one hour. His task completed and in keeping with tradition, the hangman threw lengths of the rope into the crowd. The knot hit the horrified little girl on the chest – an act that would haunt Catherine for the rest of her life. However, she could not have realised that forty-six years later, she would be the one standing on the Aberdeen gallows.

Neglected as a child, Catherine was left to fend for herself from an early age and was poorly educated, attending neither school nor church. When she was sixteen she married James Humphrey, an Englishman who was serving as a private in the army. For the last five years of his service he was attached to the Aberdeen Militia and on his discharge he decided to stay in the town. He opened a butcher's shop, but later took over a public house on Bowl Road.

Catherine became pregnant soon after they were married but sadly the child died in infancy and the couple remained childless. At first the marriage was a happy one but gradually their relationship deteriorated. She became dependent on alcohol and matters grew even worse when James also began to drink heavily. Catherine became convinced, wrongly, that her mild-mannered and inoffensive husband had been involved in a series of adulterous affairs throughout their married life and she grew to hate him.

In the early spring of 1830, Catherine purchased a quantity of sulphuric acid. A few days later, James was asleep and woke suddenly as he felt a sudden excruciating pain in his mouth, which he afterwards described as liquid fire. Liquid had indeed been poured into his mouth as he slept but he managed to spit it out and, as he did so, he noticed that it burnt the bedding and his nightshirt. Catherine was in the room and told him he must have

'sudden excruciating pain'

drunk a glass of tainted beer. James, however, realised at once that she had attempted to pour poison into his mouth and was heard by neighbours to shout, 'Oh woman, woman, you've tried to do it many a time, but you've done it now.' Catherine replied that she did not know what he meant.

Mrs Smith, who lived next door, heard the raised voices and, fearing something was amiss, she rushed to the inn, carrying her child. On entering the bedroom she put the child down and gave it the glass to play with, not knowing it was the one Catherine had used to pour the liquid into her husband's mouth. Within moments, the child screamed out in pain and Mrs Smith put it to her own lips to taste, experiencing a burning sensation immediately she did so. Catherine suddenly grabbed the glass from her hand and ran into the street and from the window Mrs Smith watched her smash it into small pieces on the pavement.

Mrs Smith now suspected something was seriously wrong and was convinced that an attempt had been made to poison James. He was treated by Dr Jamieson, who, on arrival at his bedside, thought James was already dead. However, he slowly opened his eyes and complained of terrible pains in his mouth, throat and stomach. Dr Jamieson's first act was to open a vein but there was no improvement in his condition. He arranged for a stomach pump to be brought to the house but was unable to force the tube down his patient's badly swollen throat. The next day, James continued to experience severe pains throughout his body and the doctor, on observing that his patient's mouth was more swollen and his lips showed evidence of having been badly burnt, concluded he had ingested a highly corrosive substance.

The police were made aware of the suspicions of Mrs Smith and the doctor. They retrieved the shattered pieces of glass, which were gathered up from the pavement, and they were sent for examination. Tests confirmed the presence of sulphuric acid. The doctor told police that he believed three spoonfuls would have caused the symptoms shown by James, and they were aware that Catherine had purchased a quantity that would have been more than enough to cause them. She was arrested shortly after her husband died on 18 April and charged with his murder.

Catherine's trial was held before the Circuit Court of Judiciary in Aberdeen on Monday 13 September. The Crown's witnesses were persuasive and the jury had little difficulty in convicting her of wilful murder. She was sentenced to death and the judge ordered that afterwards her body was to be dissected in public by Dr Skene of the town's Marischal College. He warned Catherine that given the nature of her crime she should not expect a reprieve. The day after her conviction she confessed to administering the sulphuric acid, but insisted she did not meant to kill James. Her purpose was only to hurt him as punishment for his alleged ill treatment of her and his adulterous ways. However, there was no public support for her and no meaningful petition was organised.

Her execution was set for 8 October and she was visited daily by a number of clergymen including prison chaplain the Reverend Mr McCombie, who, in view of her illiteracy, read to her from the Gospels. Two days before her appointment with the hangman, Catherine bade an emotional farewell to her family and friends. Throughout her time in prison she remained quite calm, despite being able to hear the scaffold being erected outside her cell.

She slept little on the eve of her execution but when visited by the town's magistrates in the morning, she was composed and appeared ready for her forthcoming ordeal. When asked if she had anything to say, she replied, 'Gentlemen, you who have it in your power should look to those public houses in the quarter where I lived, for many of them are in a bad state and have much need to be looked after.'

The last execution to have taken place in Aberdeen was on 14 January 1785, when Elspet Reid was hanged for theft. The town therefore did not employ an executioner and it was necessary to call on John Scott of Edinburgh to perform the task. As the trap opened, Catherine was heard to say, 'Oh my God'.

DEATH OF A SERGEANT MAJOR

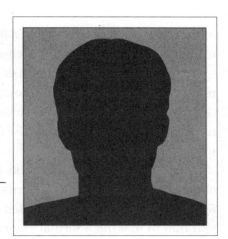

Suspect:	James Bell
Age:	Unknown
Crime:	Murder

Private James Bell was unhappy serving with the 69th Rifles and wished to leave the regiment as soon as possible. He therefore told his senior officers that a private also named Bell, who was serving in the 5th Dragoon Guards, was his brother. This was a lie but it was not discovered until much later, by which time his request for a transfer had been granted. He joined his new regiment in Dublin in 1833 and two years later, on Saturday, 16 May 1835, the 5th arrived at their new posting at Piershill Barracks in Edinburgh.

The next morning Bell was keen to see the sights of the town, a place he had not visited previously. He sought permission to leave the barracks but his request was refused by Sergeant Major William Moorehead, who advised Bell that nobody would be allowed to leave the barracks that day as there was still much work to do since their arrival less than twenty-four hours earlier. Bell's comrade, Private George Smith, was present and heard his friend mutter something under his breath but thought nothing more of it. He also heard Bell ask Captain King for a pass and again made some unfavourable remarks about the sergeant major, which were heard by the captain. In response, the officer told him, 'I am not the man to refuse anyone leave, but since you have said this, you shall not have liberty.'

Rather than learn from this incident, Bell's sense of injustice at his treatment, for which he held the sergeant major responsible, intensified and his resentment towards him grew. At one o'clock that afternoon, Mary Ann Karnan, who lived in the barracks with her husband, a private in the regiment, was present when Bell asked Major Scarlett for a transfer to another regiment, giving the reason that he felt his sergeant major was treating him unfairly. Adjutant Ash, who was at the major's side, advised him of the circumstances surrounding his move to the 5th Dragoon Guards. He added that he was something of a troublemaker and would remain so wherever he served. The major turned to Bell and told him his request would not be granted.

By mid-afternoon Bell was in his hut, which he shared with a number of other privates, six of whom were also present. Among them was Private Egan, who later told of an irate Bell attempting to persuade the others to join him in making a formal complaint about the sergeant major and his unfair treatment of them. Some sympathised with his point of view but there was no appetite to follow his suggestion and the proposal was abandoned. Bell must now have accepted that if he was to do anything, he would have to do it alone.

At 6.30 p.m., Bell walked out of the hut following an order to report to the stable block for cleaning duties. He returned forty-five minutes later and asked Mrs Karnan if she knew the whereabouts of Sergeant Major Moorehead. Unaware of Bell's intentions, she replied that she saw him walking towards the stables a few minutes earlier. It was by now almost 7.30 p.m. and Private Smith was also in the stables talking to the sergeant major. Private Smith watched Bell walk up behind the sergeant major and it was only when he raised his hand that he saw the pistol. Before he could give a warning there was the sound of a gunshot and the sergeant major fell to the ground, crying out 'My God' as he did so. Bell glared at the wounded man and shouted, 'You're down. If I have not done good for myself, I have for my comrades.'

Sergeant Major Moorehead was treated by Dr Logan, the regimental surgeon, but died of his wounds eight days later. Sir George Ballinghall, professor of Military Surgery at Edinburgh University, assisted by Dr Logan, performed a post-mortem, which confirmed the ball had shattered the deceased's spine, as a result of which he had lost a large quantity of blood. The dead man was a widower whose wife had died six months earlier, leaving him with sole care of their one child, who was now an orphan. The sergeant major was able to make a deathbed deposition, in which he told of having to reprimand Bell regarding his behaviour on several occasions in the weeks leading up to the shooting. The Crown believed Bell had simply reached the end of his tether at what he perceived to have

'he had lost a large quantity of blood'

been unfair treatment and had decided there was only one way of putting an end to it. At Bell's civilian trial, which opened on Monday 22 June at the High Court of Judiciary, it seemed as though the victim's reputation was being put on trial by the defence.

Many of the regiment's senior officers and their wives were in the packed courtroom to hear Bell enter a plea of not guilty. He accepted that he shot his victim but claimed he was insane at the time he did so, which was rejected by the prosecution. Following his arrest, he made two statements, the first of which was taken immediately after the shooting. In it he declared he shot the sergeant major in the back deliberately, as he had been tormenting him over a lengthy period. In the second statement, which was taken some time later, he insisted he did not mean to kill the sergeant major, and had only wanted to frighten him.

As the trial progressed it emerged that Sergeant Major Moorehead was not universally liked by his men. However, the Crown rejected totally the proposition put forward by Bell's defence barrister that his client was an excellent soldier, who was driven temporarily insane by the behaviour of a martinet. Privates George Smith and John Callaghan described the sergeant major as a fair-minded man, who was liked and respected by his men and superior officers. These witnesses and their comrades Corporal Baxter and Private Egan all testified that they had served with the accused since he joined the regiment and none of them had seen any signs of insanity. This view was supported by Sheriff Tait, who questioned Bell after his arrest and he testified that the accused spoke openly and freely. Professor Traill, who treated the insane, was called by the prosecution as an expert witness. He had examined Bell and although he found signs of an old head injury, there was no evidence of mental problems.

The defence called Private Graham, who gave a wholly different view of the victim and the accused. He described the sergeant major as someone who treated his men unfairly and harshly. The private also stated that he saw Bell immediately after the shooting and he had looked wild-eyed, which convinced the witness that he was insane at the time. An important defence witness was Captain Beville, who was Bell's superior officer for eight months, and he testified that he posed no disciplinary problems whatsoever during the whole of that period. Privates Duffy and Fagan had served alongside Bell and they too described him as a good soldier.

Bell's lawyer also called three serving prisoners, Alex Alexander, Charles Cameron and Daniel Hannay to give evidence on his behalf. They had all shared a cell with him at different times as he was waiting in Calton Gaol for his trial to start. They spoke of his bizarre behaviour, which included insomnia, whistling and singing for long periods, constantly laughing out loud for no apparent reason and washing his handkerchief in dirty water. Furthermore, he would often attempt to drill the other prisoners and would call out for his horse and sword.

Claiming to have been insane at the time of committing a murder was often used as a plea when the evidence against the accused was overwhelming. This was the view of the Crown in this case and the prosecutor warned the jury to disregard this evidence and pointed to the fact that despite their supposed concerns regarding his behaviour, none of the witnesses asked to be moved from the cell they were sharing with him at the time. They were accused of lying to the court in the hope of obtaining some form of reward from Bell. Their evidence and that of the other defence witnesses was dismissed by the jury, its members taking less than a minute to reach a unanimous guilty verdict, following which Bell was sentenced to hang on Monday 13 July.

Bell rose at five o'clock on the morning of his execution and read his Bible for three hours, before being taken to have his arms pinioned by the hangman, John Williams, whose third execution this would be. Nevertheless, Williams had already gained a reputation as an incompetent drunkard who was unable to perform his duties efficiently. He had great difficulty pinioning Bell's arms, although his prisoner was co-operating, and the watching officials were appalled to see Williams crying like a baby.

Bell remained calm throughout the procedure and as he and the officials stepped on to the scaffold, the crowd of 20,000 met the appearance of Williams with yells of derision as they realised he was drunk. To his credit, Bell gestured to the spectators to be quiet. However, Williams was shaking so much that he had great difficulty in positioning the rope properly and the crowd grew restless and angry as there was a great deal of sympathy for the condemned man. Eventually, an exasperated Mr Brown, the Superintendent of Public Works, pushed Williams aside to adjust the rope himself, before stepping back and allowing the hangman to continue with the execution.

Bell signalled that he was ready but Williams botched the simple task of pulling the lever. After an agonising delay of several seconds, Bell fell through the drop, but took several minutes to die. The enraged crowd shouted 'Shame' and 'Cut him down', which led the officials to think there could be a serious riot or possibly a rescue attempt. Normally, the magistrates and clergymen would step off the platform, leaving the hangman alone to complete his task. However, they sensed the hostile nature of the crowd and noticed many of them were picking up stones to throw at Williams. They decided to remain on the scaffold, believing that if they did so the spectators would not wish to harm them and would not throw any stones. They proved to be correct and despite calls for them to step aside they stayed and probably saved Williams from suffering very serious injuries.

After being cut down, Bell's body was buried in the grounds of Calton Gaol. Williams managed to leave the town relatively unscathed although he was spotted by a group of boys, who pelted him with stones. It proved to be the last execution the hapless Williams would perform as he decided to resign from the post, his brief career at an end.

CASE TEN   1839

THE THORTER ROW MURDER

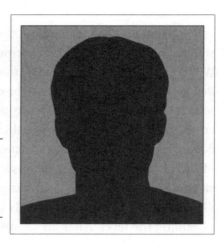

Suspect: Arthur Woods
Age: Unknown
Crime: Murder

Duncan McNab, a member of the Dundee watch, was on patrol in the early hours of Sunday, 5 August 1839. It was a few minutes after one o'clock when he entered Thorter Row, a court onto which opened the doors of three public houses and several dwellings. It was deserted and although he heard raised voices it quickly fell silent again and he continued on his way. He returned to Thorter Row thirty minutes later and saw what he thought was a drunk lying on the ground. He approached the man, intending to help him stand before sending him on his way. However, he realised immediately that he was looking not at a drunkard but at a corpse. The dead man was lying on his back inches from the bottom of six steps leading to the home of Arthur Woods and his wife Henrietta.

As he examined the body, which he could not identify, McNab was joined by local tailor William Annal, who was on his way home. He agreed to stay with the body while the watchman sought assistance. Within a few minutes he returned with his colleagues, Peter Forbes and Sergeant James Low, who arranged for a cart to take the body to their offices, where it was examined by Dr Webster and surgeon Adam Moon.

The deceased had suffered a fractured skull, the blow from which would have rendered him unconscious. The doctors also discovered ligature marks to his neck and they concluded that he had been strangled to death after suffering the head injury. There was no doubt that the man had been murdered.

The corpse was recognised by Peter Forbes as that of twenty-one-year-old pedlar John Drew Woods, the son of Arthur Woods and stepson of his wife, Henrietta. Sergeant Low called on them and was a little surprised to find the couple fully dressed despite the hour. When asked if they knew

'he had been strangled to death'

the whereabouts of their son, Arthur replied, 'He's not here, he shan't be here.' His wife added, however, that he had visited them about an hour earlier, demanding to be let in, but they did not open the door and refused him entry. When asked if they knew what became of him, she said she thought she heard him fall down the steps as he left. His father added, 'It wasna me that did it.' Their answers were highly suspicious and led the sergeant to look on the couple as possible suspects.

The police focused the enquiry on Thorter Row as they were convinced the solution to the mystery was to be found in this small court. Mrs Mitchell, landlady of Wright's Tavern, which opened out into the court, told officers that she had heard a violent argument the preceding week, in the Woods' home. She had walked over to find father and son fighting inside and watched as they both fell to the floor. She could not separate them and called out to neighbour Andrew Mill, a sailor on shore leave, for assistance. When questioned, he told of seeing Henrietta attempt to strike her stepson with a poker. She continued to hit out at him after father and son were parted and as John was being escorted out of the house. Andrew recalled being told by John that his stepmother was responsible for causing a great deal of friction between him and his father.

Mrs Summers, landlady of another local tavern, told police that the victim knocked on her door one hour before his body was discovered. He appeared to be drunk and asked for alcohol but she refused to let him in, saying it was far too late to serve him. Mrs Mclean, whose house was on Thorter Row, heard an argument, apparently in the Woods' home, a little later. This, the police realised, would have been only minutes before the body was discovered by Duncan McNab.

However, by far the most incriminating statement was provided by Mrs Scott, who also lived in Thorter Row. On the night in question, she was standing at her door and spoke to John. He complained that Mrs Summers had refused to serve him with alcohol and she watched as he staggered towards his father's house. A few minutes later, she heard raised voices coming from inside the Woods' house, one of which she recognised as that of John who screamed, 'Don't choke me father!' She then heard his father's voice shouting, 'I'll be your butcher before I sleep.' All went quiet and after a few moments she noticed the watchman stroll through the courtyard. Once he had left Thorter Row, the Woods' door opened and Arthur and Henrietta emerged, carrying John. The couple carried him down the steps and placed him on the ground before returning indoors. Mrs Scott, assuming John was drunk, went back inside her house.

A search of the Woods' home was made and several lengths of rope were discovered hanging from a hook on the pantry door. When they were aligned with the ligature marks on the dead man's neck, one of them was found to correspond exactly. The police were aware that the relationship between father and son had become strained following Arthur's marriage to Henrietta, whose presence in the home was greatly resented by John. There were frequent quarrels and it seemed that it was during one of these that the murder occurred. The physical evidence, together with the statement made by Mrs Scott, led to Arthur and Henrietta being charged with John's murder.

Their trial was delayed until 25 February 1840, due to Henrietta giving birth to a baby in December the previous year. At the conclusion of the evidence, the jury retired for thirty minutes and returned with a guilty verdict against Arthur, but decided that the case against Henrietta was not proven. She was released immediately and Arthur was sentenced to death.

Nevertheless, many believed Woods to be innocent and even those who thought he had killed his son felt the crime was not premeditated and had been committed only after a great deal of provocation. Several well-supported petitions seeking a reprieve were received by the Secretary of State. These included a petition signed by forty Dundee tradesmen, another supported by fifty-seven local worthies and one was received from nineteen of Edinburgh's leading citizens.

Mrs Scott, whose testimony was of crucial important to the Crown, had declared when taking the oath that she was married to Mr Scott.

However, Wood's supporters discovered that the couple had never married. It was therefore argued that she lied under oath to the court and her evidence could not be trusted and should therefore be ignored. If her testimony was stricken from the court record, the Crown's case was seriously undermined. It was also claimed that Mr Neaves, who acted as the condemned man's counsel, was incompetent. These arguments were not accepted by the trial judge when his opinion was sought, but the execution was nevertheless postponed so that consideration could be given to the petitions. However, it was decided that the execution should go ahead on Monday 25 March.

Given the strength of support for Woods, the authorities feared the possibility of a rescue attempt being made or, at the very least, a demonstration of some kind at the scaffold. A detachment of the 1st Royals therefore arrived in Leith on the eve of the execution on the steamship *Caledonia* to reinforce the local volunteer forces should their intervention prove to be necessary. Fortunately, the troops were not required as there were no crowd problems.

As he was being pinioned in the gaol, Arthur Woods thanked the prison officials for their kindness and support. On the scaffold, he gave a short speech to the vast crowd in which he continued to claim his innocence. As hangman John Scott was removing the condemned man's neckerchief, Woods asked him to send it to Henrietta as a keepsake, a request Scott readily agreed to before sending him to his doom.

CASE ELEVEN   1853

THE NEW VENNEL OUTRAGE

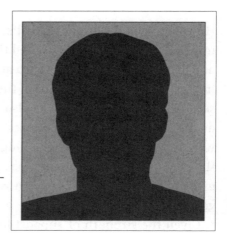

Suspects: Hans Smith
McFarlane
& Helen Blackwood

Ages: Unknown

Crime: Murder

Forty-year-old ship's carpenter Alexander Boyd had lived in the Chilean port of Valparaiso with his wife and three children for several years, but returned to his home town of Glasgow to administer the estate of his mother, following her recent death. On the morning of Saturday, 11 June 1853, he met his old friend James Law, also a carpenter, and the two men spent the day drinking and reminiscing. They visited a number of public houses and by the time they reached the New Vennel district, a notorious slum, both men were extremely drunk.

It was believed that within an area of 100 square yards, in excess of 1,000 people lived in squalid tenements. In recent months several men had been found drugged, stripped to their underwear and robbed of their clothes, valuables and cash. The victims were either too embarrassed to

'drugged, stripped to their underwear and robbed'

report the matter to the police or were so drunk at the time that they had no memory of the events which led to them being discovered in such a condition.

However, in 1853 one victim did remember what happened to him and what is more, knew the identities of those responsible. Rather than report the matter to the police, he decided to take his own revenge by setting light to the room of the man he blamed, Hans Smith McFarlane. The fire brigade managed to extinguish the flames and the damage was restricted to the door. Nevertheless, this did not prevent McFarlane continuing with his criminal activities and it was he, his common-law wife Helen Blackwood and their friends Mary Hamilton and Ann Marshall, who approached Alexander and James when they wandered into the New Vennel area. Enticed no doubt by the promise of sex and alcohol, the two men were led to McFarlane's room, which was situated on the top floor of a three-storey tenement.

Later that night, Constable William Campbell was in the area when his attention was drawn to a large crowd, which had gathered outside the tenement he knew to be occupied by McFarlane. As he approached the scene he realised that the body of a man dressed only in his stockings and underwear was spread-eagled on the ground. It was Alexander Boyd, who had fallen more than thirty feet and suffered extensive injuries to the back of his head, from which a large amount of blood was flowing. He was clearly dead. Close to the corpse were the pieces of a smashed drinking cup.

Several witnesses described hearing a woman's voice shouting from the building that Alexander had fallen accidentally from a window. However, Campbell and his colleague Constable David Henderson, who had arrived at the scene, suspected foul play. They entered the building and made for McFarlane's room, in which they found James Law sound asleep and still unaware of his friend's death. Alexander's clothes were on the bed and there were bloodstains on the fireplace. Neither McFarlane nor his associates were to be seen, but a search was begun following a discussion with Jane Leitch and Mary Kelland, who provided the officers with important information.

The friends witnessed the two men being approached by McFarlane and the women, and overheard Helen Blackwood say to Mary Hamilton, 'It is a good chance.' Realising that the intention was to rob the men, Jane and Mary decided to follow the group to McFarlane's room. Although the door was closed, there were gaps in it as it had not been repaired after the earlier arson attack and through it they saw the events, which ended with Alexander being thrown out into the street. Furthermore, they were adamant that he was alive at the time for he was still breathing as he was carried to the open window.

Additional officers were called to the area and visited surrounding premises. One of those interviewed was Hugh Gray, whose room was on the ground floor of the tenement in which McFarlane lived. Hugh said that he had been enjoying a pipe of tobacco before bedtime, when his window shook with what turned out to be the force of the impact of Alexander's body hitting the ground. A few minutes later, an anxious McFarlane rushed into his room, wringing his hands and asking repeatedly, 'What have I done Hugh?' but he left without waiting for a reply. Hugh watched him head towards the room of another neighbour, Charles Scott, a bone gatherer. Charles later informed the police that McFarlane told him that he invited two men to his room and one of them had fallen from the window accidentally. As McFarlane left, he muttered, 'What am I to do? What are Helen and I to do?'

More devastating evidence against the four suspects was provided by eleven-year-old William Shillinglaw and his nine-year-old brother, James. The boys' father was dead and they were now more or less homeless and having to fend for themselves. They attended the local ragged school as it provided them with shelter and food, but at night McFarlane allowed them to sleep under a bed in his room whenever they needed to. They were allowed to come and go as they liked and at nine o'clock that evening the boys fell asleep in their usual place, unnoticed by the adults when they returned to the room with the two drunken men.

They woke up to see Mary Hamilton enter the room, leading in a drunken James Law. They were followed by McFarlane, Blackwood and Marshall with Alexander Boyd. The brothers watched as James fell asleep almost immediately and heard Blackwood ask Alexander for money with which to buy whisky. He handed over some coins and more alcohol was brought into the room, which was passed around in a jug.

The brothers saw Mary Hamilton take a packet from her pocket, which she unwrapped before pouring the powder it contained into a cup of whisky, which she handed to Alexander. He drank from it and within a matter of seconds he staggered to his feet, clutching his throat and gasping for breath. He seemed to have realised that his drink had been drugged and threw himself towards Helen Blackwood, who struck him on the side of his head with a chamber pot. He fell backwards, striking his head on the stone hearth as he did so and rendering himself unconscious.

Blackwood asked the others what they should do with him and the group decided to strip him down to his underwear after taking what cash they could find in his pockets. The boys heard McFarlane suggest they throw him out of the window but they could see that although seriously injured, Alexander was still breathing. Blackwood and McFarlane each took an arm as Marshall lifted his feet and they carried him to the window from which they threw him out, followed by the cup from which he had been drinking. Marshall leaned out of the window feigning distress and shouted, 'Oh my man's dead; he went to the window and fell over it.' Blackwood then blew out the candle and the four of them left the room, locking the door as they did so and leaving behind James, who was still asleep, and the two boys, whose presence they remained unaware of.

The police circulated the names and descriptions of McFarlane and the women, which led to their arrests within a matter of hours. McFarlane claimed he was not present when the deceased fell from the window. He insisted he was drinking in a nearby inn and was on his way home when he heard that a man had fallen to his death. Helen Blackwood told police that the two men were brought to the room by Ann Marshall and Mary Hamilton and that Alexander died as a result of an accidental fall from the window. Marshall and Hamilton also protested their innocence, the former admitting that she was in the room when the deceased fell but insisting she was making the bed at the time and saw nothing. Hamilton said she saw the man fall from the open window but nobody was near him and it was an accident.

A post-mortem was performed by Dr Easton of Glasgow's Andersonian Institution and Dr McGregor of the Royal Infirmary. They described a powerfully built man who had suffered several fractures to his skull and severe internal injuries, especially to the liver, any one of which could have proved fatal. The stomach contents yielded no trace of any toxic substances but the doctors said this did not disprove the police theory that some such substance was administered to the deceased in the shattered cup found by the body, as one that was vegetable based would have passed through the stomach and into the blood very quickly, making detection almost impossible.

The trial of the four accused took place on Thursday 21 July, at which the jury returned a verdict of not proven in respect of Mary Hamilton, who was released from custody. The others were found guilty of murder, but the jury added a strong recommendation for mercy in Ann Marshall's case. The three prisoners were sentenced to death and as Helen Blackwood was led from the dock she screamed, 'We have not got justice. There is a higher judge for me, I am innocent.'

Marshall was subsequently reprieved, which left only McFarlane and Blackwood for execution on Thursday 11 August. William Calcraft was the hangman and 25,000 spectators gathered in Jail Square to witness the event. It was decided to wait until the two condemned prisoners were standing on the drop to give them the news that Marshall would not be joining them.

CASE TWELVE   1855

THE BODY IN THE LOCH

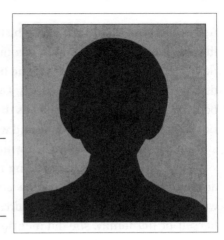

Suspect: Agnes Cameron
Age: 25
Crime: Murder

As grocer Daniel Hossack strolled along the bank of Duddingston Loch at two o'clock on the afternoon of 14 July 1855, he noticed a bundle floating on the surface of the water, protruding from which appeared to be a baby's leg. He shouted to two nearby anglers for their assistance and using their rods, the bundle was pulled from the water. When it was unwrapped the men discovered the body of a female baby, swathed in an apron and wearing a cap and chemise.

The local policeman, Constable Peter Murphy, was unable to find any identifying marks and not having the experience or resources to investigate the matter further, he arranged for senior colleagues from Edinburgh to collect the body and make the necessary enquiries. A post-mortem was performed by Dr Littlejohn and Dr Duncan, who believed the baby to be only a few days old and to have been in the water for between twelve and twenty-four hours. However, they were unable to determine the cause of death.

Detective Michael Reilly was given the task of solving the puzzle and he realised that it would first of all be necessary to identify the mother if he was to make any progress. The post-mortem revealed that the mother had received a high standard of professional care when giving birth and the detective therefore visited the local maternity hospital, where he spoke to a number of doctors and nurses, all of whom were shown the body. Nurses Johnstone, Thomson and Burns recognised the baby and the clothes she was wearing and were able to provide information about the mother. They told of a young woman who admitted herself on 25 June, giving the name

Agnes McDonald, and who gave birth to a daughter on 3 July. It was her first born and despite being in labour for twenty-eight hours, mother and daughter were healthy and left the hospital on 13 July, the day before the discovery of the body in the loch. During her stay, the medical staff had become increasingly concerned as the young woman made it clear she did not wish to bond with her baby and was reluctant to even hold her. She told staff that arrangements were being made for a nurse to foster the little girl.

When arrangements were being made for the mother and child to be discharged, Agnes refused to allow contact to be made with her family and would not provide a forwarding address. Despite not giving any details about herself or her family, she did mention that her father was an instrument maker who lived and worked close to the hospital, but she did not give his name. However, Detective Reilly traced one such man named Cameron, who, when questioned, confirmed he had a twenty-five-year-old daughter named Agnes, but he was adamant she had not given birth to a baby. Nevertheless, when Agnes was traced and seen by hospital staff, she was identified as the mother of the baby girl, whose body was now lying in the mortuary.

Detective Reilly learnt that on the day she left hospital, Agnes rented a furnished room at a weekly cost of half a crown from Sarah Cassidy on Old Assembly Close. Sarah did not see the baby but her daughter, Mary, did and the new lodger told the youngster she would be taking her to a nurse in the near future. Agnes left the house with the baby at nine o'clock that night and did not return until three hours later, this time alone.

Agnes was charged with her daughter's murder, which she denied. She told the police she was working as a servant for a Mrs Campbell in Kilberry but left in March because of her pregnancy. She returned to her native Edinburgh and supported herself until it became necessary to enter the maternity hospital. She gave her mother's maiden name as she wished to conceal her true identity. On the day she left hospital she told police of meeting a woman whose name she did not know and whose whereabouts she was unaware of. Agnes had asked her if she knew anyone who would be suitable to look after her baby. The stranger replied that she too had recently given birth and for a single payment of £3 she would take the little girl and raise her as her own. Agnes agreed to these terms, asked for no further information, and handed her baby and the cash to the stranger.

She explained that she decided not to tell her family, employer or friends of her pregnancy because she was too ashamed to do so. She met the baby's father only once and did not know his name or address and was thus unable to call on him for support. She insisted that she knew nothing of the body discovered in the loch and, having been taken to view it, said she was not convinced it was her child.

At her trial on Monday 12 November Agnes pleaded not guilty, but her own barrister acknowledged that the jury might believe there to be strong circumstantial evidence against the prisoner. However, her defence was based on what was claimed to be the Crown's failure to prove that a murder had even taken place. He drew the jury's attention to the equivocal medical evidence and the testimony of Dr Littlejohn given under cross-examination, in which he acknowledged the possibility of a baby being asphyxiated accidentally. He had described one such case in which a mother had placed her child in her lap face down, as a result of which the child suffocated without the mother having realised what had happened. It was argued that the Crown had not been able to show if the baby was dead or alive when put in the loch, nor had it been demonstrated how she had met her death or if it had been caused accidentally or deliberately. It was possible therefore, that the deceased had met her death due to a tragic accident, but whatever had happened, their client was not responsible.

A single woman who became pregnant in mid-Victorian Britain and who could not rely on the support of the father faced a difficult future for herself and her child. Families were often willing to help but this was not always the case. In these circumstances the choices were stark; the workhouse, abortion or infanticide. A number of young women were executed in the nineteenth century for murdering their newborn babies, but in many cases juries were

'murdering their newborn babies'

often sympathetic. At the close of the evidence in the case of Agnes Cameron, the jury deliberated in their seats for a few moments before returning a unanimous verdict of not guilty. The judge ordered her immediate release from the dock but this was delayed for a few minutes as she had fainted.

CASE THIRTEEN 1857

THE OLDMELDRUM MURDER

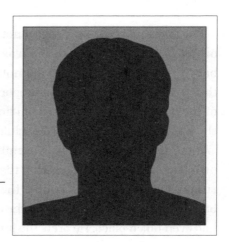

Suspect: John Booth
Age: 37
Crime: Murder

John Booth, a thirty-seven-year-old pedlar, lived in Oldmeldrum with his wife Mary and their children; a nine-year-old son and a daughter aged three. His parents-in-law owned a small provisions shop on Weavery Lane in the village, which was only a few minutes walk from the Booths' cottage.

Booth was often away from home for several days at a time, visiting markets and fairs, at which he sold his goods. On 21 July 1857, he returned from the market at St Sairs and was due to travel to the fair at Aikey on the following day. A number of pedlars arranged to meet in Oldmeldrum on the 21st to make their way to Aikey in a group the next day. These included Thomas Moncur and Alexander Laird, who met Booth that afternoon in Margaret Strachan's public house on North Road in the village. The three men spent the next few hours drinking and at first they seemed to be enjoying themselves. At nine o'clock, however, Mrs Strachan heard raised voices coming from their table and could see they were arguing.

As they were leaving, the landlady saw Booth strike Moncur and it emerged later that the assaulted man had taunted his assailant with accusations about his wife's alleged immoral behaviour whenever he was away from home. Moncur had made matters worse by suggesting that he might visit her in the near future when Booth was away, as he would be sure to receive what he described as 'a warm welcome'. It was now 9.30 and Booth made his way home, determined to confront his wife with the rumours about her adultery.

Unaware there was a problem when he walked through the door and that she would soon face his wrath, Mary readily agreed to unfasten her husband's boots when he asked her to do so. However, as she knelt down, he accused her of being unfaithful when he was away from home, a charge she angrily denied. He refused to listen to her pleas of innocence

'He refused to listen to her pleas of innocence'

and without warning pulled out a knife, with which he cut her several times. Screaming loudly and wearing only a nightdress, she rose to her feet and ran from the cottage in the direction of her parents' home.

Her mother and father lived in just one room, which served as both their living space and the shop. Also staying with them that night was their grandson James, John and Mary's son. They were all asleep when Mary's desperate hammering at the door woke them up. Her father, James Barclay, let her in and she told him of the attack she had suffered at the hands of her husband. Her mother Jane rose from her bed, lit a candle which provided a little light and attempted to comfort her distraught daughter.

Jane was able to calm her down and was treating her knife wounds when, twenty minutes later, Booth forced his way in, still brandishing the knife. James ushered Jane and Mary behind the counter before placing himself between them and Booth, hoping to shield his wife and daughter from harm. However, Booth pushed him aside to find Jane standing in front of Mary, thereby preventing him from reaching her. Frustrated and still in an uncontrollable rage, he began to stab his mother-in-law.

In a desperate attempt to stop him injuring his wife, James grabbed a shovel with which he struck his son-in-law several blows. The men began to struggle and Jane took the opportunity of running towards the door, crying out as she did so, 'Mary, run for your life, for this man has murdered me.' Jane collapsed to the floor a few feet from the door but Mary managed to reach it, where she was joined by her son James, who was now standing at his mother's side and crying out repeatedly, 'Granny is dead.'

Worried neighbours, alerted by the screams, hurried to the scene, where Alexander Smith found John Booth sitting quietly on the ground outside the shop. From inside, another neighbour shouted that Jane was dead. Without any prompting, Booth admitted responsibility to Alexander, adding that he regretted that it was not his wife who was dead as he had wanted to kill her. Local carter John Melvyn, who was travelling along Weavery Lane, stopped to offer assistance. He also spoke with Booth, who once again admitted responsibility for attacking his mother-in-law.

James Tarves, the village constable, arrested him within minutes of the killing and Booth made a verbal statement admitting his crime. This was the third spoken confession made within a short time and later, those who heard him make them confirmed that Booth was in full control of his emotions and did not appear to be under the influence of alcohol. Surgeon John Ingram was at the scene within minutes but was unable to help Jane. However, he treated Mary's knife wounds, from which she was to make a full recovery. He also examined the killer, who was covered with blood, none of which was his own, and found that he had suffered no injuries of any description.

Mr Ingram performed a post-mortem on Jane, assisted by Dr Francis Ogston. They found eight knife wounds to her head, arms and chest, and agreed that a great deal of force must have been used to produce such devastating injuries. The most serious of these stab wounds passed between the fifth and sixth ribs before piercing the right side of her heart, and which was the cause of death.

Booth was held overnight in a nearby inn and taken to Aberdeen the next afternoon, where his trial took place on Thursday 24 September. He denied murder but pleaded guilty to culpable homicide, which the Crown refused to accept, for this was considered to have been a ruthless and deliberate act. Booth called nobody to testify in his defence but provided one character witness, John Alexander, a hardware dealer who had known the accused for more than twenty-five years. Alexander described his friend as a quiet and inoffensive man, whom he would have considered incapable of murder. His barrister claimed that Jane's injuries were caused accidentally and that Booth did not intend to kill her. However, this version of events was rejected by the jury and he was found guilty of murder. Booth received the decision calmly but asked the judge if he could address the court before sentence was passed. The judge agreed and Booth offered an explanation for the crime.

In a long rambling statement he accused the deceased of being an immoral drunkard, who for many years had set an appalling example to Mary by encouraging her to behave in similarly unacceptable ways. Booth told of a number of occasions on which he discovered both women in bed together, entertaining men in his own home. Whenever he confronted them they would become violent towards him. More recently, his son James had begun to misbehave and his attempts to discipline the nine-year-old were unsuccessful. Booth blamed his mother-in-law as his son was spending a great deal of time with her during his regular absences from home. He blamed Jane for his unhappiness and matters had come to a head on the night of the killing.

On sentencing Booth to death the judge warned him that he should hold out no hope of a reprieve. Nevertheless, a number of petitions seeking to spare his life were signed by hundreds of people in Oldmeldrum, Aberdeen and the surrounding districts. They were unsuccessful and the execution was set for 21 October. Booth spent his final days reading the Bible and in prayer. He was also visited in the condemned cell by his wife and father-in-law, with whom he was able to make his peace.

Standing on the gallows outside the Aberdeen Town House, Booth urged the crowd of spectators to ignore what he had said at his trial about the alleged immoral behaviour of his wife and mother-in-law, saying, 'As what would a man not say to try and save his life.' After hangman William Calcraft withdrew the bolt, Booth struggled briefly at the end of the rope, but was dead after a few moments. This would prove to be the last execution in Aberdeen for more than a century.

CASE FOURTEEN 1862

A DUTIFUL DAUGHTER

Suspect:	Mary Struth
Age:	31
Crime:	Murder

John Struth, a retired sailor in his late seventies, lived in rooms on Silver Street in Kincardine with his thirty-one-year-old daughter Mary and her one-year-old son, John Simpson. John senior had been unable to work for two years following an accident and he received a weekly payment of two shillings and sixpence from the parish. Nevertheless, he was an active man who, until the closing weeks of 1861, was often seen by his friends and neighbours walking in the town and surrounding countryside. Mary worked as a labourer on local farms when she could find employment, but much of her time was spent helping to care for her father.

It was a far from comfortable existence, but despite living close to the poverty line the family seemed happy and Mary was considered by those who knew her to be a caring and dutiful daughter and a loving mother, who coped well in difficult circumstances. Therefore, when her father died on 26 January 1862, townspeople were astonished to learn that Mary had been arrested and charged with his murder.

In early December John was known to have been well and on the 5th he was seen walking through the town by his friend Agnes Shand, who rented rooms in the same house as John and his family. The next morning, Agnes heard him retching and obviously in distress. His sudden deterioration was also witnessed by Elizabeth Maxwell, an old friend of Mary's, who was lodging with her temporarily as she had found casual employment on a nearby farm. Elizabeth was leaving for work in the fields when she saw

John vomiting. He was in bed and complaining of severe pains in his chest and bowels and claimed that Mary had forced him to drink a glass of water which tasted unpleasant and which he suspected contained poison.

Agnes called on John later in the day to find him apparently feeling better and out of bed. Nevertheless, he described his daughter as a vagabond and once again accused her of giving him poison. Mary, who was present, denied the accusation and Agnes left, convinced that he was simply confused. However, by the time Elizabeth returned from work that evening, John had been taken ill once more and was again lying in his bed.

John's health did not improve and he continued to be poorly over the following weeks, often complaining of a great thirst. On one occasion, after Mary went out on an errand, Agnes called on Elizabeth and the two women decided to pour some of the liquid John had been given by his daughter a few minutes earlier into a phial, which Agnes took to her room. By this time another neighbour, Jessie Ainslie, had become a frequent visitor to John's bedside, having also become concerned about his worsening health. On one visit, he called out to her in agony, 'Oh there's boiling lead rushing up my throat,' and once again he accused Mary of attempting to poison him.

As the New Year approached, Elizabeth was out walking with another friend, Jane Drysdale. They met Mary, who asked Jane to buy a pennyworth of sugar of lead for her. She explained that she did not wish to go to the

'Oh there's boiling lead rushing up my throat'

chemist as she was dirty and wearing her oldest and most threadbare clothes and felt too embarrassed to visit the shop herself. She assured the two women that she intended using it to apply to Elizabeth's leg, which had been injured a few days earlier. However, she did not subsequently offer to treat her friend's leg and this led Elizabeth and Agnes to became even more concerned for John's welfare, especially as his condition seemed to be worsening by the day. Matters came to a head on the morning of 11 January, when Mrs Shand heard John vomiting almost continuously and called on him twice to see how he was. Mary insisted he was well but at nine o'clock that night she heard Mary shouting at her father, 'Take that medicine father. Mr Steel went to the doctor himself and sent it down for you, so you must take it.' Mrs Shand could hear John apparently attempting to resist before eventually agreeing to take a little of whatever it was she was trying to give him.

Alexander Steel was the official in charge of poor relief in the district and Mrs Shand rushed to his house to advise him of her concerns, taking with her the phial of liquid collected earlier. Mr Steel was aware of John's poor health and had visited him at home on a number of occasions over the previous two weeks. However, he was alarmed at what Mrs Shand told him, especially as he had not recommended any medicine to be taken by the ailing man. He decided to visit John immediately and was told by the elderly man that he was experiencing great pain throughout his body, leading Mr Steel to send Mary for Dr Crawford. As they waited for the doctor, John told Mr Steel that he was convinced Mary was slowly poisoning him and asked to be taken elsewhere to be looked after for his own safety.

Mr Steel made a search of the rooms and found a cup containing a suspicious-looking substance, which he showed to Dr Crawford on his arrival. The doctor tasted a little on the tip of his finger and insisted it was not cream of tartar as Mary claimed. Suddenly, Mary knocked the cup from the doctor's hand, crying out, 'Do you think I would poison my father?' Mr Steel replied, 'There's no person blaming you for it. You're only taking guilt for it yourself.' He knelt down and retrieved some of the liquid and, as he was doing so, Mary admitted that it was in fact salt of sorrel, but she would not have given it to her father as she knew it was toxic. She claimed she intended to use it to remove stains from her clothes.

Arrangements were made by Mr Steel to have John taken to the home of Janet Strang, a neighbour who provided him with a nourishing diet and where he was prescribed magnesia by Dr Crawford. His condition improved rapidly and on 16 January, Mary was arrested and charged with the attempted murder of her father. The police believed they knew the motive for the crime following discussions with Edward Innes, a plasterer in the village who also acted as secretary for the Kincardine Society for Deaths.

John was a member of the society, whose weekly subscriptions had been paid regularly on his behalf by his daughter. Thus, she would have been eligible to receive the sum of £6, which was payable on his death. The subscriptions were collected by David Miller, who recalled a conversation with Mary in early December, when she asked if her brother William was entitled to a share of the payout should her father die. David assured her that as the only person to have paid the subscriptions, she alone would be entitled to any money in the event of her father's death. Poverty, it was alleged, drove Mary to attempt to murder her father for £6.

No statement had yet been taken from John because, given the good recovery he seemed to be making, it was felt there was plenty of time to do so. However, his health took an unexpected turn for the worse and it was decided that John Grahame, the local Sheriff Substitute, should visit him at Mrs Strang's home on 25 January so that a deathbed deposition could be taken. Unfortunately, this was not possible as John was unconscious when Mr Grahame arrived and he died the following day.

Dr Crawford performed a post-mortem, assisted by Dr Forrest of Stirling. They found John's heart to be enlarged but the liver, spleen, kidneys and lungs to be healthy. However, his stomach and bowels were inflamed, which the doctors believed indicated that he had been poisoned. Furthermore, both suggested salt of sorrel as a likely cause of death. No trace of poison was found in the body but the doctors said that if, as seemed likely, he had received the last dose on 11 January, it would have been eliminated from his body by the time of his death and would not be evident at the subsequent post-mortem.

Dr Douglas Maclagan made a chemical analysis of the internal organs, the stomach contents, the liquid in the phial obtained by the dead man's concerned friends, and that recovered by Mr Steel. Traces of the poison were found in the latter, but Mary had already acknowledged this to be the case and results from the contents of the phial were inconclusive. Traces of lead were found in the organs but this was consistent with the amount Dr Maclagan would have anticipated being present from drinking the local water. This led him to conclude that sugar of lead had not been used and he agreed with his colleagues that the likely cause of death was salt of sorrel.

Mary's trial took place on Monday, 2 June 1862, at which she entered a not guilty plea. Among the few defence witnesses called to speak on her behalf was Mary's friend Elizabeth Scotland. She told the court that she had known the prisoner and her family for more than twenty years and in that time she had impressed her as a loving and caring daughter, incapable of murdering her father. At the conclusion of the evidence the jury retired at 8.20 p.m. and returned just eight minutes later, announcing a verdict of not guilty to a stunned courtroom. Mary had maintained her composure throughout the hearing but smiled broadly on being told she could leave the dock immediately. Outside, she was greeted by a large group of friends and well-wishers.

CASE FIFTEEN 1862

SLAUGHTER AT SANDYFORD PLACE

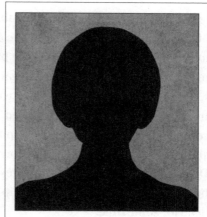

Suspect: Jessie McLachlan
Age: 28
Crime: Murder

John Fleming was a successful Glasgow accountant who lived at 17 Sandyford Place and whose business premises were located in St Vincent Place. He also owned a villa in Dunoon and every year he and the other family members moved to the coast, where they spent the summer months. A full-time servant remained in Glasgow and two local women were hired to help with domestic chores in Dunoon. During the working week, John and his son, who was also named John, would stay at the house in Sandyford Place, but every Friday afternoon they returned to Dunoon to spend the weekend with the family.

On Friday, 4 July 1862, father and son left their Glasgow office and travelled to Dunoon, leaving eighty-seven-year-old James Fleming, father of John senior, at Sandyford Place with the family servant Jessie McPherson, who lived on the premises. On the following Monday morning, John and his son made their regular journey from the coast to the office in Glasgow. After work, young John went to Sandyford Place, where he arrived a short time before his father. He rang the bell and to his surprise, the front door was not opened by the servant but by his grandfather, who told him that Jessie was out, adding that he had not seen her since Friday evening.

John senior arrived some time afterwards and later told the police that the first he knew something was amiss was when his son said, 'There's no use sending anything for dinner here today as the servant has run off and there is nobody to cook it.' This came as a great surprise to his father, as

Jessie had always been most reliable. Her room was on the ground floor of the three-storey house and the door was locked. The key could not be found, but it was known that the pantry door key also unlocked the door to her room and this was used to gain entry.

The shutters at the windows were closed and the room was in darkness but when they were opened, the corpse of Jessie McPherson was revealed lying on the floor. Her upper body was covered with a carpet but she was naked from the waist down. John senior rushed to the home of Dr William Watson, who, minutes later, was kneeling at the side of the body. He put his finger on her hip and declared, 'Quite cold, she's been dead for some time.'

A post-mortem was performed in the house the next day by Dr George McDonald and the police surgeon, Dr Joseph Fleming, who believed that the extensive injuries were caused by a cleaver or similar implement. Her shoulders, hands and arms were cut and bruised and these were thought to be defensive wounds. The most serious injuries were to her head and face and she was badly disfigured. Her jaw was shattered and her brain exposed in several places. More than twenty injuries had been inflicted by her killer while standing over her as she lay face-down on the floor, for there were several lacerations to the back of her neck. Her right ear was almost sliced off and the doctors concluded that there had been a relatively lengthy

'Her right ear was almost sliced off'

struggle, which they suggested meant the perpetrator was probably quite weak and may have been either a woman or an elderly man.

There were bloodstains on the kitchen door and mat and leading out of the kitchen there were streaks of blood along the length of the lobby, although an attempt had been made to clean them up. These indicated that Jessie met her death in the kitchen, after which her body was dragged to her bedroom, where it was discovered. Close to the body, there were three bare footprints in the blood and the floorboards on which the impressions had been left were removed and examined by Dr McLeod.

The victim's best clothes were missing from her wardrobe and a number of silver spoons and ladles had been taken from the dining room sideboard, but the police were not convinced that robbery was the motive for the crime. They believed that the killer was hoping to disguise the real reason and initially they were convinced the murderer was James Fleming, whose account of what had happened over the weekend was considered to be highly implausible. He claimed to have been woken up by loud screams at four o'clock on Saturday morning and believing a group of drunken revellers to be responsible, he went back to sleep without investigating further. He could not explain why, despite hearing the screams, he had not thought it possible they were linked in some way to the fact that his servant was missing, which became obvious a few hours later with the discovery of the bloodstains in the house, clear signs that a struggle had taken place. On 9 July, James was arrested and subjected to a four-hour examination by the Sheriff, after which he was charged with the murder and held in custody.

A description of the missing silver was circulated, which led to pawnbroker Robert Lundie visiting the police with the items. He told them that a woman who gave the name Mary McDonald and her address as 5 St Vincent Street visited his shop at noon on Saturday 5 July and had pawned the items for £6 and fifteen shillings. She told Robert she was there on behalf of her mistress, who needed the cash to pay the rent. Needless to say, the police found that these details were false.

However, the police learnt that the description of the mystery woman matched that of a former servant in the Fleming household, who had remained on friendly terms with the dead woman. She was twenty-eight-year-old Jessie McLachlan, who lived with her husband James, a sailor, at 182 Broomielaw Road and both were detained on 14 July and examined by the sheriff. James was second mate on a steamship and was able to prove he was on board his ship in the Irish Sea over the weekend the crime was committed and was released. However, his wife was unable to provide a satisfactory explanation of her whereabouts at the relevant time and was kept in custody pending further enquiries.

The detained woman had worked as a servant for the Flemings for two years, until she left in September 1857, after which she remained friends with the deceased and they met often. She told the police that she last saw her friend on the evening of 28 June and knew nothing of her murder.

She claimed to have visited another friend, Christina Fraser, on the night of Friday the 4th and was home by 11.15 p.m. She slept, as she always did, in the same bed as her three-year-old son and woke at seven o'clock the next morning. She continued by saying that James Fleming had brought the silver to her home early on Friday and asked her to pawn it on his behalf. He told her he needed the cash for a trip to the Highlands and did not want to visit the bank or to ask his son for the money. She pawned the items on the Saturday, giving false details as he had instructed her to do, and he later paid her for her trouble.

Her version of events, however, was found to be untrue. Her friend Christina had in fact visited Jessie at her home on Broomielaw Road, where she remained until ten o'clock, when they left the house together before going their separate ways a few minutes later. The McLachlans' lodger, Margaret Campbell, was interviewed and she confirmed that her landlady did not return home until nine o'clock on Saturday morning. She knew her landlady was not at home during the night because her three-year-old son cried out for his mother in the early hours and when Margaret went to the bedroom to comfort him she realised his mother was absent. Later, Margaret had to let her in because Jessie had forgotten her key. She also noticed that she was wearing a different dress to that which she was wearing when she left the previous evening. The police believed this dress was the property of the dead woman.

The case against Jessie McLachlan was strengthened when her husband approached the police with more incriminating information. He claimed to have a guilty conscience but it is likely that he feared becoming implicated in the crime, which, by this time, he may have believed his wife to be guilty of. He told the police about a box containing some of the dead woman's clothes, which his wife asked him to take to his sister's home in Greenock a few days after the murder. Hitherto, the detained woman had claimed not to have possessed any of the victim's clothing at any time, but when advised of her husband's statement, she admitted that they did belong to Jessie McPherson, who gave them to her to have altered and dyed. When their description appeared in the press, she panicked and asked her husband to dispose of them.

More of the dead woman's clothes were discovered in undergrowth near Hamilton and the police were confident they were able to link them to Jessie McLachlan. Nine local residents came forward following press reports and identified her as having been in the locality on 8 July, carrying items of clothing, and all claimed to have spoken to her. The suspect admitted she had been in Hamilton on the 8th but denied any knowledge of the hidden clothing and insisted the clothes she was seen with were her husband's and not Jessie McPherson's. Furthermore, the police believed their suspect could be placed at the crime scene. Dr McLeod compared her footprints with those found in the blood at Sandyford Place. To make the comparison, she was required to place her feet in bullock's blood, after which she made an impression on a piece of wood. As far as the doctor and the police were concerned they were identical, thus strengthening the case against her.

Eight days after his arrest, James Fleming was released. The police believed that, despite his protestations of innocence, it was highly probable that he played some role in the crime. However, Jessie McLachlan was thought to be the actual killer and the elderly man's willingness to testify for the prosecution, although not admitting to any involvement himself, was considered to be a price worth paying for her conviction.

Jessie McLachlan's trial opened on Wednesday 17 September before Lord Deas and she pleaded not guilty to murder and robbery, with an unusual addition. She told the court that the person responsible for the murder was the prosecution's main witness, James Fleming, who killed the unfortunate woman after she refused to give in to his sexual advances, or after she threatened to accuse him of such behaviour. Testimony was given by witnesses regarding the accused woman's movements over the weekend in question, the silver plate, the dead woman's clothing, and the footprints found at the scene.

In her defence, it was claimed that Jessie McLachlan's lodger was simply wrong when she said that Jessie had stayed out all of the Friday night until early on Saturday morning, and that at no time was she wearing anybody else's dress. The footprint evidence was dismissed as it had not been shown beyond all reasonable doubt that they belonged to those of the accused. As for the clothes found in Hamilton, the defence claimed it had not been shown conclusively that they belonged to the dead woman and besides, their client denied any knowledge of them. If they were Jessie McPherson's, it was suggested that it was more likely that James Fleming had arranged for them to be disposed of in order to mislead the police into believing a robber took them, thereby concealing the real motive for the murder. Their client was able to demonstrate that she had come into possession of some of Jessie McPherson's clothes legitimately. The accused admitted to the police that she pawned the silver plate, but that this was done at the request of James Fleming. It was argued that her husband had a good job and she was not desperate for money; it was therefore ludicrous for the Crown to suggest that robbery was the motive for the crime.

James Fleming began his evidence by giving his version of events of Friday 4 July. He breakfasted with his son and grandson and after they left for the weekend, he walked into the town centre, leaving Jessie McPherson alone in the house. He did not see her again until eight o'clock that night, when he ate the supper she had cooked for him. He read a newspaper and retired to his bed at 9.30 p.m. She remained in the kitchen and that was the last time he saw her alive. It was at some time between four and five o'clock the following morning that he was woken up by the screams, which he thought came from outside the house, and went back to sleep.

On Saturday morning, he lay in bed waiting for Jessie to bring him his porridge, which she normally did at the weekend. However, she failed to do so and at nine o'clock he knocked on her bedroom door, which was locked, and there was no response. He acknowledged that he noticed spots of blood on a clean shirt he had left in the kitchen but did not investigate the matter at the time and forgot about it. There was no sign of Jessie throughout Saturday and at seven in the evening, her friend Andrew Darnley called at the house, only to be told she was not at home. There was no sign of the missing woman on Sunday and Andrew Darnley made another fruitless call. Andrew expressed his concerns but James Fleming still took no action to discover what might have happened to his servant.

As he was being cross-examined, the defence barrister clearly found it difficult to disguise his incredulity at James's account of what took place at Sandyford Place that weekend. How could he fail to take any action to discover what had happened to his missing servant? How could he not have realised that attempts had been made to clean up traces of blood in the kitchen? Why did he not find it unusual to see spots of blood on his recently washed shirt? It was also reported by the milkman that early on the Saturday morning, James Fleming had for the first time opened the door to him; this, it was argued, was because he realised there would be no servant available to do so as he knew at this stage that Jessie McPherson was dead.

An important defence witness was Mary Fulton, who knew both the victim and the accused and who was able to say categorically that the former had recently told her that the woman in the dock was her dearest friend. She also told of meeting Jessie McPherson on 28 June while out shopping, a few days before she met her death. She looked unwell and said, 'I do not feel happy or comfortable with old Mr Fleming for he is actually an old wretch and an old devil.' She added that she was too embarrassed to go into more detail at the time because Mary's husband was with her. Corroboration was added by the testimony of the dead woman's stepsister, who had also heard her complain of the elderly man's behaviour towards her. The inference was obvious; James Fleming committed the crime following her repeated refusal to submit to his sexual demands. When the defence barrister returned to his seat after concluding the case on behalf of the accused, there was loud applause from the public gallery.

Nevertheless, the jury was not persuaded and after an absence of just fifteen minutes returned with a guilty verdict. Before sentence could be passed, the now convicted murderer asked if a written statement, which she had prepared for such an eventuality, could be read out. Lord Deas agreed and his clerk spent the next forty minutes reading it to a hushed court.

It opened by describing the very close friendship she enjoyed with Jessie McPherson and of her frequent visits to see her at Sandyford Place. These usually took place on Friday nights after 9.30 p.m., by which time most of the Fleming family had left for the coast and James was in bed. On 4 July, she arrived to find her friend and the old man sitting by the kitchen fire. He knew the visitor from her time as a servant in the household and seemed delighted to see her. He opened a bottle of whisky and when that was empty he gave Jessie McLachlan one shilling and two pence with which to buy more from a nearby shop.

She was absent for a few minutes only and on her return she found her friend lying on the laundry floor in a large pool of blood, groaning loudly. There was a long cut across her nose and forehead, and she was insensible. Fleming refused to call for a doctor, saying she would soon recover. They put her to bed but the bleeding continued. Jessie McPherson slept for two hours and when she woke up she seemed to have improved and was able to speak. She told the accused that after she had left to buy the whisky, she and Fleming argued and he attacked her with a cleaver. She also recounted details of an incident the previous week when he entered her bedroom and attempted to sexually molest her. She protested and he left the room and apologised later at breakfast before offering her money not to tell anyone of his behaviour towards her.

Her friend continued by telling of her plans to travel to Australia and of her decision to extract as much money as she could from Fleming. She was growing tired but before falling asleep said she had decided not to report him to the police for this assault but was determined to make him pay even more. Later, when confronted, Fleming appeared to be contrite and promised to fund the injured woman's move to Australia and, if Jessie McLachlan swore on the Bible never to tell anyone about what she had learnt or witnessed, he would also provide her with enough money to buy a shop, enabling her to live comfortably for the rest of her life. She had done so and this was the major reason for the truth not emerging until now, as she did not want to break that oath.

The injured woman woke again at five o'clock on Saturday morning, by which time her condition had deteriorated. Jessie McLachlan attempted to leave the house to find a doctor but all the doors and windows were locked, preventing her from doing so. Suddenly, she heard a piercing scream coming from the kitchen. She rushed there and, to her horror, found the elderly man striking her friend repeatedly with the cleaver. There was nothing she could do to stop the attack and within a very short time Jessie McPherson was dead.

She now feared that her own life was in danger but Fleming assured her that he did not wish to harm her and that he would keep his promise to help her buy a shop. He told her, 'My life's in your power and your life is in my power.' In a panic she decided there was nothing she could do as it might well be thought that she had been a willing accomplice. She therefore helped to attempt cover up the crime by cleaning up the blood, which was on the walls, floor and clothing, which included James's shirt, as best she could. She also agreed to assist in disposing of the deceased's clothes and the silver plate, which was indeed an attempt to persuade the police that robbery was the motive.

She thus acknowledged that she was in the house when the murder was committed and had helped mislead the police into believing unknown robbers were responsible, but insisted her actions were due to a sense of panic. Lord Deas told her this account could not affect the death sentence he was obliged to pass. Nevertheless, she gained many sympathisers who believed she too had become a victim of a treacherous and evil man, who was prepared to allow an innocent woman to hang in his place. Others believed passionately that her statement was a pack of lies, constructed to fit in with the known facts, and that she was willing to see an elderly and innocent man suffer for her heinous crime.

This division of opinion was evidenced by the two following letters, which appeared in the *Dundee Courier* on 25 September 1862:

Sir, Referring to that awful and mysterious murder committed in Glasgow and the issue of the trial, resulting in the sentence of death on Mrs McLachlan, I beg of you if there has been any means taken in Dundee to memorialise the Secretary of State to get that sentence reversed and you would oblige a reader of your paper and a believer in the innocence of Mrs McLachlan.

A. NOVICE

An opposing view was expressed in a second letter:

Sir, I hope the people of Dundee will not be misled by a morbid and mistaken sympathy into an attempt to defeat the ends of justice by getting up a memorial on behalf of that wretched criminal on the grounds that any measure of credibility can be attached to her statement at the conclusion of the trial. It is clear to me that she has not only savagely murdered Jessie McPherson, but has attempted a second murder, worse than the first, in laying the guilt of her own bloody deed on an innocent man. Her own confession and the most favourable view that can be taken of her case, leaves her in the position of one who was really art and part in the murder in as much as she agreed for a paltry bribe to conceal what she had witnessed. What motive had she to screen old Fleming at such imminent risk to herself? Was it the fear of being implicated in the crime? Then why did she not give the true story when she found herself implicated? It is inconceivable that when she was charged with a crime which she had seen another commit, had she been really innocent, she would not have told what she had seen, instead of confirming the crime against herself by inventing impossible lies. She has, in so far, shown herself to be a person capable of such a crime. Her conduct, on her own confession, affords a strong presumption that, even supposing Fleming to have had a hand in it, she was more than a mere innocent witness of it. Now, there is so much presumption against the old man. It cannot be said of him that if, according to his own confession, he did so much, it may be presumed that he did the whole deed. The statement of the prisoner has indeed a startling appearance of truth, from the circumstantiality and minuteness of detail and its seeming correspondence with the facts brought out in the evidence ... I am yours A.

Opinion would continue to be divided but support for Fleming wavered when it became known that he was the father of a nine-year-old daughter. The girl's mother, who had been a servant in the Flemings' household, died in childbirth. Across Glasgow, 'Hang Old Fleming' was daubed on walls and many hundreds of Jessie's supporters signed petitions in her support. A mass meeting took place in the City Hall on the night of 29 September at which a resolution was passed urging Sir George Grey, the Home Secretary, to order further enquiries be made into the case and in the meantime grant Jessie a respite. A similar meeting was held that night in Edinburgh's Upper Queen Street Hall, at which a great deal of support was also shown for the convicted woman.

The pressure on the government intensified, which led to her execution, scheduled to take place on 11 October, being postponed. Eventually, on 6 November, she was advised that her sentence had been commuted to penal servitude for life. Five days later she was transferred to the prison at Perth, where she spent the next fifteen years. At the end of November her husband left their son with a sister-in-law and emigrated.

Jessie was due to be released in late 1876 but she assaulted a prison officer and it was not until 5 October 1877 that she walked out of gaol a free woman. She took temporary lodgings in Greenock before travelling abroad. She died on 1 January 1899 in Port Huron, America, still protesting her innocence. This was many years after the death of James Fleming, who was never charged with an offence related to the death of Jessie McPherson.

THE KILLER DOCTOR

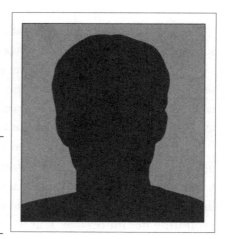

Suspect:	Dr Edward William Pritchard
Age:	39
Crime:	Murder

When Dr Edward William Pritchard's wife, Mary Jane, was taken ill in December 1864, he diagnosed gastric fever. As the weeks passed she showed no signs of recovering her health and her mother, Jane Taylor, therefore travelled from her home in Edinburgh to help with the care of her daughter, son-in-law and their five children at 131 Sauchiehall Street in Glasgow.

Unfortunately, not long after she arrived, seventy-one-year-old Mrs Taylor also became ill and on Saturday, 25 February 1865, she died. Her son, who was also a doctor, travelled to Glasgow as soon as he heard the sad news and said he was not surprised given his mother's age and poor health. She was being treated by Dr Paterson but the Registrar, James Struthers, asked Dr Pritchard to complete the death certificate, on which he gave apoplexy as the cause of death. The body was returned to Edinburgh and Mrs Taylor was buried in the Grange Cemetery. Dr Pritchard was present at the burial and afterwards returned home to resume caring for his wife.

There was no improvement in Mary Jane's condition, despite what the couple's friends described as his wonderful and loving care of her. She was also seen by his colleagues, Dr Gardiner, Dr Cowan and her brother, but she could not be saved and died on 17 March, just three weeks after her mother. Her husband signed the death certificate and her body was taken to Edinburgh, where she was buried alongside her mother. On the day of her death, Dr Pritchard wrote the following entry in his diary:

Died here at one a.m. Mary Jane, my own beloved wife, aged thirty-eight years; no torment surrounded her bedside, but, like a calm, peaceful Lamb of God, passed Minnie away. May God and Jesus, Holy Ghost, one in three, welcome Minnie. Prayer on prayer till mine be o'er, everlasting love. Save us Lord, for thy dear Son.

Although the two deaths were not thought suspicious, an anonymous informant contacted the police suggesting they should be investigated more thoroughly. Dr Pritchard was subsequently interviewed and enquiries were also made into his background. Doubts were raised about his qualifications, especially when it was learnt that he studied for his degree in medicine at a German University. However, he had begun his studies at King's College, London in 1846 and was qualified to practice medicine in the United Kingdom. He served as a surgeon in the Royal Navy in the Pacific and Mediterranean but left the service when his ship was ordered to the Africa Station.

He had read papers at a number of prestigious venues including those on Longevity, Normal Sleep, and Cholera at the King's College Medical Society between 1844 and 1846. Among his published works were *On the Guaco Plant, Observations on Filey as a Watering Place, Tobacco – Its use and Abuse* and *Tincture of Guaco in Gout*. After leaving the navy he set up his practice in Hunmanby and, later, in Filey. The police discovered that he left Yorkshire to come to Scotland due to rumours regarding his alleged immoral behaviour.

Following the press reports of Dr Pritchard's questioning by the Glasgow police, Jessie Nabb came forward with more information regarding his somewhat dubious past. She once worked as a servant for the Pritchards and had formed a close bond with her late mistress. Jessie told of an improper relationship between the doctor and another housemaid, seventeen-year-old Mary McLeod. Jessie believed the adulterous affair had been going on for three years and she was convinced that when the young servant was absent due to ill health, she was in fact recovering from an abortion.

Jessie also recalled an occasion when Mrs Pritchard told her of discovering her husband and Mary in an apparently compromising situation, but he managed to persuade her that nothing untoward had occurred.

She believed him and the young servant was allowed to keep her job. Later, Mary boasted to Jessie that the affair was continuing and that if anything happened to Mrs Pritchard, she would step into her shoes. Jessie informed Mrs Pritchard of these comments but her mistress replied, 'Mary is given to telling stories and should not be believed in everything she says.' Mary McLeod was questioned by the police and admitted that she and Dr Pritchard had been having an affair. However, she claimed to know nothing of a plot to murder his wife and was released without charge.

The police, however, now had two possible motives for the murders. Firstly, it was thought Dr Pritchard intended ridding himself of his wife, leaving him free to marry his young lover. Secondly, it was learnt that the doctor was experiencing financial difficulties and although there were no insurance policies on the lives of either his wife or her mother naming him as a beneficiary, he did stand to gain from their deaths. In her will, Mrs Taylor left £2,000 to her daughter and it was stipulated that should Mary Jane predecease her husband, two trustees were to ensure that the money was used solely for the benefit of the children. However, despite this safeguard it was believed that the doctor would have anticipated having control over how the money was spent. Enquiries made at the Clydesdale Bank revealed that his account was overdrawn and, furthermore, he had recently insured his own life for £1,500, against which he had borrowed £255. It also emerged that his mother-in-law had loaned him £500 with which to purchase the Sauchiehall Street premises, and with her death he no longer had to continue making the repayments on the loan.

Another servant, Mary Paterson, recalled Mrs Taylor telling her that she was suspicious of the food the doctor was giving to her daughter and she took on the responsibility of preparing her meals. The decision of his mother-in-law to come and help care for her daughter put at risk his plan of murdering Mary Jane slowly and, on learning of her suspicions about the food, he decided to dispose of her first. Although her murder was not part of his original plan, it did provide unexpected financial benefits. Once she was out of the way, he was free to continue with his scheme to murder his wife.

Given the absence of physical injuries on the women's bodies, it was believed that Pritchard poisoned both of his victims. Enquiries were made locally and led the police to the shop of John Curry, from whom they learnt that Dr Pritchard had bought significant amounts of morphine and aconite during February and March. John Campbell, manager of the Western Branch of the Glasgow Apothecaries Company, also revealed that for the past eight months the doctor had purchased large quantities of antimony, aconite, laudanum, digitalis and strychnine from him.

On the Monday before Mrs Pritchard died, Mary Paterson tasted a small piece of cheese prepared by the doctor for his wife and immediately experienced a severe burning sensation in her throat. Two days later, the doctor asked Mary to prepare an egg flip for her mistress, to which

'a severe burning sensation in her throat'

he added some 'sugar'. She took it to Mrs Pritchard, who refused to take it and when she put a little to her own lips, Mary felt a searing pain in her mouth after which she vomited. Catherine Latimer, another servant in the Pritchard household, described her mistress suffering severe pains throughout her body a number of times and on one occasion heard Mary Jane say to her husband, 'Don't cry, for if you do so you are a hypocrite.'

The bodies of both women were exhumed and post-mortems performed, but there was no immediately obvious cause of death. However, the contents of their stomachs were given to Dr Andrew Maclagan, Professor of Medical Jurisprudence at Edinburgh University, for chemical analysis. Large amounts of antimony were found in the organs of both women, far in excess of what would have been prescribed for any medical reasons. It was concluded that in the case of Mrs Pritchard it had been administered over a period of several months and that other poisons had also been fed to her. Her mother, however, had been poisoned over a much shorter timescale and it was concluded that she had been given massive amounts of antimony in tapioca and beer. Opium was also discovered, but not enough to have contributed to her death. She was known to have taken 'Battley's Sedative', which contained the drug, for medical purposes but it was determined she could not have died as a result of an accidental overdose of opium.

Dr Pritchard's trial, at which he entered not guilty pleas, was held in late June. An attempt was made to place responsibility for the crimes on the shoulders of Mary McLeod, but the doctor was found guilty and sentenced to death. Mary testified on behalf of the Crown and her evidence proved to be crucial in securing his conviction. She revealed that she had indeed become pregnant but told the court that she had suffered a miscarriage. When asked if Dr Pritchard had assisted in causing the miscarriage, the judge intervened, saying she should not answer as that would be a crime he was not charged with. Mary also stated that Pritchard had promised to marry her if his wife died and had even given her a ring. He also gave her a locket containing his photograph as a token of his love but following his arrest she had destroyed it. Under cross-examination by the prisoner's barrister she continued to deny any involvement in the murders in the strongest possible terms.

Dr Pritchad was found guilty of murder and on 11 July, while in gaol awaiting his execution, he confessed to the two murders but again implicated Mary McLeod. However, on the eve of his execution, he left the following letter:

I, Edward William Pritchard, in full possession of all my senses and understanding the awful position in which I am placed, do make free and open confession that the sentence pronounced upon me is just; that I am guilty of the death of my mother-in-law, Mrs Taylor and of my wife Mary Jane Pritchard; that I can assign no motive for the conduct which actuated me beyond a species of terrible madness and the use of ardent spirits.

I hereby freely and fully state that the confession made to the Reverend R. Soldham on the 11th day of this month was not true and I hereby confess that I alone and not Mary McLeod poisoned my wife in the way brought out at my trial. Mrs Taylor's death was caused according to the wording of the indictment.

It was hoped that he would confess to another murder he was suspected of having committed in May 1862, when his home in Berkley Terrace was destroyed by fire. The only occupant at the time was a young servant, Elizabeth McGirn, who was found burnt to death in the attic. Her death was thought suspicious at the time as it was proven that she had not moved as the flames engulfed her and it was believed that she must have been drugged before the fire started. However, no motive for her killing could be established and there was insufficient evidence to charge Dr Pritchard with any crime. The Caledonian Insurance Company, however, refused to pay the full amount of £700 at which the property was valued and Pritchard had to settle for less than a third of that amount. As he waited for his appointment with the hangman, he refused to admit his guilt of that murder.

The Pritchard case led to widespread concern regarding the matter of professional etiquette within the medical profession. This followed the revelation that Dr Paterson, who attended to Mrs Taylor in her final moments, suspected that she had been poisoned. As a result of his concern, he refused to sign a death certificate and wrote to James Struthers, the Registrar, explaining his reasons. This was why the Registrar had asked Dr Pritchard to issue a death certificate, which he was more than pleased to do. Many were bemused that Dr Paterson took no other action but he insisted he had fulfilled his professional obligations in writing to the Registrar. In defending himself, the Registrar pointed out that Dr Paterson could have proposed a post-mortem or that a second opinion be sought, but he did neither. Nevertheless, it was a widely held view that if something more had been done at the time, the murder of Mrs Pritchard might have been prevented.

Dr Pritchard was hanged on Friday 28 July at Glasgow before a crowd of 100,000 spectators. After his execution, the doctor's eldest daughter wrote to the authorities asking if it would be possible to have a lock of her father's hair. Her request was agreed to but the person given the task of obtaining it was too late, as his hair and beard had already been shaved off and burnt as the visiting magistrate had ordered. However, it was discovered that the executioner, William Calcraft, had taken some, no doubt intending to sell it later as a morbid souvenir. When asked to surrender some of it for the daughter he refused initially but was eventually persuaded to provide her with the lock she wanted so much.

CASE SEVENTEEN   1868

THE END OF AN ERA

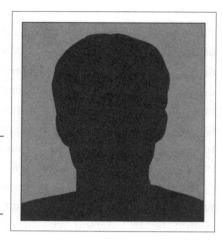

Suspect: Robert Smith
Age: 19
Crime: Murder

John Scott, a shoemaker by trade, lived with his wife and eleven children at Burnside Cottage, on the outskirts of the village of Cummertrees. The cottage also served as a shop from which groceries and household wares were sold. The Scotts purchased their stock in Annan, a little over three miles away and at eleven o'clock on the morning of Saturday, 1 February 1868, their eight-year-old daughter, Thomasina, was sent there to buy a few items needed for the shop.

Although it had rained earlier it was a clear morning and she was told that if the weather remained good she was to walk back, but if it began to rain she should catch the train, which would arrive in Cummertrees at ten minutes past four. Her mother handed ten shillings to the little girl with which to make the purchases and waved her off, not realising she would never see her daughter alive again.

Thomasina had walked about a mile when the rain began to pour down but she was close to Longfords Cottage, the home of farm worker Robert Crichton and his wife Jane. Robert was at work but the little girl was welcomed warmly by Jane – who knew her well – when she knocked on the door seeking shelter. Also in the cottage was nineteen-year-old Robert Smith, who made his living by whitewashing cottages in the district and if that work was scarce, as a farm labourer. He was a friend of the Crichtons and a regular visitor to their home. After the rain stopped, Thomasina set off once more for Annan, accompanied by Smith, who said he was heading in the same direction.

At some time between three and four o'clock that afternoon, Smith returned to Longford Cottage, where he found Jane on her knees, scouring the floor. Suddenly, she heard what she immediately recognised to be a gunshot, felt a tremendous blow to the side of her head, and realised that she had been shot. Smith had indeed shot her but had loaded the gun incorrectly, which saved her life. As she struggled to remain conscious, Smith began to beat her. He knew the layout of the cottage and dragged

'she struggled to remain conscious'

her out of the kitchen, which was visible from the road outside, into a more secluded room at the back. He stabbed her in the neck and attempted to strangle her with his bare hands. Jane put up a fierce struggle but could feel herself weakening and felt as though she was succumbing.

Suddenly, there was a loud banging at the front door, which startled her attacker. Smith made his way to the door, flung it open and rushed past two startled young men, who had stopped at the cottage to ask for a drink of water. They noticed blood on Smith's hands and clothes and on discovering the badly injured Jane, raised the alarm. She responded well to medical assistance, which required the removal of three pellets from her head, and was soon able to tell the police what had happened to her and who was responsible. Smith had meanwhile left the district but he would not remain at liberty for long.

As the search for Smith was beginning, the Scotts were becoming increasingly concerned as Thomasina had not returned home. She was not on the train that arrived in the village at ten minutes past four, which led her parents to send one of their other children to see if she was walking home along the Annan road. When it became clear she was not, a family friend travelled to Annan, where enquiries at the shops Thomasina would have called at revealed she had not done so. Realising she did not arrive in Annan, her parents became even more alarmed. Meanwhile, the news had reached Cummertrees of the murderous assault on Jane Crichton. Mr and Mrs Scott hurried to her cottage and learnt of their daughter's visit earlier in the day and that she had left with Smith, the wanted man.

Her father began a frantic search by torchlight and was joined by many of his worried neighbours. After three hours, at eleven o'clock that night, a group of searchers entered an area known locally as Crofthead's Plantation, in which they discovered the girl's body. Her purse, which had contained the ten shillings given to her by her mother, lay discarded and empty at her side. Bruises to her neck indicated that she was strangled manually and this was later confirmed at a post-mortem. Other distinct marks to her neck led to the conclusion that an unsuccessful attempt was made to hang her from the branch of a nearby tree. It was also revealed that Thomasina had been raped, meaning robbery and sexual gratification were the motives for the murder of the little girl. Smith was the obvious suspect and it was believed he returned to the cottage to kill Jane Crichton in order to prevent her from naming him as Thomasina's killer.

The wanted man was orphaned when his parents died eleven years earlier, after which he had been largely self-reliant. It was learnt that he was lodging at 35 Queensberry Street, Dumfries, where he was arrested on the Sunday morning. The print of a heavily nailed boot was found close to Thomasina's body and was a perfect match with one of Smith's, found in his room. He confessed almost immediately to rape, murder, robbery and attempted murder. He admitted using the ten shillings taken from Thomasina to buy a pistol at the shop of Mr Hamilton, an ironmonger in Annan, before returning to shoot Jane Crichton. As he was unable to load it properly he attempted to beat and strangle her and thought he had been successful in doing so when he was disturbed and ran from the cottage.

He was held in the gaol at Dumfries as he waited for his trial to start, and on 24 February he wrote the following letter to his surviving victim:

Dear Jane Crichton,

I write you a few lines to let you know that I am well at present, hoping this will find you and all your family enjoying the good health, thank God for it. Dear Jane, I was a great blackguard when I could have taken away the young girl's life so most wickedly and then to come and boldly to your house again and then to fire a pistol at you and then to seize you by the throat for to choke you and then to take my knife and to try and cut your throat. If the Lord had not been merciful to you and saved your life – if it had been the other way round – it would have been a most horrible case for me to have done. But I thank God that he was merciful to do so to you. Dear Jane, you and your friends may be mad at me for it, but you can tell them all that it is against me that I would let any of them do anything to me now after I have seen it, for the Lord's hand is mightier than the Devil's, for the Lord saved your life that day, but I heard you were getting better for I hope that when you receive this you will be all better and going about again the same as usual. Dear Jane, I had many a thought of taking away your life. I wanted to rob your house and I did not know how to do it until that day the young girl came in. I thought if I had a pistol I could soon have taken your life away. I thought it was a good job when I got the ten shillings from the young girl and got the pistol. I thought it was all right for I thought that the shot would have ended your days too, and then, there would not have been any could have informed the police bout me and I would have got clear from the hands of men in the meantime. But the Lord proved merciful to me and you. But the young girl is resting in the grave and I will be there to soon and I well deserve it and something far worse. Dear Jane, the Lord was great to save your life, the Devil is great but thanks be to God for he is greater than the Devil. Dear Jane, I have no more to say at present. Give my kind love to all the neighbours, to your son John and all the men and tell them that I will not see none of them on Earth but I trust in God that I will see you and yours and them in heaven.

Robert Smith. My address is Dumfries County Prison. Write soon, Dear Jane and let me know how you are now.

Despite his earlier statement to the police and the contents of his letter, Smith pleaded not guilty to all charges when his trial opened at the High Court in Dumfries on 21 April, claiming to have been insane at the time. Having heard all of the evidence, the jury retired for just seven minutes before finding him guilty of wilful murder. He was sentenced to death and the execution was arranged for Tuesday 12 May. William Calcraft was supposed to conduct the proceedings but a few days beforehand he wrote to the local council saying he was unavailable. Arrangements were quickly made to replace him with Thomas Askern of York, who demanded a fee of twenty guineas.

It was a wet and miserable morning when, at eight o'clock, the condemned prisoner walked up the steps of the gallows. The appalling weather meant there was only a small crowd, estimated to number less than 400, to witness Scotland's last public execution.

CASE EIGHTEEN   1868

TRULY MAD OR SIMPLY BAD?

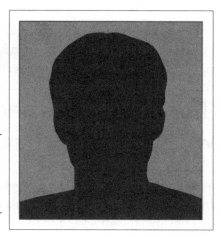

Suspect: William Cargill
Age: 35
Crime: Murder

It was a few minutes to four o'clock on the afternoon of Thursday, 10 September 1868 when Ann Swankie called at Jean Vannet's public house on Ladybridge Street in Arbroath and asked for a drink of water for herself and her two daughters, Jean and five-year-old Ann. Mrs Vannet was more than pleased to give them the water and the two women chatted at the door for a few minutes with fisherman Thomas Cargill. They became alarmed, however, on hearing a woman's voice cry out, 'Oh dear, it's done now.' Immediately, Ann realised that little Ann was no longer standing at her side.

A few feet away there was an open door which led to a back room, towards which Ann hurried. Inside, she was appalled to see her daughter being beaten in a most savage manner by a man wielding a poker. Thomas Cargill had to restrain the desperate mother as the man turned towards her and screamed, 'Come forward now, I've done for her and I'll do for you!' Ann recognised the attacker as thirty-five-year-old William Cargill of Auchmithie, whose brother was married to her sister, although she scarcely knew him.

Several men had by this time heard the raised voices and rushed to the spot. The passage from the street to the room was too narrow for anyone to enter easily and stop the attacker, who was continuing to beat little Ann about the head, which was by now soaked in blood. The floor, walls and door of the room were also splattered with her blood and it was clear to everyone, except apparently her attacker, that she was dead.

When told what was happening, William Cargill's wife rushed to the room, which she and her husband were renting, but she was unable to persuade him to stop and he threatened to kill her also. One of the men

'The floor, walls and door of the room were also splattered with her blood'

standing helplessly at the door took a knife from his pocket and prepared to run inside, but he was restrained by the others. Another man threw his dog towards the attacker, but to no avail. Eventually, William began to tire and was disarmed before being dragged out into the street. He remained in a terrible rage and had to be carried by several men to the nearby police station, struggling violently all the way there.

A post-mortem was performed by Dr David Arratt, who found a major wound in the middle of the little girl's forehead and several other smaller ones. Her head was crushed almost to a pulp and a number of the skull's bones had been forced downwards into the brain. There were injuries to the rest of her body but the cause of death was given as brain damage due to the cumulative effects of the head injuries, which had been inflicted with the poker.

Dr Arratt was also asked to examine the arrested man at the police station as his strange behaviour following his arrest gave cause for concern. On his arrival, the prisoner was immediately handcuffed as he was in a highly agitated state and was foaming at the mouth, screaming, 'Kill me, hang me,' repeatedly. When he had calmed down, Superintendent John Milne attempted to question him, but the prisoner simply stared into the corner, in which he claimed he could see several little devils. The doctor was of the opinion that although Cargill had been drinking he was not drunk and added that William genuinely believed he could see the devils.

Cargill was detained overnight and was closely watched by Constable Alexander Jones. The prisoner slept very little and spoke to the officer several times, saying at one stage, 'They told me that the child was dead, but I know better. There is crying yet.' On another occasion he acknowledged he had killed Ann but later in the night claimed it was the Devil who had carried out the act. News of the killing spread throughout the community and during the early hours of the morning, a large group of children assembled outside William's cell window and mocked the prisoner with their chants and ribald comments.

During the night, Constable Jones noticed that Cargill was holding a folded piece of paper, which had not been spotted earlier. Reluctantly, the prisoner handed it to the officer and when unfolded it was revealed to be a cheque for £19. Cargill insisted it was a present from the Heavenly Father and as long as he had it in his possession he could do whatever he wanted. Therefore, he had permission to kill the Devil, who had appeared to him in the form of little Ann. If he had not done so, mankind would have been lost. He became very excited once more and would not settle until another piece of folded paper was handed to him, which he was told was the cheque.

In the morning, Cargill was calm but when told he was to be put on a train to Dundee at 11.10, he simply laughed and said he knew very well that he would be travelling on Noah's Ark. As he was being led out of the cell, he said, 'Come along father, there's room for us all.' It had been agreed that he would remain in Dundee Gaol until an assessment was made of his mental condition. However, the Arbroath police officers, after looking after him for the night, were convinced he was genuinely unhinged.

Cargill was examined by Dr Rorie, the medical superintendent at the Dundee Lunatic Asylum. The prisoner told him he knew he had killed a child but he was convinced at the time that he was killing the Devil. He explained that ten days earlier, Jesus had appeared at his bedside to say how happy he was with him as he was leading a more settled lifestyle, was working hard and had stopped drinking heavily. However, later that same day, the Devil appeared before him and attempted to lure him back into his old ways. On the morning of the attack, Cargill was on his boat, fishing for herrings, when the Devil reappeared but said nothing. That afternoon he was back at his lodgings and was convinced he could hear the Devil on the roof. He went outside to investigate and at that moment, the little girl approached him and he began his attack, convinced she was Satan.

During his interview with Dr Rorie, it became clear that Cargill had suffered two fits in his life. The first occurred three years earlier and the second only a few weeks before the killing. The doctor believed these were due to epilepsy and were a major contributory factor in his deteriorating mental health. The doctor felt that for the ten or so days leading up to the killing, the prisoner was labouring under a religious mania and therefore did not know right from wrong.

However, opinion regarding Cargill's mental state was divided. When he first arrived in the gaol at Dundee, he was put in a cell with another prisoner, who on the second night reported that Cargill attempted to strangle him for no apparent reason. William was put in chains but released from them ten days later when his condition had apparently improved. Within a short time, however, he threatened the prison chaplain during a visit to him in his cell. Interestingly, a group of prisoners approached the governor, Alexander McQueen, to say they had been observing him and believed he was sane and putting on an act so as to avoid probable execution. The governor was also of the opinion that his prisoner was feigning insanity and urged that he be put on trial for the murder of the little girl.

It was decided that the issue of his sanity should be put before a jury and Cargill's trial opened on 8 December 1868, with an admission by the accused that he was responsible for Ann's death but was insane at the time. The Crown insisted the accused was drunk when he committed the crime and was not mad. Evidence was heard from those who were at the scene of the attack and others who had been able to observe his behaviour since his arrest. Although the perpetrator and his victim were related by marriage, no rational motive could be found for what he did and the trial focused on the single issue of his sanity. Cargill's defence team brought witnesses to provide details of his strange behaviour in the past.

Mrs Brown, the post-mistress in Auchmithie, had known Cargill since he was a little boy and recalled one occasion some years earlier. She kept the keys to the village church and he had asked her for them. He unlocked the doors and began to sing revivalist hymns. When villagers came to see what was happening he urged them to go to their boats and carry them into the church. He also told them that he could see the sky in the south-west opening up to reveal the gates of Heaven.

Cargill's brother, James, had worked alongside him on their fishing boat, of which the accused was the captain, and he swore that William had often shouted out bizarre commands to the crew. On one occasion he began to shout, 'Glory, glory to the Lamb,' and ordered the crew to assemble at the mast. On this and on other such occasions, his crew obeyed him without hesitation as they feared what he might do if his orders were not carried out immediately. This fear was not groundless for William had once thrown one of his crew overboard for no apparent reason, but fortunately the man was rescued from the sea. On another trip, the skipper claimed to have seen Jesus walking on the sea, close to the boat. James also testified that his brother's behaviour deteriorated badly in the two days they were at sea immediately preceding the killing of Ann. Cargill was adamant that the Devil was tormenting him and as the boat approached the harbour at Arbroath, he told James that when the boat was sailing close to Bell Rock he made a Bible out of a mackerel.

At the conclusion of the defence's evidence, the Solicitor-General rose to his feet and addressed the court on behalf of the Crown. He said that having heard all of the evidence, he was satisfied that the prisoner had not acted when drunk and accepted he was insane. The judge agreed and directed the jury to return such a verdict. It was ordered that the prisoner was to be detained subject to Her Majesty's Pleasure and as he was being led from the dock, Cargill laughed heartily.

CASE NINETEEN 1869

ROBBERY AND MURDER AT THE BLACKHILL TOLL BAR

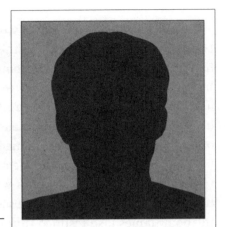

Suspect:	George Chalmers
Age:	45
Crime:	Murder

The Blackhill toll bar was situated in a deserted spot, 300 yards from the junction of the Comrie Road and that leading to Crieff. It was three quarters of a mile from Braco and several hundred yards from the nearest cottages. John Miller, a sixty-four-year-old bachelor in poor health, who required a stick with which to walk, was the keeper and he lived there alone. John was a well-known and popular character, who enjoyed passing the time of day with local people and strangers who were passing by. At 7.30 on the evening of Tuesday, 21 December 1869, shepherd Walter McLaren was walking home to Inverardoch and was invited inside by John. The two men sat by the fire and chatted as John carried on knitting a stocking. John checked his silver pocket watch and as it was almost eight o'clock, Walter left and continued on his way homewards.

At 6.30 the next morning, farm labourer Peter McLeish met Archibald McLaren, a miller, close to the toll bar and they both expressed surprise that John was not up and about as he usually was by that time. They knew he had been complaining of feeling ill for some days and decided to knock on the door to make sure he was well. There was no reply so they called on his sister, Mary Bayne, who lived in Braco, to advise her of their concerns. She and the men returned to the toll bar and tried unsuccessfully to force the door open. They therefore broke a window, which

Archibald climbed through. Inside, he discovered John's body; he had clearly been the victim of foul play.

He was lying on his back, his stick still firmly held in his left hand. There was a massive amount of blood at his head, which had frozen in the icy weather. When the police arrived they concluded that his killer had watched John from outside and waited for him to sit down to eat his supper, as there was a plate of uneaten bread and cheese

'There was a massive amount of blood at his head'

together with a glass of porter on the table. The killer had then probably entered quietly and a post-mortem performed by William Hutton Forrest of Stirling confirmed that his attacker struck John three fierce blows across the back of the head with a crowbar which lay at the side of the body. Great force was used and the first strike had probably been enough to kill him.

There was little doubt that robbery was the motive for the crime. John was known to be careful with his money and was rumoured to be very well off. However, he kept his money in the bank and it was believed the murderer would have only found that day's takings from the toll bar, which, it was estimated, would have been about £1. John's silver pocket watch and chain had been ripped from his waistcoat and the cottage had been ransacked before the killer left, locking the door behind him and throwing the key into an overgrown part of the garden, where it was found by the police.

The officers investigating the crime received several reports of three suspicious-looking tramps seen in the vicinity of the toll bar earlier in the day of the murder. Their descriptions were circulated throughout the district, which led to the arrests of two men the next day at a lodging house in Crieff and, a few hours later, their companion was detained in Comrie. They were questioned by Sheriff Graham in Dunblane but they were able to convince the authorities of their innocence and all three were released without charge.

Another sighting of a tramp in the vicinity of the toll bar on the afternoon of the murder was reported by Braco shoemaker John Dewar. The solitary vagrant was described as being a short man with a curved back who walked with a limp and spoke with a stutter. A search was made but there was no sign of the man, who was identified as George Chalmers. He had been released from Alloa Gaol the day before the murder after serving a sentence for a public order offence.

Five months after John's murder, Constable Edward Billington stopped and questioned a suspicious-looking character in Dundee, who explained that he was on his way to Arbroath. The officer had no reason to detain the man and allowed him to continue on his way. Back at the police station, the constable mentioned the encounter to his sergeant, who, from the description of the man, believed it was similar to that of Chalmers. A search was begun of the area but there was no sign of him.

Constable Billington was annoyed with himself for allowing the suspect to escape from his grasp and when he came off duty at six o'clock the next morning he opted not go to bed as he normally did. He changed into plain clothes and set off towards Arbroath in pursuit of the man. Eventually, he caught up with his prey and arrested him on suspicion of the murder at Blackhill toll bar. When interviewed at the police station, the detained man acknowledged that he was George Chalmers but denied all knowledge of the crime. He insisted that following his release from prison, he had travelled to Edinburgh, where he remained until early January. He then made his way to Glasgow and from there to England, where he had spent the last three months.

The time that had elapsed since the killing was not wasted by the police, who were able to amass a good deal of evidence which incriminated Chalmers. It was realised a few days after the murder that some of the clothes found at the scene did not belong to the dead man. It also became clear that some of John's clothes were missing. The inference was clear: the killer abandoned his own threadbare clothes at the murder scene and changed into those belonging to the dead man. The killer's clothes found at the toll bar included a coat, a pair of trousers and a vest, in the pockets of which were discovered an awl, a pair of scissors, a small knife and two pipes. When arrested, Chalmers was found to be in possession of a pawn ticket for the sum of two shillings, issued to a man giving the name John Smith in November 1869, and Falkirk pawnbroker George Barr was able to identify Chalmers as the man who had used that name when he visited his premises.

Constable John Robertson, who arrested Chalmers in Alloa for the public order offence which led to his brief stay in gaol, was interviewed together with William Wallace, a prison warder who knew Chalmers. Both confirmed that they had seen the suspect wearing the clothing abandoned at the toll bar when arrested for the public order matter and when released on the day before the murder was committed. When arrested on suspicion of the murder, Chalmers was not wearing the victim's grey tweeds, boots and shirt taken by the killer, but the police believed he had probably sold those and they considered there was more than enough evidence to link him to the crime.

The suspect was forty-five years old and was a native of Fraserburgh. For many years he had used the alias James Wilson to avoid detection after stealing a great deal of money belonging to a relative some years earlier. He had worked as a cobbler, farm labourer and as a crewman aboard whalers. He would also sing on the streets and in public houses to earn money and, of course, he regularly turned to crime to supplement his income.

His trial opened at the Perth Circuit Court on Tuesday, 6 September 1870, at which he pleaded not guilty. He claimed to have been nowhere near the crime scene, as he had slept for two nights in a shed at a Bannockburn pit following his release from prison. William Muirhead, an employee at the pit, was called by the defence and he confirmed that Chalmers did have permission to sleep there at about that time. However, under cross-examination he was unable to give the precise dates Chalmers had stayed at the pit.

As for the abandoned clothes and other items such as the awl, which the Crown claimed belonged to Chalmers for use when he found casual work when on the tramp, he denied they were his. He also stated that he had given away or bartered the clothes he was wearing when released from gaol, but could not give the names of those to whom he had handed them over.

The jury found Chalmers guilty by a majority of thirteen to two and he was ordered to be held in the condemned cell at Perth Prison and fed on bread and water until 4 October, the date set for his execution. There was little support for a reprieve and on the eve of his hanging he wrote the following letter to his sister:

My Dear Sister,

I received both your letters; the first was read to me by the governor of the prison and the last one by Sheriff Barclay. And oh I felt very sad when listening to your kind and faithful words, while tears ran down my cheeks as I know they are the last letters I will get from you. I confess with sorrow that I have been a most wicked man for the past twelve years. I disobeyed all the good counsel of our dear father and mother.

I left my home and took to a wandering life, which led me into every kind of evil company and which I do now bitterly regret.

Oh my dear sister, strong drink has been my ruin, it has been the cause of all my troubles. Oh that I had taken your many advices and kept free from that accursed drink. It has brought thousands of men and women to shame and misery and so it has brought me. I now see the folly of all my sinful ways and what my reckless life has brought me to.

I feel thankful to the Rev Mr Fleming, the Rev Dr Manson, Sheriff Barclay and also to the Chaplain of the Prison for all their Christian labours on my behalf.

I have also to thank the Governor of the prison as well as all the other prison officers, for their uniform kindness to me while here.

My dear sister, I wish you would allow this letter to be made public after my death for the benefit of my fellow creatures, that they may take warning from my sinful and profligate life and its melancholy end.

So farewell my dear sister, while I remain your loving but unfortunate brother.

George Chalmers.

P.S. I must add my thanks to my counsel and agents, who did all they could for me.

This was the first execution in Scotland to be carried out within the prison walls and out of view of the public. Nevertheless, an element of ritual was retained. The Lord Provost and local magistrates assembled at the Town Hall before walking in a solemn procession to the prison, where 200 people had gathered at the gates. The official party was met by the Sheriff, who handed the death warrant to the Lord Provost.

The dignitaries proceeded to the condemned cell where prayers were read out. When asked if he wished to make a confession, Chalmers declined to do so. The hangman, William Calcraft, entered the cell and pinioned the prisoner before escorting him to the gallows. As the white cap was being pulled down over his face he uttered his final words, 'Goodbye to you all. Thank God. I am innocent.'

The following month, Constable Billington was presented with a reward of £50 for the initiative he had demonstrated in capturing Chalmers.

MURDERED
BY HER PIMP

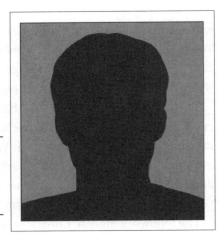

Suspect:	William Cunningham
Age:	Unknown
Crime:	Murder

William Cunningham was a shoemaker by trade but in the late 1860s he met Julia McLean, a prostitute, and very soon afterwards he chose the easier life of a pimp living off his paramour's earnings. In early 1870, they were renting a squalid, single ground-floor room at 19 Broadoak Close off High Street in Glasgow.

Cunningham was a violent man who subjected Julia to regular beatings and on 21 January she arrived in a distressed state at the home of her sister, Mary, telling her, 'Oh Mary, I had to run for my life. William threw a stool at me and if I had not stooped it would have split my skull.' Evidence of the assault was already visible as Mary could see a bruise on the side of her sister's head and another close to her eye. Julia stayed the night with Mary but returned to Cunningham the next morning, ignoring her sister's desperate pleas not to do so.

Mary's fears were well-founded, for the following week Julia was lying badly injured in the Royal Infirmary. At two o'clock on the afternoon of Saturday 29 January, she was discovered on a piece of waste ground near to her lodgings, moaning and bleeding from her chest. Medical student James Wall was on hand to provide emergency treatment to three stab wounds. She was carried to her room, where she told neighbour Margaret Paterson that Cunningham was responsible for her injures, but adding that she would not press charges. Indeed, only a few minutes later when Dr McGill, who was treating her wounds, asked who had attacked her, she replied that she did not know.

Nevertheless, Cunningham was arrested a short time later as he drank in William Wright's spirits bar in North Albion Street, no more than 20 yards from where Julia was discovered. There was no blood on

'moaning and bleeding from her chest'

his clothes or his hands and when told the reason for being detained he simply said, 'Nonsense.' On being charged with wounding her, he broke down and began to cry, saying he would rather harm himself than his beloved Julia.

During a visit to see her sister in hospital, Mary asked Julia directly if Cunningham was responsible for her wounds, to which she replied, 'Yes, he is a cruel man and he will suffer for it,' adding that the stabbing followed an argument, the reason for which she did not explain. However, when interviewed by the police, Julia was more circumspect, telling them she was very drunk at the time; others were present and as she had no clear memory of events one of those might have stabbed her.

Initially, Julia made excellent progress and was expected to survive her ordeal. Sadly, this proved not to be the case and her condition deteriorated rapidly, resulting in her death on the following Saturday. A post-mortem was performed by Dr Moore, the Medical Legal Examiner for the Lower Ward of Lanarkshire, assisted by Dr Donald Dewar. They reported that the three stab wounds were inflicted with great force and with an extremely sharp knife. One was to her right hand, another to her left arm, and the third and fatal wound had entered her left breast and penetrated her heart. Despite their efforts, the police were unable to find the weapon used to murder Julia and although her account was somewhat equivocal, Cunningham was brought to trial.

The trial took place on Monday 7 March and lasted for six hours. Two of the Crown's most important witnesses were Margaret Barr and George King. Margaret was a prostitute who had been staying with the accused and her friend Julia for several weeks. She told the court that on the night of Friday 28 January, she and Julia went out looking for business. They were drinking heavily and at eleven o'clock Margaret met George King, a sailor on shore leave. He was dining with his brother on

Sauchiehall Street but returned to the room on Broadoak Close, where he and Margaret went to bed together.

Margaret and George woke the next morning at seven o'clock to find Cunningham and Julia sitting by the fire. Nobody had enough money with which to buy more whisky so George handed his coat and waistcoat to Cunningham to pawn and to purchase more alcohol with any cash he was able to raise for them. Cunningham left with Julia and they returned with a bottle of whisky, which was emptied within a short time. George and Margaret returned to bed but awoke some time later to find Cunningham beating Julia.

George was able to separate them but they soon began to argue once more and after Cunningham struck her a particularly violent blow, George grabbed him and threw him out of the room. Cunningham next attempted to climb back in through a window but George was able to prevent him from doing so and, believing there would be no more trouble, the sailor went back to bed and was soon asleep once more.

His sleep was once again interrupted by Margaret's screams and, looking out into the street through the open door, George saw Julia lying on the ground looking extremely pale and could also see that her dress was saturated in blood. He ran for help and approached two police officers to whom he attempted to explain what had happened. However, he was so drunk that he was incapable of doing so and could not find his way back to the scene. He was arrested for being drunk and taken to the police station, where he gave a false name. When Julia was later found, he was held for two days as he was considered to be a suspect. His claims not to have been involved were eventually believed and he was released after explaining that he did not at first give his true name as he was embarrassed at being involved in the affair and hoped, foolishly, to hide his true identity.

George did not see Cunningham stab Julia but the attack was witnessed by Margaret, who was awake when he climbed through the window and regained entry to the room. She admitted that she was suffering from the effects of alcohol at the time but was adamant that she watched the accused walk calmly to a dresser, take a shoemaker's knife from a drawer and stab Julia three times before walking out of the room, still holding the knife. Julia was left gasping for breath but was able to follow him out of the door, before collapsing as soon as she was outside.

The defence barrister, Mr J. Gibson Starke, called no witnesses and relied on his closing speech to the jury, in which he reminded them that the only alleged eyewitness to the crime was a woman of low morals, who had been drinking heavily. He insisted that her unsupported testimony was not sufficient to convict his client and send him to the gallows. Furthermore, he argued that the murderer was more likely to have been George King.

The jury returned a guilty verdict after fifty-three minutes by a majority of eleven to four but added that they believed the crime was not premeditated and was committed under considerable provocation and, on those grounds, recommended him to the mercy of the court. However, the judge passed the mandatory death sentence and Cunningham's execution was set for 28 May.

That a man had been provoked by his wife or a woman he had been in an intimate relationship with was often put forward as a mitigating factor in the hope of the charge being reduced from murder to manslaughter or, as in this case, as a means of obtaining a reprieve. Provocation did not necessarily mean a response to an act of violence but could equally refer to an act of defiance, no matter how minor it might have been. In Cunningham's case, it seemed that the fact Julia had the temerity to argue with him, despite the cause not being known, was thought enough to save him from the noose.

The jury's recommendation for mercy and the absence of a majority verdict formed the basis of the petition sent to the Home Secretary asking for mercy. It was given added weight by the signature of Mr McHutcheon, the jury foreman. The petition was successful and on 17 March, Cunningham was advised that his sentence had been reduced to one of life imprisonment.

CASE TWENTY-ONE 1871

KLEPTOMANIA, MURDER AND ATTEMPTED SUICIDE

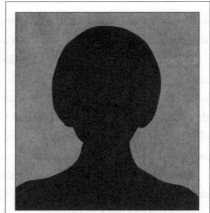

Suspect:	Eliza Clafton
Age:	25
Crime:	Murder

The trial of twenty-five-year-old Eliza Clafton opened in Edinburgh on Monday, 19 June 1871. There was standing room only in the courtroom, which reflected the massive interest in this tragic case. Eliza was placed in the dock and listened intently as the indictment was read out, charging her with the murders of her three-year-old-son Daniel and her daughter Isabella, who was eleven months of age at the time of her death, on Monday 6 March. The accused was said to have attempted to kill herself afterwards with the same razor she used to slash the children's throats, at the family home in Millbank near Stow.

When asked to enter her pleas, Eliza was still unable to speak because of the injuries to her throat and it was left to her representative to plead not guilty to all charges on the grounds that she was insane at the time. The accused was

'with the same razor she used to slash the children's throats'

the wife of weaver Samuel Clafton and the couple had been living in their home for five years. She had always impressed her neighbours as a quiet and sober young woman, devoted to her husband and a loving mother to her children.

The Crown's first three witnesses were grocer Robert White, his wife Elizabeth and their daughter Christina. Their premises comprised two storeys, with the shop being located on the ground floor and the family's living area on the upper floor. When the door at street level was opened, a bell usually rang to alert the family, one of whom would come downstairs to serve the customer. However, on the day of the killings, the bell was broken, but when Eliza called in at five o'clock carrying her baby daughter, Robert and Christina were already behind the counter and Eliza was served with a loaf of bread. Eliza promised to pay for it at the end of the week as usual, when her husband received his wages. She left and Robert and Christina returned upstairs.

Forty-five minutes later, Christina went down into the shop for some wood and at first she saw nobody and presumed it was empty. However, when she went behind the counter she was surprised to find the prisoner crouching on her knees as though attempting to hide. When Eliza stood up, Christina noticed that she was holding a bar of soap of the type kept on a shelf behind the counter. There was also a packet of tea on the counter and the drawer of the till was open. When asked for an explanation, Eliza insisted that Christina had served her with the items, which the latter denied. Eliza called her a liar and Christina called out to her parents.

Elizabeth White was astonished to hear her daughter's account for she regarded Eliza as a good friend, who often visited the shop. She told the accused, 'This will never do Eliza,' at which Eliza became extremely distressed and cried out, 'I have taken nothing' as she walked out of the shop. Elizabeth called her husband who checked the contents of the till, from which nothing had been taken. Nevertheless, he believed that had Eliza not been interrupted, she would have stolen the cash it contained. He was convinced that when Eliza had called in earlier she realised the bell was not working and returned, hoping to take advantage by not alerting the Whites to her presence, and intending to steal cash and other items. Robert decided Eliza's behaviour could not be ignored and that her husband should be told.

Robert walked to the mill at which Samuel Clafton worked and the two men walked back into the village together. They reached the Claftons' cottage and paced up and down outside for several minutes as they discussed the incident. Robert told the court that Eliza must have seen them from the window, for within a few seconds the men heard a piercing scream from inside the cottage.

The next two witnesses called to give evidence were James Roebuck and Isabella Crosby. James was a weaver who knew the Claftons well and, alerted by the screams, he entered the cottage. He found Eliza sitting on a chest and when he asked her what had happened, she made no reply. Then he noticed her daughter, motionless on the floor and young Daniel sitting upright in front of the fire, struggling to breathe and clutching his throat, from which blood was pouring.

James ran to fetch Isabella Crosby and on their return to the cottage she immediately approached Eliza, who sat staring ahead of her without making any response; they then realised that blood was flowing from a wound to her throat. The little girl was obviously dead and emergency treatment was given to mother and son. As they awaited the arrival of the police and medical help, the following note, written by Eliza, was found:

Dear Husband, I write you a loving farewell and my children, give my kind love to mother and sister and all inquiring friends, be good to the bairns. I hope you will forgive me as God will forgive me. Kirst White has done all this. She swore that I had taken siller which was false, but they hang everybody. I have nothing to live for; I have no friends in this world. [sic]

Daniel died but Eliza clung on to life. Police Sergeant Peter Milne spent the night at her bedside and prevented two further suicide attempts. She regained consciousness and took a phial of poison she must have hidden earlier under the pillow, but was prevented from drinking any. She appeared to drift off to sleep but later she suddenly grabbed at her throat and pulled out a tube, which had been inserted to help her breathe. She was again unsuccessful and despite her serious injuries, she survived.

Sergeant Milne accompanied her to the children's funerals on the following Thursday and Eliza told him that she could not explain why she killed them. She repeated this assertion in a short written declaration made on 12 April, which was read out when her trial began: 'I remember trying to cut my own throat in the beginning of last month, but I do not remember touching the children. I remember writing the letter to my husband, the letter now shown me.'

As chance would have it, there happened to be three doctors in the village at the time of the tragedy and they were called to the scene. Doctors Buchan, Middleton and Littlejohn all gave evidence regarding the initial treatment given to the wounded and of the subsequent post-mortems. There was nothing that could be done for baby Isabella, whose jugular vein and windpipe had been severed, and she was already dead by the time the doctors arrived. Daniel was still breathing, despite having lost a large amount of blood. However, his jugular vein had not been damaged and it was hoped he might survive. Sadly, he died at four o'clock the following afternoon and for most of that time his father had been at his side, holding his hand. The post-mortems later confirmed that the children's deaths had been due to the throat wounds, which had been inflicted with their father's razor.

At issue throughout the trial was the question of Eliza's sanity. The Crown refused to accept that the prisoner was insane and asked all its witnesses to offer their views on her mental state, despite the fact that none of them was qualified to do so. The White family described her as a pleasant young woman and had not noticed anything odd in her behaviour prior to the day of the killings. James Roebuck and Isabella Crosby described her as a good friend, neighbour and mother who had never appeared to be suffering emotionally. Sergeant Milne, who spent many hours with Eliza in the aftermath of the deaths, told the court, 'I did not see anything during the whole period to indicate that she was insane.'

The prosecution barrister argued that the accused was not insane at the time she killed her children. Her husband was not a violent or unreasonable man and she had nothing to fear from him after being accused of attempted theft by the Whites. It was claimed that when she saw him in conversation with Mr White, she had been overcome by shame and guilt. Unable to face her neighbours and family, she decided to kill herself. It was acknowledged that from the contents of the letter left for her husband, she may not have intended to kill the children initially. However, she did so and no matter how apparently irrational her behaviour might seem, she was not mad.

The defence called friends and neighbours, who provided conflicting anecdotal testimony regarding the prisoner's emotional state. Jane Cronby had known Eliza since childhood and described her as being 'dull in spirits' in the recent past. James Thompson, a Stow millwright, said he had seen her with 'a troubled look'. Local weaver Robert Elder saw her shortly after she cut the children's throats and said she 'had a wild look'. Mrs Paterson, the wife of Samuel's employer, visited the cottage on the night of the tragedy and felt that Eliza, who was being held there, had a 'sorrowful look on her face'. Dr Buchan confirmed that he treated the accused during her pregnancy. He was aware that in the past she had suffered from a ruptured bladder, which was still causing her great physical distress. He believed that this could have caused her to become depressed and therefore not able to think rationally.

Since the Victorian age, it has been widely recognised that a rare acute mood disorder known as puerperal mania sometimes occurs in women after childbirth, characterised by a severe manic reaction. Eliza had been breastfeeding Isabella and Dr Buchan believed this could have exacerbated her fragile emotional state. Dr Watson had treated Eliza's bladder rupture in 1866, but she discharged herself from the infirmary before she was fully cured. Having learnt that she later breastfed her son for eleven months, he believed that she would be prone to 'fits of mental melancholy' since then.

The final defence witness was Professor Laycock of Edinburgh University, who had many years' experience working with those suffering mental health difficulties. He was convinced that given her personal history since the birth of her son, Eliza would be prone to episodes of 'mental excitement'. He testified that kleptomania was a manifestation of a worsening mental state and he believed that a sudden violent emotional experience, similar to one she may have experienced when accused of dishonesty by the Whites, would have pushed her over the edge and explain her subsequent actions.

The jury retired for five minutes and the foreman returned with the following verdict: 'The jury unanimously find the panel not guilty and therefore acquit her of the crime charged against her; and the jury find the panel was insane at the time of committing the crime charged and therefore declare that she is acquitted of the charge on account of such insanity.' The judge drew the proceedings to a close by directing that Eliza be detained during Her Majesty's Pleasure.

CASE TWENTY-TWO   1883

A DEADLY POACHING AFFRAY

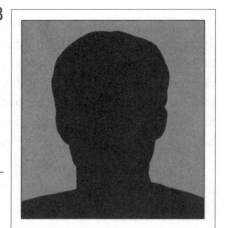

Suspects:	Robert Fletcher Vickers & William Innes
Ages:	37
Crime:	Murder

Lord Roseberry's estate was situated five miles from the village of Gorebridge and in late 1883 poachers ceased to be merely a nuisance and had become a major cause for concern. The head gamekeeper, James Grosset, who had worked on the estate for almost thirty years, was determined to put an end to the problem. Therefore, on the night of Friday 14 December, James, his assistant John Fortune and John McDermid, a rabbit trapper, set off in the darkness and headed towards Edgelaw Farm one mile distant as poachers had been active in that area for some time. The men were not armed and were carrying only their walking sticks.

They hid at a spot where they hoped poachers might show themselves but after waiting for some hours nothing untoward had happened and they decided to go home. However, after walking only a short distance, they heard a shot, which seemed to come from the direction of Edgelaw Farm. As they retraced their steps, a second shot rang out and moments later they saw two men walking towards them.

The three men concealed themselves by lying on the ground and when the two suspicious characters were 10 yards away, they leapt to their feet to confront them. James recognised the men as Robert Fletcher Vickers and William Innes and called out to them, 'There is no use going on like that. Stand still, I know who you are.' In response, Innes swore and shouted, 'Stand back,' and, nodding in their direction, said to Vickers, 'Take that one on the left and I will do for that one on the right.' Vickers raised his gun, there was a shot and John McDermid fell to the ground clutching his right arm.

Instinctively, James turned towards his wounded companion and as he did so Innes fired at him and he felt a bullet enter his left shoulder. Seconds later there was a third shot, which was fired by Vickers, causing John

'John McDermid fell to the ground clutching his right arm'

Fortune to stumble to the ground clutching at his stomach and crying out, 'What will my poor wife do?' One of the poachers, whose identity James could not be certain of, approached him and, pointing the gun at his head pulled the trigger, but fortunately it misfired.

Innes called out to Vickers, 'Load again and don't let him get away.' However, James was able to take advantage of the opportunity he had been given to flee, having managed to rise to his feet, albeit with great difficulty. As he ran from the spot, he heard the poachers say they would catch up with him very soon at a nearby bridge. James therefore changed direction and made it to Robert Simpson's farmhouse at Edgelaw. The poachers were satisfied that the other two men were dead and left them to make an unsuccessful search for James, which they later abandoned, presuming he lay dead somewhere nearby.

Despite his injuries, James was able to raise the alarm, return to the scene of the shootings and arrange for his friends to be carried to his cottage, where medical treatment was given by Dr Edwin Bailey. John Fortune was thought to be the most seriously injured of the three and in the days that followed, fifty-two pellets were removed from his abdomen. Dr Bailey was confident he would recover and did not consider it necessary for him to make a deposition to the police until he had recovered fully. However, he did make a verbal statement in which he named Innes and Vickers as the men who were responsible for his injuries and those of his two friends. Unfortunately, he succumbed to his wounds and died on 18 December.

Dr Bailey removed a number of pellets from John McDermid's right arm, between the wrist and elbow, before dressing his wounds. Although it was believed he would survive the ordeal, it was feared he might lose his arm. A written deposition was not taken from him but he identified Vickers as one of the attackers when the poacher was brought to his bedside on Boxing Day. Despite his apparent improvement, he began to bleed heavily as the dressing was being changed on 8 January, and he died from blood loss soon afterwards. The post-mortems were performed by Dr William Spalding, who confirmed the two deaths were caused by gunshot wounds inflicted at close range. James made a complete recovery and he also named Innes and Vickers as being responsible.

The suspects were notorious poachers, who had acted together for many years. As far back as 1880, Sergeant George Adamson arrested them for poaching on the neighbouring estate of the Marquis of Lothian, and it was the sergeant who assisted with their arrests in the current shootings. He first of all visited the home of Innes in the early hours of Saturday morning and found that he had accidentally shot himself in the face while attempting to hide the gun and had suffered a badly injured jaw. A neighbour, James Storie, told the sergeant that he heard the shot and had run to help. He was surprised to find the injured man fully dressed, which suggested he had only just returned home. Innes was taken to the Royal Infirmary for treatment before being detained in police custody.

Sergeant Adamson and his colleagues called at the cottage in which thirty-seven-year-old Vickers, a miner, lived with his wife on a number of occasions on the Saturday, but did not find him at home until the early hours of Sunday morning. Following his arrest he denied any involvement in the shootings. He acknowledged that he was with Innes earlier on the Friday evening, in Allen's public house, but insisted he had gone home at ten o'clock, was in bed within the hour and did not leave the cottage until after daybreak.

When they could at last interview Innes, who was also a thirty-seven-year-old miner, he too said that he had been with Vickers on the Friday evening but they parted at about ten o'clock, when he made his way home. Despite his self-inflicted facial wounds – the circumstances surrounding which he refused to explain to the police – Innes insisted that he had not possessed any powder or shot for more than a month. However, when his home was searched, bags of shot and flasks of powder were discovered hidden away. His gun was eventually discovered and shown to David Brotherston, an experienced gamekeeper, who pointed to freshly made marks of clay and other indications that it had been taken out and used in the recent past. He also examined the gun belonging to Vickers, which again had been used recently. He conducted tests by firing the guns into plasterboard from various distances and estimated the victims were shot from a distance of 6 or 7 yards as they had described.

The trial very nearly did not start as scheduled. First, the lawyers discovered that due to an administrative error, the wrong date had been entered on the indictment. However, the prisoners agreed to a handwritten amendment so the case could proceed, as they did not wish to remain in custody for a further fortnight. Then, as the jury was being sworn in, Alexander Ramsay, a Leith spirit merchant, rose to his feet to advise the judge he was over sixty years of age and should not therefore have been asked to serve. An exasperated judge admonished him for not declaring this earlier, but an indignant Mr Ramsay assured the judge that he had done so when first written to by court officials.

When the trial finally began, the most important of the Crown's witnesses were the surviving gamekeeper and the gun expert. The men in the dock were portrayed as experienced poachers, who, on realising they could be identified and arrested, had been determined to avoid capture. They therefore took the decision to shoot their defenceless victims in cold blood. Although two had later died, they were able to identify their murderers.

The defence argued that the case against the two men rested entirely on the question of identification, as it had not been demonstrated that their guns were the murder weapons. It was further claimed that the accused had alibis and the jury was reminded that no written depositions were taken from the two deceased, despite there being the opportunity to do so before they died. This, it was argued, was a serious lapse on the part of the Crown as deathbed statements were crucial in such circumstances. It was claimed that the statements described by the prosecution should be treated as hearsay evidence and therefore with a good deal of caution. Furthermore, it was suggested that the testimony of the surviving man,

James Grosset, was insufficient in a capital case. It was not suggested that he was lying, but it had to be recognised that he survived an extremely distressing experience and in his understandably confused state of mind, he convinced himself, wrongly, that the well-known poachers Innes and Vickers were the attackers.

The law prevented their wives being called as defence witnesses, but Vickers' son and daughter provided alibi evidence. Others called to testify for the defence included miners and their families from the close-knit community of Gorebridge. John Wallace swore that on the night in question he was with Vickers in Allen's public house from 8.30 p.m. and remained in his company for over an hour, when his friend went home. Innes was also present, but the two men were not in each other's company. Under cross-examination, the witness conceded that he had been convicted of poaching with Innes in the past.

Elizabeth Young and Ellen Wilson testified that they saw Vickers arrive home that night at a little after ten o'clock. Mrs Young said that she walked over to his cottage to speak with Mrs Vickers, but did not knock on the door as she heard her friend putting her husband's supper on the table and did not want to disturb them. Mrs Wilson told the court that she had suffered from toothache throughout the night in question, which kept her awake, and was in a position to say that Vickers could not have gone out during the early hours as she would have heard him do so.

Thirteen-year-old Jessie Vickers recollected that night clearly, as her father was in the cottage and had shouted at her for returning home late. Her fifteen-year-old brother also recalled eating supper with his father, who afterwards locked all the doors and did not leave again that night. At five o'clock the next morning, he and his father set off to work together at the local mine. David Walkinshaw and his wife, who lived opposite Innes, testified that they saw him arrive home before midnight, heard him lock up and insisted that he could not have left again at any time during the night without them hearing him do so.

Following the closing statements by the prosecuting and defence lawyers and the judge's summing up, the jury was absent for fifty minutes before returning with guilty verdicts by a majority of nine to six. The prisoners were sentenced to death and returned to Calton Gaol to await their executions on 31 March 1884. However, the majority verdict gave the men and their family's hope that the well-supported petition seeking a reprieve, which was forwarded to the Home Secretary, would be successful; however, it failed.

The authorities faced a major problem as the execution date approached. The leading hangman of the day, Bartholomew Binns, had very recently faced public condemnation following a botched execution at Liverpool. He was said to have been drunk and to have placed the noose incorrectly around the condemned man's neck. This had led the unfortunate individual to take eight minutes to die by strangulation. It was therefore decided not to employ Binns on this occasion and applications were invited for the task of hanging the two men. One of those who applied to the Mayor of Edinburgh was James Berry, a former policeman from Bradford in Yorkshire. In his letter he described watching William Calcraft execute three men in Manchester and since then had met his successor, William Marwood, from whom he had bought a rope and pinioning straps on his retirement. Despite his inexperience, Berry was chosen and this was to be the start of his long career as the nation's main executioner.

Robert Fletcher Vickers and William Innes, who reportedly made full confessions shortly before they were hanged, embraced before they were escorted to the gallows. Their executions went ahead without any difficulties.

THE BABY FARMER

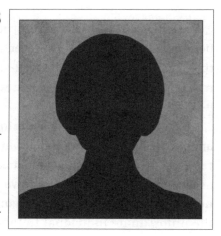

Suspect:	Jessie King
Age:	27
Crime:	Murder

On the afternoon of Saturday, 26 October 1888, a group of boys came across a bundle on Cheyne Street in the Stockbridge district of Edinburgh, which they began to use as a football. After a few minutes they became curious as to its contents and when they pulled open the waterproof garment, the mummified body of a baby, its head covered with a piece of cloth, fell out on to the ground. A post-mortem later revealed it to be the body of a boy, about twelve months of age. What

'the mummified body of a baby'

appeared to be a piece of apron string was tied tightly around his neck and strangulation was given as the cause of death. The murder investigation that followed led to the discovery of Scotland's most notorious baby farmer.

Detectives James Clark and David Simpson were given the responsibility of solving the crime and began by arranging for house-to-house enquiries to be made in the immediate neighbourhood. The police learnt from a number of residents that a Mr and Mrs McPherson moved into rented rooms in the home of plasterer James Banks and his family on Cheyne Street five months earlier. In September, Mrs McPherson was seen with a baby on one day only and when asked by curious neighbours where the child was, she assured them that the little boy had been adopted by a respectable family.

When police visited her, Mrs McPherson denied all knowledge of the dead baby boy. Nevertheless, when a request was made to search her rooms, she became obstructive and appeared to be especially reluctant to hand over the key to the door of the cellar in which the McPhersons stored their coal. It was only after the officers threatened to break it down that she relented. On entering, the officers discovered the body of a baby on one of the shelves and Mrs McPherson was heard to murmur under her breath, 'It's all up.' She and her husband were arrested and charged with murdering the two as yet unidentified children. A post-mortem revealed that the second body was that of a girl aged about two months and she too had been strangled.

Following further enquiries into their backgrounds, it was discovered that 'Mrs McPherson' was actually twenty-seven-year-old Jessie King and 'Mr McPherson' was Thomas Pearson, a fifty-nine-year-old gardener. They had lived as man and wife since May 1887, having initially rented rooms on Dalkeith Road where they stayed for several weeks. They later moved to Ann's Court, Canonmills, where they lodged with Elizabeth McKenzie before arriving in Cheyne Street.

The sensational circumstances surrounding their arrests led to a great deal of publicity and after reading some of the press reports, a concerned Janet Anderson of Prestonpans approached the police. Her sister, Elizabeth Campbell, died one week after giving birth to a son, Walter Anderson Campbell, in May of the previous year. David Finlay was Walter's father and agreed to provide financial support for his upkeep for three months, during which time Janet looked after the baby. In mid-August, David advised Janet that he could no longer afford to pay towards Walter's upbringing and had paid £5 to a Mrs Stewart to adopt him. The woman calling herself Mrs Stewart collected Walter from Janet's home a few days later and was accompanied by an older man, who introduced himself as the woman's father.

The police took a statement from David, who told them that Mrs Stewart was one of several people he interviewed who had replied to an advertisement he placed in a local newspaper, seeking adoptive parents for his son. It was David's intention to sever all contact with Walter and to take no further interest in his upbringing. Mrs Stewart assured him that the payment of £5 was to cover initial costs only, after which Walter would be raised as her own. Later, Janet and David identified King and Pearson as the couple who had taken the little boy.

Several former neighbours on Dalkeith Road remembered the couple living as uncle and niece and using the name Pearson. Elizabeth Penman and Jane Bookless recalled the arrival of a baby boy who disappeared after several weeks, and when they enquired after him, they were told he was being fostered by an aunt. Further confirmation that a male child, almost certainly Walter, had been in the care of the Pearsons was given by another neighbour, former nurse Margaret Reid. She had looked after him for three days on behalf of the couple she identified as those now under arrest. The police suspected that Walter had been a victim of the couple but it was now known that the mummified body found on Cheyne Street was not him. The boy had been identified as that of Alexander Gunn, a child the couple assumed care of while living in Ann's Court.

In early 1887, Catherine Whyte gave birth to illegitimate twin boys, Alexander and Robert Gunn, who were born in the home of Mrs Mitchell. Mrs Mitchell was a respectable woman who arranged for a nurse, Euphemia McKay, to assist with the births. Catherine received no support from the boys' father and as she was in domestic service, placed them with Margaret Henderson, who provided excellent and professional care. During their stay with Margaret, Catherine visited the boys regularly.

Some months later, Catherine decided with much reluctance that it would be in their best interests if the twins were adopted. She sought the help of Euphemia McKay, who agreed to advertise for prospective adoptive parents and to interview them. The boys were eventually separated and a Mrs McPherson took Alexander and a fee of £3. He was taken to Ann's Court and at the beginning of August, Euphemia decided to visit him to check on his progress. However, when she arrived, she was told that the McPhersons had moved away without leaving a forwarding address.

Catherine contacted the police having read of the arrests. She never met the McPhersons but when shown the shoes worn by the little boy whose body was found on Cheyne Street, she recognised the pair she had bought for Alexander. Furthermore, Euphemia, who had interviewed Mrs McPherson, identified Jessie King as being the same woman. Also, their former landlady, Mrs McKenzie, recalled the accused couple bringing a baby boy to the house, as did a little girl named Janet Burnie, who had helped to look after him. Both told police that they heard the couple call him Alexander and after he disappeared suddenly, the McPhersons said he had been adopted by another woman. The police were in no doubt, however, that Alexander had been strangled, possibly by Pearson or, more likely, by King.

The press coverage of the case led to a Mrs Tomlinson contacting the police. She told them that her unmarried daughter, Alice, had given birth to a baby girl, Violet, on 11 August 1888, after which an advertisement was placed in a local newspaper for an adoptive parent. Alice suffered poor heath and could not afford to keep Violet, and the baby's father would not help financially. Mrs Tomlinson selected a woman calling herself Mrs Burns, who agreed to take the child for only £2 as she was in very good health and would not be so expensive to feed. In the weeks that followed, Mrs Tomlinson attempted unsuccessfully to see Violet but Mrs Burns had moved away from the given address. The body of the baby girl found two months later in the Cheyne Street coal cellar was so badly decomposed that it was not possible to recognise her facial features, but the distraught grandmother recognised Violet's distinctive hair.

Isabella Banks, the daughter of the couple's landlord on Cheyne Street, had seen King with a baby girl in September, at the time Violet was said to have been handed over. The woman had thrown the baby into the air, saying affectionately, 'My bonnie wee bairn,' and told Isabella that the child's mother was due to arrive at any moment to take her home. The baby was never seen again and the police believed that within minutes of taking Violet, King strangled her and the body was put on the shelf in the coal cellar.

Pearson denied all knowledge of the deaths but King was more forthcoming. She told Police that she had collected Alexander in April and had kept him until the end of May. Initially, Pearson refused to accept the child into the home but as time passed he grew fond of him. King insisted that she attempted to find a children's home in which to place him but all had refused to accept him because he was illegitimate. When they could no longer afford the costs of keeping the little boy, she confessed to strangling him when Pearson was not at home.

She wrapped the body in a cloth, put it in a box and placed it in a cupboard, where it remained until she and Pearson moved to Cheyne Street. She took the body with her and later wrapped it in Pearson's waterproof to prevent any smell drawing attention to it. She placed the bundle on a piece of spare land, where it was later found by the boys, who used the parcel as a football. Again she insisted Pearson knew nothing of these events and when he asked her where his waterproof was, she told him she had thrown it away as green mould had appeared on it. She continued her statement by saying that she collected Violet and took her home on a day Pearson was at work. The baby cried continuously so King gave her whisky to quieten her. However, the little girl began to gasp for breath and so she decided to choke her by covering her mouth. Afterwards, she placed the body on the shelf, where it remained until discovered during the police search of the premises.

Despite confessing to the two murders, King refused to say anything about the death of Walter, whose body had still not been found. Nevertheless, at her trial, which opened on Monday, 18 February 1889, she was charged with the three murders but that relating to the killing of Walter was withdrawn part way through due to the lack of evidence. Furthermore, given her insistence that Pearson knew nothing of the murders, it had been decided to drop all charges against him on condition he testify on behalf of the Crown. This he did, denying all knowledge of the murders from the witness box and his testimony did not add anything to the case against King.

Jessie King entered not guilty pleas to the murders, but the evidence linking her to the children and the self-incriminating statements she gave following her arrest meant the prosecution had a strong case. No defence witnesses were called and her barrister, Fitzroy Bell, relied solely on his address to the jury at the close of the proceedings. He attempted to cast doubt on the assumption the children had been murdered by suggesting that the bodies were so badly decomposed that it was not possible to say with certainty that their deaths had been caused deliberately. Secondly, as an alternative explanation, he asked the jury to consider the possibility that King had been acting under the control of Pearson. Fitzroy Bell believed that if he had persuaded the members of the jury that King did not commit any murders, she could be found guilty of the lesser offence of culpable homicide. In support of this argument he suggested, rather cruelly, it was the appropriate sentence as the families who had left their children with the prisoner must accept some of the responsibility for what happened to them.

In his summing up, the judge acknowledged the growing public awareness of the horrors of baby farming and stated that the trial had left, 'The most grave suspicion that underlying the system of supposed child adoption was a state of things most dangerous in the moral welfare of society.' The murder of children by baby farmers was a peculiarly Victorian and Edwardian phenomenon and followed the introduction of the Bastardy Clause to the New Poor Law in the 1830s. This absolved the fathers of illegitimate children of all responsibility for their upkeep, which became the responsibility of the mother alone. If she did not have the support of her own family, she faced terrible choices, for charities were often reluctant to provide assistance to illegitimate offspring. The mother could opt for an illegal and dangerous abortion, choose to abandon the baby, enter the workhouse, or commit infanticide, an offence for which several young women were hanged during the nineteenth century.

It was against this backdrop that baby farmers emerged, targeting these vulnerable women. They offered to take a child for a payment but rather than care for it as promised, simply murdered it or allowed it to starve to death, thus making a financial profit. The practice flourished as the field of childcare and adoption was largely unregulated until the early years of the twentieth century, when more enforceable legislation was introduced.

The judge also raised a similar point to that of the defence, when he told the jury, 'It appears to be quite a common thing for guilty parents practically to get rid of their offspring for the payment of a few pounds without having the slightest idea of what becomes of the children afterwards or seeming to care.' These comments appear particularly harsh considering the actions of the mothers and other family members in this case. The children were not simply abandoned, which often happened, and attempts were made to find suitable homes for them. Judged by the standards of the day, even David Finlay showed some concern for his son by acknowledging paternity, offering financial support, albeit limited in nature, and by at least attempting to find good adoptive parents, which many putative fathers did not do.

The judge said he was leaving it to the commonsense of the jury members to decide on King's guilt or otherwise, but advised them that he could see no grounds for convicting her of culpable homicide. If they believed she had killed one or more of the children, these must be viewed as deliberate and premeditated acts and a verdict of wilful murder was the only option available to them. The jury retired for four minutes before returning with guilty verdicts to wilful murder. As the judge was placing the black cap on his head, King turned pale and began to sob uncontrollably. She had to be supported by the prison warders standing with her in the dock as she listened to the death sentence being passed and again as she was being taken down to the cells below.

King's mental health was not an issue at her trial, but she made several serious suicide attempts whilst in the condemned cell. One of these involved unpicking the thick seam from her prison dress, which she attempted to convert into a rope with which to hang herself, but it was discovered by prison staff. It was decided to have an assessment of her mental health made by Professor Sir Douglas Maclagan and Sir Arthur Mitchell, both of whom declared her to be sane, thus removing any obstacle to her execution.

Despite the nature of her crimes, 2,000 signatures were collected in support of a petition seeking a reprieve, but to no avail. On 9 March King was told that the Secretary of State for Scotland, the Marquis of Lothian, had decided there were no grounds to ask the Queen to intervene. In the days that remained to her, she received a number of visitors, including a woman for whom she had worked seven years earlier. Her former employer said she would have visited earlier but did not realise who she was from the press coverage, as she had known her by the name of Kean. The condemned woman confirmed that when arrested the police had wrongly registered her name as King, and that fault had not been rectified in the official records.

Following her arrest, King had given birth to a baby son who was now five months old and who had remained with her during the trial and, subsequently, in the condemned cell. A few days before her execution, he was taken from her and placed into the care of the Roman Catholic Church, who would arrange for his adoption.

As the execution date approached, the prison governor was worried that the execution on Monday 12 March might be more harrowing than usual, given King's reaction in the dock on hearing the verdict and sentence at the end of her trial. However, she remained calm on the morning and bade an emotional farewell to the female warders who had watched over her and most of whom were crying. In a breach of custom, the hangman, James Berry, placed the cap over her head before she walked out of the cell to spare her having to gaze on the gallows, which he knew could be a distressing experience. She died bravely and Berry later wrote that as he was pinioning her she told him she had killed the children because she could not bear to hear them crying.

Jessie King was suspected of murdering many more babies but, prior to her execution, she confessed only to the two of which she had been convicted. She was one of eight women hanged in the United Kingdom for baby farming between 1870 and 1907.

DID THEY HANG JACK?

Suspect:	William Henry Bury
Age:	29
Crime:	Murder

There were many who believed at the time, and some who still do, that Jack the Ripper was executed in Dundee Gaol on the morning of Wednesday, 24 April 1889. The man suspected of being the notorious serial killer was twenty-nine-year-old William Henry Bury. Some weeks earlier, at seven o'clock on the evening of Sunday 10 February, he walked into the town's central police station to report that his thirty-three-year-old wife, Ellen, had committed suicide. He told officers that five days earlier he woke up to find her body on the bedroom floor, after she had apparently strangled herself by placing a noose around her neck and tightening it. He concluded his account by insisting that upon seeing her he had been overcome by a strange and inexplicable impulse to mutilate the corpse.

Afterwards, he feared being wrongly accused of being Jack the Ripper because of the nature of the mutilation and decided to hide the body. He placed it in a crate, which he put in the cellar of 113 Princes Street, where the couple were lodging. He intended leaving the crate there and making good his escape, but had been overcome with grief and guilt and chose instead to report the matter to the police.

Detectives Lamb and Campbell were ordered to investigate these bizarre claims and visited the premises with a key provided by Bury, who, in the meantime, was placed in a cell to await the outcome of their enquiries. He and his wife had been living in two sparsely furnished rooms but the detectives went first to the cellar, in which they found the crate which was thirty-six inches in length, twenty-eight inches wide and twenty-five inches deep. They lifted the lid and removed a sheet to reveal the decomposing and horribly mutilated body of a naked woman. Her head had been forced to one side, her left leg had been broken to ensure it fitted into the confined space and was twisted in such a fashion that the foot was resting on her left shoulder. Her right leg had been broken in several places before being pushed down into the crate, thus enabling the lid to be fully closed. It was only after the body was removed and was laid out on the floor that the true extent of her injuries became clear. There was a large red mark to her neck, knife wounds to her body, and her abdomen had been slashed open, from which twelve inches of her intestines spilled out.

A search of the rooms yielded a long-bladed and blood-stained knife, together with a piece of rope to which strands of a woman's hair were attached. An ulster which had apparently been cut with a knife was also

'twelve inches of her intestines spilled out'

found with the remnants of a corset, and a number of buttons in the fireplace. Doctors Templeton and Stalker performed a post-mortem and believed that approximately four days earlier, the victim was beaten semi-conscious by a blow to her left temple, where they had discovered a large bruise, and afterwards the rope was used to strangle her. The knife wounds were inflicted after she had been stripped naked. It came as no surprise that both doctors were of the opinion that it would have been impossible for her to have strangled herself.

Outside the house, written in chalk on a wall, were two messages: 'Jack Ripper is At the Back of the Door' and 'Jack Ripper Is In This Seller'. The London police were advised of these discoveries and given details of the mutilation suffered by Ellen and of Bury's account. Inspector Frederick George Abeline, one of the leading investigators on the Whitechapel case, interviewed family members and acquaintances of Bury and his wife in London. Arrangements were also made for her sister, Margaret Corney, to travel to Dundee to make a formal identification of the body. This she did and she was also able to provide the police with a great deal of background information. They quickly ruled out Bury's version of events and were determined to charge him with his wife's murder.

Ellen was popular with those who knew her and in the recent past had been working as a needlewoman, making waterproof clothing, before moving to new job in a jute factory in the East End of London. In the past she had also worked as a servant in a brothel, but it was not known if she had ever been a prostitute. Seven years before she met her death, Ellen's aunt died and left her £300, which she invested wisely, buying shares in the Union Bank of London. She met Bury in early 1888 and after a brief courtship they were married at Bromley parish church on 4 April. This came as a great surprise to her friends, as she seemed to be the only one not to realise it was her money that attracted him.

Bury was born in Stourbridge in Worcestershire on 25 May 1859, the youngest of three children. Twelve months later, his mother was declared insane and entered the Worcester County and City Lunatic Asylum, where she remained until her death in March 1864. His father, a hard working and respectable fishmonger, was killed in an accident in August 1859. A family friend agreed to raise the three Bury children and, despite this difficult start to his life, the prisoner enjoyed a stable upbringing. He later moved to Wolverhampton to live with an uncle and where he worked as a hawker in household goods.

Bury moved to London in 1887 and settled in the East End, where he found employment as a sawdust and sand seller for James Martin of Quickett Street, Bromley. He was later discovered to have stolen money from his employer and was sacked, although the matter was not reported to the police. When his former employer was interviewed following his arrest in Dundee, he advised the police that he had witnessed a drunken Bury assault his wife on three separate occasions when he had demanded money from her.

In the early days of their marriage the couple lived in lodgings with Elizabeth Hayes in Swaton Street, Bow, who, when questioned by the police, also provided evidence of his violence towards her. Within days of the wedding, Elizabeth heard Ellen screaming and when she rushed to their room she saw Bury kneeling on his wife, who was spread-eagled on the floor, holding a knife to her throat. He was threatening to kill her and when their alarmed landlady said she was going to alert the police, Bury calmed down, apologised to his wife and handed the knife to Elizabeth. Later, Ellen told her the attack followed her refusal to provide him with cash.

Shortly after this incident, the couple moved to other lodgings in the East End, firstly in Blackthorne Street and later in rooms rented from William Smith on Spanby Road, who told police that throughout their stay Mrs Bury seemed to be desperately unhappy. In December 1888, Bury asked his landlord to make him the crate in which his wife's corpse was later discovered, explaining that they were emigrating to Australia, where they planned to settle in Brisbane. However, on 19 January, the couple boarded the steamer *Cambria*, which sailed overnight to Dundee. They were waved off by Margaret Corney, who, even at this late stage, attempted to persuade her sister not to make the journey with her husband. However, Bury had shown his wife and her family a letter purporting to offer him a job with Dundee jute merchants Malcolm, Ogilvie & Co. He was to receive a weekly wage of £2 and Ellen would also be offered work with the company, for which she would be paid £1 weekly. The contract was supposedly for seven years and Ellen told her sister that she and her husband would be able to make a fresh start in Scotland.

On arrival in Dundee the couple rented rooms from Mrs Robinson at 43 Union Street, but left after only a few days, saying the weekly rent of eight shillings was far too high. They moved to their final lodgings on Princes Street. A neighbour, David Duncan, told investigators that in the early hours of one morning in early February, he heard screams coming from their rooms but it soon fell silent and he thought nothing more of it. Ellen was not seen alive again and the police believed the screams were made as Bury murdered his wife. In the days that followed, Bury was seen drinking in a number of public houses. He invited several men to his lodgings and they told of playing cards and using the crate as a makeshift table. They also recalled their host repeatedly raising the Whitechapel murders in conversation.

Nevertheless, the London and Dundee detectives did not believe Bury was Jack the Ripper and the motive for the murder was not to prevent Ellen reporting her suspicions about him. Although the truth behind the messages written in chalk was never discovered, officers from both police forces were convinced the dead woman did not write them. It was felt that Bury may have done so in the hope of lending credence to his fear of being mistaken for the Whitechapel murderer. His references to the Whitechapel crimes to his card-playing companions were thought to have probably been made for the same reason.

The true motive was believed to be greed, as Bury had been determined to get his hands on what remained of Ellen's inheritance. It was a premeditated crime as evidenced by his ordering the crate in which he later hid her body and which he probably intended to dispose of before deciding to try and persuade everyone that she had committed suicide. The jute manufacturers were contacted and confirmed that they had never heard of Bury or his wife and had certainly not offered them employment. Forging the correspondence offering work in Scotland was believed to have been a ruse to lure Ellen away from her family and kill her in a place where she was not known. This formed the basis of the Crown's case when his trial opened on the morning of Thursday, 28 March 1889 before Lord Young.

The prosecuting lawyer, Mr McKechnie, made no reference to the Whitechapel murders and presented a strong case for the jury to consider. Mr Hay, who represented the accused, had arranged for a second post-mortem to be performed by Doctors Lennon and Kinnear. They agreed with the Crown medical experts regarding the cause of death but claimed that the injuries could have been self- inflicted or caused by accident, and they were of the opinion she did kill herself. However, under cross-examination, Dr Kinnear acknowledged that he had been qualified for just six months and admitted that suicide by self-strangulation was rare. Eventually, under intense questioning, he confirmed that he had never heard of another similar case.

At the conclusion of the evidence, the jury retired for twenty minutes before returning with a guilty verdict, but adding a strong recommendation for mercy. A puzzled Lord Young asked the foreman on what grounds the recommendation was made. He replied that the jury members felt there was a great deal of conflicting medical evidence and the prisoner should be given the benefit of any doubt. Unsurprisingly, the judge refused to accept their decision as it stood, leaving as it did an element of doubt as to whether the jury was truly satisfied of his guilt. The jury retired once more and after deliberating for an additional five minutes, returned to the courtroom with a unanimous guilty verdict without a recommendation for mercy. Despite finishing at eleven o'clock at night, a crowd of more than 5,000 had gathered in the streets surrounding the court building and when the verdict and subsequent death sentence were announced, the news was greeted with loud and prolonged cheering.

William Bury was hanged by James Berry on the morning of Wednesday, 24 April 1889 and became the last person to be executed in Dundee. Despite the London police being sceptical about his involvement in the Whitechapel murders, two detectives were sent north to witness the execution lest there should be a confession on the drop. No such confession was made but Berry remained convinced that he had executed Jack the Ripper. As he pinioned him, he later reported that Bury had hissed, 'I suppose you think you are clever to hang *me*.' The hangman had little doubt that the emphasis on the final word meant he was admitting that he was the notorious Whitechapel murderer.

MURDER ON GOAT FELL

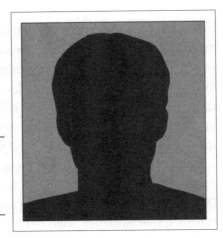

Suspect: John Watson Lawrie
Age: 25
Crime: Murder

Thirty-two-year-old Edwin Robert Rose was a single man who lived with his parents in Upper Tooting. His employer, James Goodman of Brixton, for whom he worked as a clerk, agreed he could take two weeks holiday and on Thursday, 5 July 1889, Edwin left for Scotland. He had booked into the Hydropathic Hotel at Rothesay, but did not return from a trip to Arran on the 12th, and he was not seen again at the hotel. His family became anxious when he did not return home on the 18th as planned and con-firmed on a postcard sent to his father from Scotland, on which he wrote, 'Dear F, I shall return to London by train arriving at St Pancras 2.40 on Thursday. All well. Do not write, time will not permit. This is a charming island. Ned.'

Thinking Edwin may have decided to extend his stay in Scotland by a few days, his family waited until the 22nd of the month before advis-ing police in Rothesay of their concerns for his wellbeing. His brother travelled north to discover the last sighting of Edwin was on Goat Fell on Arran. A search was begun on the following Sunday, in which the police were assisted by many local residents and holidaymakers. The search centred on Goat Fell, but no trace of him was found on that day or during the following week. It was therefore decided to widen the search area and a notice was published seeking more volunteers to help. There was a marvellous response and more than 150 men, women and children met at the kennels in the grounds of Brodick Castle, where they were split into three groups.

Local fisherman Francis Logan discovered Edwin's body in Glen Sannox, having been drawn to the spot by the stench of the decomposing corpse, which was not immediately visible as it had been carefully hidden under

'the stench of the decomposing corpse'

more than forty stones. However, this had not prevented a great deal of his flesh from being eaten by rats and other wild animals. His pockets had been gone through and all his cash and valuables stolen save for a handkerchief. His jacket had been placed over his head as though the guilt ridden killer was attempting to avoid having to gaze on the terrible head injuries he had inflicted.

A post-mortem revealed that Edwin's shoulder was dislocated and he had sustained several severe skull injuries. It was recognised that these could have been caused accidentally due to a fall, but the deliberate attempt to conceal the body and the fact that many of his belongings had been taken led the police to initiate a murder investigation. They were particularly keen to interview a stranger to the district who was known to have befriended Edwin in the final days of his life and who had not been seen since the deceased was first missed.

It was learnt from a party of young women, who were also staying at the Hydropathic Hotel, that a few days into his holiday Edwin boarded the steamer *Ivanhoe*, which sailed to Brodick. During the voyage, Edwin was seen to have fallen into conversation with a man calling himself Annandale. He returned to the hotel that night but the next day, Edwin was once more on the boat, together with fellow hotel guests Francis Nickel and William Thom. Also on board was Annandale, with whom Edwin again spent the day. When Francis and William were boarding the boat to return to Rothesay, Edwin advised them he would not be accompanying them as he had decided to spend a few days with Annandale at his lodgings with Esther Walker.

Two days later, William Thom returned to Arran, where he met Edwin, who, during their conversation, told of a surprising incident. After purchasing a bottle of brandy, Edwin invited Annandale to take a sip as he was complaining of a toothache. However, Annandale put the full bottle to his lips and drank the entire contents within seconds. William met Edwin for the last time on Arran on Monday 15 July, when they ate lunch together. William told him he had some misgivings about Annandale, who Edwin was due to meet later that afternoon as they had arranged to climb Goat Fell together. Edwin had suggested that he too had doubts about his new friend and told William he would not spend any more time with him. They parted at 3.15 and William did not see Edwin alive again.

Despite assuring William that he would not go to Goat Fell with Annandale, Edwin and he were seen by two men who knew them to commence the climb later that same day. Part way through the climb, they overtook the Reverend Robert Hind, who remembered them vividly as he noticed that it had begun to rain heavily yet they did not seek shelter and continued to climb. At the peak, they were spoken to by two brothers, the last people to see Edwin alive. Later that night, shepherd David McKenzie saw a man he later identified as Annandale emerging alone from Glen Sannox. This proved to be the last sighting of the main suspect.

On 22 July, John Watson Lawrie, a twenty-five-year-old pattern maker, returned to work at Sharp, Stewart & Co. in Springburn at the end of his holidays. A few days later, newspapers reported details of the 'Goat Fell Mystery', which included a description of the mysterious Annandale and his workmates joked with Lawrie that he matched the description. On 31 July, Lawrie called at his workplace and asked for the wages he was owed, saying he had been offered a job in Leith, which he had accepted. He left his lodgings on North Frederick Street, telling his landlady Mrs Corrie and his girlfriend the same story.

However, someone contacted the police to say how much Lawrie fitted the description of the wanted man, revealed his absence from work during the relevant period, and of his suddenly moving away. A visit was made to his former employer and a photograph taken by a holidaymaker on Arran of the man calling himself Annandale was shown to the employees. The man in the snapshot was identified as being Lawrie by his former workmates. Officers investigating the crime contacted Lawrie's family, who clearly regarded him as a disappointment. It became clear that he had always lived way beyond his means, which had led him to accumulate massive debts, and in March 1889 he had been arrested and charged with stealing jewellery from the landlady with whom he was staying at the time. His father paid the victim the full amount for the lost items and Lawrie escaped with an admonishment. However, relations with the family worsened and it was made clear to him that he could not rely on their help in the future. It was believed that Lawrie planned the murder with the intention of robbing his victim, financial gain being the motive.

There were a number of false sightings as the weeks passed and many believed Lawrie had committed suicide, as he had attempted to poison himself in the past. Meanwhile, members of Edwin's family travelled to Arran to thank the residents for their help and for their messages of support throughout their ordeal. The islanders erected a stone cairn at the spot Edwin's body was found as a memorial.

On Tuesday 31 August, Constable Gordon was waiting for the 2.10 p.m. train at Ferniegair when he was approached by the station manager. He told the officer that a stranger had asked for a ticket to Larkhall but had left the station in a hurry after spotting the policeman, who was wearing his uniform. The manager thought the man fitted the description of the wanted man Lawrie. Coincidentally, Constable Gordon knew Lawrie and from his vantage point on the platform he could see the fleeing man and was able to identify him as the suspect.

He immediately gave chase and Lawrie ran into a wood, hoping to lose his pursuer. However, the constable was joined by a group of labourers working nearby and several miners on their way home from a nearby colliery. Within a matter of minutes, Lawrie was discovered and arrested. He had cut his throat, but the wound was superficial and required only minimal treatment.

His trial took place over two days in early November before trial judge Lord Kingsborough. The Crown acknowledged that nobody had seen the accused push Edwin off a precipice, which is what was alleged. The prosecuting barrister also made it clear that the evidence presented would be circumstantial. They called those who could confirm that the accused was indeed the man who had passed himself off as Annandale and those who had seen him with Edwin on Goat Fell. In her evidence, Lawrie's landlady, Mrs Corrie, told the court that on his return from holiday he was wearing a yachting cap, tennis jacket and tennis shoes, all of which were identified as having belonged to the deceased and who was seen wearing them on Arran.

The defence called a guide, who knew Goat Fell, and he described it as a treacherous place, especially when it rained as it became extremely slippery. Edwin did not know the area and it was more than possible that he had lost his footing and fell to his death. This theory was given added weight by two surgeons, including Dr Heron Watson of Edinburgh, who confirmed that Edwin's injuries could have been caused accidentally following a fall. It was claimed by the prisoner's lawyer that Edwin's death was an accident and Lawrie afterwards took advantage of the situation by stealing his money, other items of value and his clothes. His only crime was theft and he was innocent of the charge of murder. Nevertheless, the jury convicted him of the more serious crime and he was sentenced to death.

The judge ordered that he should be hanged on Saturday 30 November. However, there was a well-supported petition seeking mercy and on the eve of the scheduled execution the hangman, James Berry, was inspecting the gallows when it was announced that a reprieve had been granted. The official notification, sent by Lord Lothian to the prison authorities, read as follows:

> Sir, I am to signify to you the Queen's command and beg that the execution of the sentence of death passed on John Watson Lawrie, presently in Her Majesty's Prison in Greenock, be reprieved until further signification of Her Majesty's pleasure. I am Sir, you obedient servant.
> Lothian

Lawrie was sentenced to life imprisonment. He spent the first twenty years of his sentence in Peterhead Gaol before being transferred to the prison at Perth. He died in the gaol's Criminal Lunatic Department twenty-one years later on 4 October 1930, still claiming that he was innocent of Edwin's murder.

CASE TWENTY-SIX 1890

DEATH AT
THE WEDDING

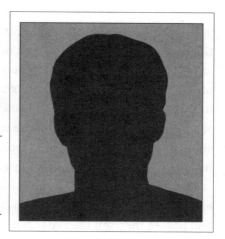

Suspect: Loritto Palumbo
Age: 24
Crime: Murder

Laurence Lonni, a young man of Italian descent who worked in Glasgow as an ice-cream seller, married his sweetheart, Margaret Powell, on Saturday, 3 November 1890. That evening, the couple celebrated their union in the tenement home of Margaret's family at 19 Rodney Street. As midnight approached, neighbours became aware of an argument involving a number of guests attending the party.

Jane Reid and her sister Mary Thompson lived in the rooms directly above those on the ground floor, in which the party was being held. At 11.30 p.m. they heard someone kicking loudly on the Powells' door. From the stairwell they saw two men at the door, who were speaking Italian until one of them said in English, 'By Christ, the first one that comes out, I'll do for them.' As he spoke these words, the door was opened by a young man the sisters recognised as Andro Luciano. Immediately, the man who had uttered the threat struck him in the face without any warning. The men struggled and as they did so they tumbled out into the street, followed by a number of other guests.

From their window Jane and Mary watched as several more guests left the party and joined in the melee outside. They saw Luciano fall to the ground and also saw another young man, Michael Gizzi, grab at his leg and scream out in pain. The police were quickly at the scene but Luciano was dead and Gizzi had suffered a serious stab wound to his upper leg. The guests provided the police with the names of two men said to have been responsible: Luigi Marcantonio, who was detained at the scene, and Loritto Palumbo who had by this time fled.

Police officers made several visits to Palumbo's Renfrew home during the next two days but there was no sign of him. A watch was also kept at his place of work, Fusal Brothers, who were ice-cream manufacturers on Wilson Street, but he did not go there. He was known to have friends in Dumbarton, where he had been employed in the ice-cream trade two years earlier. It was there that he was seen and arrested in an ice-cream shop, in which he was seeking work. Initially, he insisted that the police had the wrong man but eventually acknowledged his true identity.

The post-mortem performed on Luciano by Dr Samuel Moore confirmed that death resulted from a single knife wound to the chest, which had passed through the breastbone and penetrated the heart. The doctor added that a great deal of force must have been used by the assailant. Gizzi was taken to the Royal Infirmary, where he was treated by Dr Robert Steel. He had suffered a deep knife wound to his right thigh, very close to the main artery. This had led to the loss of a great deal of blood and he was not expected to survive, but fortunately he made a full recovery.

Although Marcantonio was found in possession of a double-bladed penknife when arrested, it was not the murder weapon and the knife used to commit the fatal stabbing was discovered later on waste ground close

'a single knife wound to the chest'

to Rodney Street. It was distinctive as it was a large, three-bladed knife and enquiries revealed that such a weapon was purchased at the shop of Arthur Wallace for one shilling on the afternoon of the wedding by a man fitting Palumbo's description, which indicated that the attack was premeditated. Detectives investigating the stabbings were by now aware of a history of bad blood between Palumbo and the deceased. Nine months earlier, Palumbo had threatened Luciano with an open razor. Those who knew them believed the two men had settled their differences but clearly Palumbo must still have harboured a grudge, which led him to buy the knife on the day of the wedding and, furthermore, be willing to use it in such a deadly fashion.

Interviews with the wedding guests enabled the police to piece together a picture of the events which immediately preceded the stabbings. Palumbo had been drinking earlier in the day with Luciano, his brother Giuseppe and Gizzi in a public house. They left, apparently on friendly terms, and made their way to the wedding celebrations. Palumbo was invited but he was not a well-liked individual as he was regarded as something of a troublemaker. The bride and groom invited him only because they feared he would cause trouble otherwise. At the party, he was drunk and began to make a nuisance of himself by deliberately attempting to trip up other guests. Luciano told him to leave and he did so, but on his way out he said angrily, 'I'll go, but we'll do you tonight.'

He returned an hour later with his brother-in-law, Marcantonio, and the two men forced their way back into the party. They spent some time drinking wine in the kitchen but caused no further problems. They left of their own volition a little later but when they attempted to regain entry, they were prevented from doing so by the groom, which was witnessed by sisters Jane and Mary. Unfortunately, an already angry Palumbo was outraged to see his girlfriend, Fanny Hamill, sitting with Luciano and he shouted, 'Send out Fanny, I want to knife her,' adding, 'Send out Luciano, I'll kill him too!'

Luciano went to the door, hoping to calm the situation, but this proved to be impossible and instead he was stabbed. Luciano's wife, Catherine, heard the cries of 'Murder!' and was immediately concerned for her husband's safety. She rushed outside but by the time she reached her husband he was dead. Gizzi told the police that it was Palumbo who stabbed him after he had plunged the knife into Luciano.

The only witness to offer an alternative account of the night's events at the trial of the two accused was Fanny Hamill. She confirmed that she and Palumbo were courting but admitted they had argued a few days before the wedding. Nevertheless, she claimed they were again on friendly terms and were together at the party. She insisted he made no threats towards anyone and was not misbehaving in any way, adding she would have seen or heard anything untoward. She claimed Palumbo had remained at the party until 4.30 in the morning and left on good terms with everybody. She concluded her evidence by telling the court that all of the prosecution witnesses had been drunk, so they could not possibly recall the night's events and as such their statements could not be relied upon.

The Crown accepted that Palumbo felt a large degree of personal antagonism towards Luciano, but Gizzi was not necessarily an intended victim. However, Palumbo had returned with the intention of causing mayhem and it was also believed that he may possibly have wanted to attack Fanny, ironically, the sole witness to speak in his support at the trial, for sitting with Luciano. Most members of the jury disbelieved her and accepted the Crown's case. Palumbo was convicted of wilful murder by a majority verdict but before the death sentence was passed, Marcantonio, who had been found not guilty, was asked to leave the dock. Before doing so, he and Palumbo embraced and kissed.

There was a great deal of support for a reprieve, especially from within the Italian community, and the following letter appeared in the *Glasgow Herald* on 7 January:

Sir, Loritto Palumbo, an Italian youth 24 years of age is lying in our city prison under sentence of death. The writer of this appeal fears that owing to the youth being a foreigner, his case may not excite the pity usually extended to our own countrymen and women in like dire extremity. She therefore solicits the attention of the citizens of Glasgow to the following extenuating points in order that the petition for the commutation of the sentence, which will be placed in many of the public resorts of the city during the next few days, may be signed without hesitation or delay, the date fixed for the execution being the 19th of this month:- the verdict of the jury was gained by a majority of one and it was qualified by a recommendation to mercy; second, the youth is an Italian, in whose national country capital punishment has been abolished; thirdly, the murder was committed in hot blood under the influence of drink and the facts point to a love affair being at the root of it; fourthly, Palumbo acted as a model to several of our well-known Glasgow artists for about four years and while so employed conducted himself with great propriety, giving entire satisfaction. He also acted as a servant to an artist during the past summer in the country and in that capacity he behaved in a most exemplary manner, giving him and members of the family the impression of his being a most gentle unassuming and obliging youth. It is now the almost universal opinion in this country that capital punishment should be abolished except in some very exceptional cases, premeditated or of long-continued-cruelty and it is by affording the public opportunities for giving force to this opinion by signing petitions for the commutation of the extreme penalty of the death sentence that such a desirable improvement in our penal code can be brought about. Trusting therefore that sufficient attention will be drawn to the petition to bring a reprieve for Palumbo.

I am etc.

M.N.M.

Copies of the petition were placed at the city's ice-cream parlours and in the office of the Italian Consul at 204 St Vincent Street. It was widely supported and more than 5,000 signatures were collected. Three days before he was due to hang, Palumbo was visited in the condemned cell by the prison governor and the Lord Provost, who informed him that he had been granted a reprieve and sentenced to life imprisonment. He thanked the officials and declared, 'God has spared my life and I am going to be God's man now.'

The next we hear of Palumbo is on 6 December 1900, when he appeared at the city's Central Police Court following his release from the life sentence four weeks earlier. Now a ticket-of-leave man, he had failed to inform the police that he had changed his address from that to which he was released. His lawyer explained to the bench that his client was unaware he was under any obligation to do so. His explanation and apology were accepted and he received an admonishment, thus allowing him to remain at liberty.

On release from prison, Palumbo gave an undertaking to the authorities that he would leave the country and travel back to Italy. However, ill health had prevented him from doing so as soon as he would have wished. Nothing more was ever heard of him and it is believed he did indeed return to his homeland.

DEATH BY THE SWORD

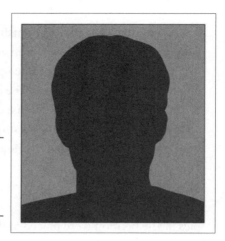

Suspect:	James Frazer
Age:	40
Crime:	Murder

The village of Polmont lies to the east of Falkirk and towards the close of the nineteenth century, at the top of what was known as the Brightons and on the road leading to Maddiston, there stood a large double-fronted villa, which had been converted into two adjoining family homes. In one lived forty-year-old James Frazer, a clerk in Glasgow's Commercial Bank, with his wife Jessie and two stepchildren. In the other property, twenty-six-year-old William Shadwell, a catering assistant at the Blair Lodge School, lived with his wife and two children. The Frazers had moved to the village two years earlier, since when the two families had enjoyed a friendly relationship. That was until a few minutes after nine o'clock on the night of Tuesday, 26 July 1892.

The Shadwells were sitting in the kitchen with their children when suddenly, without any prior warning, the door was flung open and Frazer rushed in brandishing a large sword in a threatening manner. The couple had no time to react and could not prevent their assailant first of all

'brandishing a large sword in a threatening manner'

striking William a violent blow to the head, before he turned towards Jessie Shadwell and attacked her in a similar manner. Although stunned, William and Jessie were able to push the children to safety and run out of the house into the small front garden, pursued by Frazer. He stabbed Jessie, who fell to the ground, badly injured. William attempted to position himself between his wife and Frazer, but as he did so, he too received a stab wound. William died almost immediately, but Jessie, despite suffering several terrible wounds to her body, was able to make her way to a nearby house to seek help.

Frazer, meanwhile, ran out of the garden and into the road, where he encountered twenty-four-year-old Mary Grindley, a farm worker who lived nearby with her widowed mother. Mary was making her way back home, carrying a pitcher of water, unaware of the attack on the Shadwells. Frazer signalled to her to stop, which she did, not realising he meant to harm her. He walked towards her, making sure she could not see the sword and before she could put up any resistance, he stabbed her a number of times in different parts of her body. Mary fell to the ground but managed to stagger to her feet and walk a few steps before again collapsing.

It was a warm evening and four young men, taking advantage of the fine weather, were playing cards on a patch of spare land a little distance away. They heard the disturbance and looking in its direction, saw Frazer stabbing Mary. They rushed over, intending to intervene, but Frazer took a revolver from his pocket and threatened to shoot the approaching group if they came any closer. The young men were forced to withdraw but when they saw Frazer walking away, they were able to reach Mary and carry her home, where she died shortly afterwards.

Musician Mr J.K. Gilgour was aware that there had been some kind of incident and when he saw Frazer, his friend and neighbour, walking towards him, he called out to him to ask what had happened. As the two men drew closer to each other, Frazer produced his sword and attacked the unsuspecting man. He badly damaged Mr Gilgour's fingertips, but he escaped without suffering more serious wounds.

Mrs Frazer was told what was happening and ran to the scene. Although she was in a highly distressed state of mind herself, she was able to calm her husband down and usher him back to their home, where she sat him down in a darkened room. He was quiet but was still holding the sword in one hand and the revolver in the other. She noticed that he had suffered a deep wound to his left thigh, the result of stabbing himself accidentally. A message was sent to the village policeman, Constable Porteous, of the incident and before setting off for the Frazers' home, the officer telegraphed colleagues in Falkirk to ask for assistance.

The constable was joined at Frazer's house by Superintendent McDonald and Inspector Gordon, who had made the trip from Falkirk in a gig. The three officers entered the house and disarmed Frazer, who offered no resistance. In his pockets they discovered a second revolver and a large number of cartridges. He was taken to Polmont police station, from which he was transferred to Glasgow the following day and charged with murder.

Dr Wickham had arrived at the scene of the stabbings within minutes, but there was nothing he could do for William, who had sustained a number of serious wounds, any one of which could have proved fatal. Mary Grindley had been stabbed several times, the most serious of which was to her abdomen and she too died of her injuries. Jessie was treated for wounds to her head, arms and thigh and she was also in deep shock. She was taken to Falkirk Cottage Hospital and was not told of her husband's death for several days. Against all expectations, she survived. Mary was buried in Muiravonside churchyard the following Friday and on the next day, William's remains were interred in Falkirk cemetery.

It was decided that the most suitable place for Frazer's physical injuries to be treated was the hospital wing at Duke Street Prison, under the supervision of Dr J.F. Sutherland, the institution's medical officer. Although his physical health improved, the prisoner remained subdued. His wife experienced a serious reaction to these events and suffered a major mental breakdown. She entered the Stirling District Asylum, in which she remained for some considerable time to receive treatment. She was therefore unable to visit him but he was seen regularly by his stepdaughter and many work colleagues, who, to their credit, did not desert him, despite the nature of his deeds. Reverend J. Anderson of the Polmont Free Church saw this deeply troubled man almost daily.

No motive for Frazer's actions could be discovered and it was clear there was no rational explanation. Interviews with his co-workers at the bank revealed that for some weeks he had been making uncharacteristic errors in his work and in retrospect it was apparent this had been on his mind and a source of anxiety to him. It also became known that some months earlier, he complained to the police that several of his neighbours were spreading scurrilous rumours about him and that there was secret telephone link to Polmont Post Office, which was used by those responsible for what was being said about him. He could not be reassured and he refused treatment for this delusional behaviour. However, he seemed to improve and his family and friends believed, wrongly, that he had come to his senses.

His trial for the double murder at Polmont was listed to take place in the Edinburgh High Court of Judiciary on Monday 17 October before Lord Adam. However, by then Frazer was confined in Stirling District Asylum and it had been determined that he was insane when he killed his victims, and he remained so. It was therefore ordered that he be detained during Her Majesty's Pleasure.

CASE TWENTY-EIGHT   1892

THE DISMEM-BERMENT OF ELIZABETH O'CONNOR

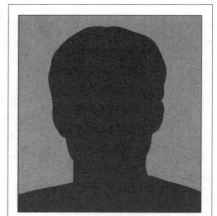

Suspect:	William McEwan
Age:	31
Crime:	Murder

West Lodge at 56 Maxwell Drive was a large villa in the quiet and attractive Glasgow suburb of Pollokshields. It was owned by Mrs Wilson, who moved to Prestwick following the death of her husband, and the building had been empty for a year as she looked for a buyer. She employed a jobbing gardener, William McEwan, to look after the property in her absence, for which she paid him a weekly wage of £1 and also allowed him to live rent-free in one of the downstairs rooms. McEwan was a thirty-one-year-old Irishman, who had been working in the district for the previous six years and was known to everyone as 'Red Wull'. Although normally a quiet and reserved individual, he was known to drink to excess at times and on these occasions he could become extremely violent.

At six o'clock on the morning of Tuesday, 11 October 1892, one of McEwan's friends, gardener Alex McDougall, called at West Lodge, where the two men often ate breakfast together. Unusually, Alex found the gate leading into the front garden to be padlocked. McEwan shouted to him from a window that he was not cooking any food that morning as he was busy. Alex went to work but returned three hours later to find the gate was now unlocked. He walked up to the front door but there was no reply when he knocked. His attention, however, was drawn to a large pool of blood on the front steps and, worried that some mishap may have befallen his friend, he notified the police. A constable arrived, made a preliminary examination and was concerned enough to believe it necessary to summon assistance. Within the hour he was joined by a number of colleagues who included senior officers and the Chief Constable. As there was still no response to repeated knocking on the front door, it was decided to enter by force.

In the room which McEwan occupied there were two beds and several other pieces of furniture. Pools of blood had formed on the floor and the walls were splattered with it. The beds and furniture were also bloodstained as were items of men's clothing, which were scattered around the room. The police also found a pair of women's shoes, a black skirt and a pair of stays. It was obvious that a fierce struggle had taken place. The police were convinced they were standing in the scene of a monstrous crime but there was no sign of an injured person or a body. However, a trail of blood led from the room and out into the garden at the rear of the property. Outside, it could be seen that a piece of ground had been disturbed recently and as the officers cleared away a few inches of earth, four holes were revealed, each one of which contained the body parts of a woman.

Later, following a more thorough search of the premises and grounds, a joiner's cross-cut saw, an axe, a large knife and a razor hidden in the ashes of a grate, were discovered, all of which had human flesh and hair attached. Newly made markings in the floorboards suggested that the still unidentified woman had been cut up with the axe as she lay on the floor. In the

'cut up with the axe
as she lay on the floor'

garden, investigators found the victim's trunk and legs in one of the holes; in the second were her left arm, lungs, heart and a kidney; in the third were the bowels and many of her internal organs; and in the fourth were her head and right arm.

A post-mortem was performed by Dr Samuel Moore, which showed the victim to have been a healthy and well-nourished young woman. Her left arm remained attached to the trunk, which had been sliced open from the neck down to the hips; all of the internal organs save the left kidney had been removed; there were cuts to the victim's face and several of her ribs were broken, which the doctor believed had been caused prior to death. He concluded that the saw and knife found at the scene had been used to dismember the body. Dr Moore was of the opinion that the woman had been first of all been stunned by her killer, who had then cut her throat, most probably with the razor found in the house. As for the dismemberment of the corpse, he believed that no special surgical skills had been required by whoever was responsible and it would probably have only taken fifteen minutes to complete the grisly task. The most difficult part would have been to separate the right arm from the shoulder socket.

The dead woman's identity remained a mystery but as her murderer had not caused any disfigurement to her face, a photograph was taken with the intention of publishing it in the press. It was hoped that somebody would see it and be able to identify her. However, this proved to be unnecessary, for news of the crime had spread rapidly by word of mouth and within hours, three women came forward. They feared the victim might be their friend who they had not seen since the previous day, which was most unusual. Their fears proved to be well-founded as they identified the dead woman as thirty-year-old prostitute Elizabeth O'Connor, who had lived in lodgings at 161 Stockwell Street. A native of County Sligo, she was renowned for her fearsome temper and was only released from prison three days before she died, having served a sentence for assaulting another woman.

Meanwhile, the police continued to search for their chief suspect, William McEwan, in whose room the murder and dismemberment had taken place. He was last seen at eight o'clock on the morning of the 12th by two young women who knew him well. They spoke to him briefly and were able to tell the investigating officers that he was walking in the direction of Paisley. The search for him concentrated on that area and he was arrested at two o'clock the next day, as he approached the Half Way House, a public house on the Paisley road.

Two gamekeepers had noticed him behaving in a suspicious manner and believing him to be a poacher, they approached him, only for him to run away. They gave chase but after running a short distance into a wood, he stopped, turned to face his pursuers and, taking a large knife from his coat pocket, slashed his own throat, opening up a massive wound. One of the gamekeepers grabbed his arm, thereby preventing him from doing himself any further harm. His companion ran to the nearby home of Dr Hunter, who was able to stop the bleeding, and an ambulance arrived to take the injured man to the Glasgow Royal Infirmary. Here, medical staff confirmed that it had been a serious suicide attempt and he was thought to be close to death. However, his life was saved and a few days later he was taken into police custody.

News of the crime caused a sensation in the city and a number of witnesses came forward who were able to provide the police with details of the suspect's movements in the hours immediately preceding the discovery of the body parts. On the night of Monday the 10th of October, McEwan visited the home of his friend, Thomas McNeilly at 97 Finnieston Street together with four other acquaintances, and the men spent a few hours in the house drinking whisky and beer. McEwan was a little tipsy and entertained the others by singing and dancing for them. At eleven o'clock the six men left the house and visited two nearby inns, where they continued drinking. Eventually they parted company and McNeilly agreed to walk home with McEwan, who was thought to be too drunk to look after himself.

Hearing of the crime, George Young, a cabman, had recognised the address at which the murder took place. At about two o'clock that morning he was waiting for custom on Bridge Street and was approached by two men and a woman, who asked to be taken to West Lodge. The witness was taken to the Royal Infirmary, where he identified McEwan as one of the men. Later, in the mortuary, he was shown the victim's head and identified her as the woman who was with the two men. The description of the second man fitted that of McEwan's friend, McNeilly, who the police learnt from his wife did not return home on the night the murder took place. He was therefore considered to be an accomplice and was arrested.

However, McNeilly denied any involvement in the crime although he acknowledged that he had spent the night in his friend's room at West Lodge, as had the victim. He insisted that he had slept alone in one of the beds and McEwan and Elizabeth O'Connor shared the other bed. McNeilly awoke at six o'clock the next morning, having overslept, and rushed out a few minutes later, leaving the couple still asleep, and headed to his work as a lamp trimmer on the SS *Furnessia*. James Graham was a storekeeper on board the ship and was able to confirm that McNeilly arrived late at a few minutes to seven that morning. He was also able to say that there was no blood on his clothes, nor did he act any differently than usual. Nevertheless, the Crown remained convinced that McNeilly was an accomplice and he was remanded in custody to await trial with McEwan, who had refused to make a statement.

The trial of the two accused opened on Tuesday 27 December, at which McNeilly entered a not guilty plea. McEwan pleaded not guilty to murder but guilty to culpable homicide. The pleas were not acceptable to the prosecution but in entering the plea, McEwan made it clear that although his victim's death had not been intentional, he acted alone and his co-defendant bore no responsibility whatsoever for her death or subsequent dismemberment. It was decided therefore not to continue with the case against McNeilly, who was allowed to leave the dock a free man.

The Crown offered no motive for the crime but argued that McEwan inflicted a fatal wound by slashing his victim's throat *before* he dismembered her body. However, in his defence it was argued that it was impossible to state categorically that any of the injuries had been sustained prior to death and expert medical evidence was called to support this view. An alternative scenario, equally plausible given the medical evidence, was that all of the wounds had been inflicted *after* she died. McEwan did not give evidence on his own behalf but his lawyer suggested that after he and Elizabeth woke up they argued over the amount of money he should pay her. They began to struggle and she died accidentally. In a panic and having lost the ability to reason properly, he decided to dismember the body and bury the parts in the garden in a futile attempt to cover up her death. The injuries to the throat area had occurred as he removed her head from the torso.

After deliberating for thirty minutes, the jury rejected the defence version of events and, following the guilty verdict, McEwan was sentenced to death. A petition seeking a reprieve was well supported and among the signatories were a number of eminent surgeons, who believed the medical evidence had not been conclusive. Nevertheless, Sir George Trevelyan, Secretary of State for Scotland, declined to recommend that the monarch should intervene.

William McEwan was hanged at eight o'clock on the morning of Wednesday, 18 January 1893 at Duke Street Gaol. The hangman was James Billington, who completed the task with more than enough time to catch the ten o'clock train to take him south.

THE MYSTERIOUS DEATH OF CECIL HAMBROUGH

Suspect:	Alfred John Monson
Age:	33
Crime:	Murder

At the Manchester Assizes in late 1893, the Lancashire & Yorkshire Revisionary Interest Company sued Mrs Annie Day of Bawtry, Doncaster, for £54 and eleven shillings. The company claimed she had signed a document agreeing to act as surety for a loan of that amount, which was taken out by her son-in-law, Alfred John Monson, three years earlier and which he had failed to repay. Mrs Day insisted that the signature on the document had in fact been forged by Monson and she therefore refused to pay any money to the company. The hearing went ahead despite both Mrs Day and her son-in-law being absent, although both had submitted written statements which were read out in court. Mrs Day was unable to attend due to her poor health and Monson could not appear as he was being held in custody in Edinburgh, awaiting trial for attempted murder and murder. At the conclusion of the evidence in Manchester, the court found in favour of Mrs Day.

In Scotland, Monson and his co-defendant, named in court as Edward Scott, were charged with attempting to murder Windsor Dudley Cecil Hambrough by drowning on 8 August in Ardlamont Bay in the Firth of Clyde and, secondly, that on the following day they murdered Hambrough in a wood on the Ardlamont Estate by shooting him. However, when the trial opened, Monson was standing in the dock alone as the police had been unable to trace the whereabouts of his co-accused, whose true identity was not known and who was rumoured to be dead or to have fled the country. In his absence, the court declared him an outlaw.

Thirty-three-year-old Monson was a married man with three children. He was the third son of the Reverend Thomas Monson, formerly Rector of Kirby-under-Dale in Yorkshire, and his mother was the daughter of the fifth Viscount Galway. Despite this impressive pedigree, Monson was considered to be something of a rogue, who had a reputation of resorting to unsavoury methods in order to finance his lifestyle.

For instance, seven years earlier he had rented Cheney Court, a mansion close to Ledbury in Herefordshire, at an annual cost of £100. He opened a private school and initially attracted a relatively large number of fee-paying pupils. Nevertheless, during the next two years there were several mysterious fires on the estate, for which he received substantial payouts from a number of different insurance companies. One of the fires in particular was remembered by those living in the district, which occurred on 1 July 1887. Alerted by smoke rising from the stables, many of his neighbours rushed to offer their assistance. When they reached the fire, they were surprised to discover that Monson had not unbolted the stable doors to release the horses. Despite being urged to do so, he refused and the animals remained locked in the building. They pleaded with him to free them but he claimed he could not do so as he had mislaid the keys. The doors were eventually smashed open by a group of men and the horses ran out to safety. It emerged later that the stables were insured by the owner of the estate, who therefore received all of the insurance money rather than Monson, who received nothing for the destruction of the building. However, the horses were owned by Monson and if they had perished in the fire, he would have received a large amount of cash. It was widely believed that he started the fire deliberately, intending that the horses should be burnt to death so that he would receive substantial compensation. In a rural community this was viewed as despicable behaviour and afterwards Monson was held in contempt.

Three months later, Cheney Court was totally destroyed by yet another conflagration. Foul play was suspected but could not be proven and Monson received £2,000 for the loss of his wife's furniture. The couple abandoned the school and moved away, leaving behind many angry shopkeepers and tradespeople who were owed a considerable amount of money in unpaid bills. Eventually, in February 1893, Monson was declared bankrupt with debts totalling £56,227.

Now, however, it was more than his reputation that was at stake as he faced a possible death sentence. His alleged victim was twenty-year-old Cecil Hambrough, the eldest son of Dudley Albert Hambrough of Steephill Castle on the Isle of Wight. Cecil was a lieutenant in the 4th Battalion, Prince of Wales Own Yorkshire Regiment, in which his father was serving as a Major. On his next birthday, the young man was due to inherit £250,000 under the terms of his late grandfather's will. When he reached seventeen years of age, his family believed Cecil needed a mentor-type figure in his life to offer him support and guidance, which his father was unable to provide as a serving soldier. A number of applicants for the post were interviewed and Monson was hired. By the time of the trial, he had acted in this role for three years, for which he received an annual salary of £300. He was the young man's constant companion and they always seemed to be on excellent terms.

In the summer of 1893, Monson rented the Ardlamont Estate, which was situated close to the village of Tignabruaich in the Kyles of Bute. The agreement also included the shooting rights. He told the owner that this was with a view to the estate being purchased outright in the near future for the full asking price of £80,000. Monson and his family arrived first and they were soon followed by his young charge. The man who would later stand accused of the young man's murder with Monson and who called himself Edward Scott arrived at Ardlamont on 8 August. George Lamont, a game-keeper employed on the estate, later informed the police that Monson told him Scott was an engineer who had been employed to look after a launch called *Alert*, which Hambrough was interested in buying.

James Dunn, a Newcastle watchmaker, and his family were spending their summer vacation in a villa owned by his sister and which stood close to the estate. At nine o'clock on the morning of the 10th, he was looking out of the kitchen window and saw Hambrough, Monson and Scott, all of whom were carrying guns, walk into a nearby wood. They separated and Hambrough took a different path to his two companions. A few minutes later, James heard the sound of a shot coming from the direction of the wood but thought nothing more of it. However, thirty minutes later he heard from a neighbour that Hambrough had been shot dead accidentally. James was present when a seemingly distraught Monson explained that he and Scott were walking in the wood together, some distance from the unfortunate young man. When they heard the gun go off, they presumed he must have shot a rabbit and headed towards where the sound of the shot had come from. They were horrified to find him lying in a ditch, clearly dead with a bullet wound to the head. The two men said they lifted the corpse on to a wall that was close by and left to report the matter.

Two hours after the shooting, Dr MacMillan of Tignabruaich issued a death certificate stating the fatal wound was inflicted accidentally. He told Monson and Scott that an inquest would not be necessary as the authori-

'They were horrified to find him lying in a ditch'

ties would be satisfied with his conclusions. Scott asked if he was required to stay for any reason and when told by the doctor that he would not, the visitor left by the boat, which sailed at five minutes past two that same afternoon. A few days after the shooting, Monson and John Stewart, an estate employee, accompanied Hambrough's body to his home in Ventnor on the Isle of Wight, where he was interred in the family vault.

What was not known at the time of the shooting was that Monson and his wife Agnes had taken out an insurance policy on the life of the dead man, in which Agnes was named as the sole beneficiary should he die. Subsequent investigations revealed that several unsuccessful attempts had been made to take out such a policy before Monson managed to do so. David Stewart of the Liverpool, London and Globe Insurance Company's Glasgow office, gave the police details of one of these failed applications.

He interviewed Monson and Hambrough together when an application was made to insure the latter's life for £26,000, naming Agnes as the beneficiary. As the interview progressed, the younger man confirmed that he was due to inherit a considerable sum when he reached twenty-one years of age. Although the man whose life was to be insured had some knowledge of the proposed policy, Mr Stewart nevertheless had serious reservations about the application. When Hambrough left them for a few minutes, Monson told the agent that he had loaned Hambrough the money with which he was going to buy Ardlamont and the policy was to protect that loan only for the limited period of time before he received his inheritance, when the loan would be repaid in full.

A similar attempt to arrange insurance, on this occasion for £52,000, was made to the Scottish Provident Institution. The company's Glasgow agent, William Wiseley, would later advise the police that he too visited Ardlamont House and met both Monson and Hambrough, who seemed content with the proposed policy. However, Mr Wiseley also became concerned when in the young man's temporary absence Monson gave his alleged loan to Hambrough as the reason for the policy and he too refused to agree to the application. The police learnt Monson made no such loan to Hambrough and that was why he waited for him to be out of earshot when he gave that as the reason for the policy to the companies' agents. It was felt that Monson probably believed this explanation gave credibility to the application for the policy but it was essential Hambrough was not aware of it.

Nevertheless, Monson did manage to secure a policy with the Mutual Life of New York Company, which agreed to insure Hambrough's life for the sum of £20,000, which was to be paid to Mrs Monson should the young man die. Again, it had been claimed the policy was essentially for the short term to cover a loan. A single initial payment was made by Monson but within a very short time the company received the death certificate signed by Dr MacMillan, stating the young man's death had been caused accidentally. As the doctor had predicted, this was accepted by the authorities but the insurance company was very suspicious and it was they who contacted the police, asking that further enquiries be made into the circumstances surrounding the death.

It did not take the police long to learn of Monson's past financial dealings and the more recent failed applications to insure the dead man's life. It was decided therefore that an investigation was justified. Among those interviewed were the estate workers who had carried the body from the wood to the main house. They were told by Monson that he and Scott lifted the body from the ditch and placed it on the wall. However, most of them now recalled having noticed at the time that there was no blood on the ground where he was supposed to have fallen, and the ditch appeared not to have been trampled on or disturbed in any way. Officers given the task of investigating the matter were beginning to have doubts about Monson's version of events, which had suggested the gun had gone off accidentally as the deceased stumbled in the ditch. Rather, it now seemed more likely that Hambrough had been shot intentionally from behind as he was standing on the wall.

Further support to the theory of foul play came when the police learnt of an incident which took place on 8 August, the day before the fatal shooting. In July, Monson hired a boat for three months from local man Donald McKellar, saying he would use it for regular fishing trips he and his friends planned to make during their stay in the area. On the evening of the 8th, Monson and Hambrough, who could not swim, went out in the boat saying they intended to fish for a few hours.

Later, Monson swam ashore alone, claiming the boat had struck a rock, causing it to capsize and throwing the two men into the water. He had searched for his young companion but failed to find him and exhaustion forced him to return to dry land. At first it was presumed that Hambrough had drowned, but he was able to clamber to safety on to a small rock and his cries for help were eventually heard. An apparently much relieved Monson took out another boat to bring the young man back to shore.

When the hired boat was recovered and returned to Mr McKellar, he was surprised to discover a roughly cut plughole in its bottom, which had not been present when he hired the boat out to Monson. More potentially incriminating information was provided by John Douglas, a gamekeeper on the estate. He told the investigating officers that he saw the boat almost every day after it was hired but he had never noticed the plughole. The police were now convinced that Monson drilled the plughole before setting off with Hambrough and opened it at some distance from the shore, intending that his companion should drown. However, after he swam ashore and it became obvious that his companion did not perish, he had no alternative other than to row out to bring him back. Hambrough, of course, had not complained of any untoward behaviour by Monson while in the boat and the investigating officers credited their suspect with having undertaken his task in such a way that his intended victim was not at all suspicious.

A major obstacle to arresting Monson was the death certificate signed by Dr MacMillan, which stated death was caused accidentally. However, when approached by the police, the doctor was honest enough to acknowledge that he had perhaps been too hasty in reaching his conclusion. He therefore readily agreed to withdraw the original death certificate, which was followed rapidly by Monson's arrest.

Permission was also granted for Hambrough's body to be exhumed and this was done on 4 September. A full post-mortem followed, which concluded that he was shot from behind and the entry wound suggested the shot had travelled in an upwards direction. There were no burn marks on the skin at the entry wound, which should have been present if the gun had gone off accidentally, close to his head. This supported the police's view that the victim was shot deliberately from below and from a distance of several feet, as he was standing on the wall.

It was decided not to rely solely on medical evidence and Edinburgh gun maker James McNaughton was asked to examine the crime scene. He was able to note and measure the damage caused by the shotgun pellets to trees and plants in what he believed was the line of fire. He also conducted a number of experiments which involved shooting a gun similar to that which killed Hambrough into models of human heads and into the skulls of recently slaughtered horses. The gun maker concluded that the victim was shot from a distance of nine feet in the manner described in the post-mortem and the fatal wound could not have been caused accidentally. These findings were corroborated by Dr Joseph Bell (already famous as Sir Arthur Conan Doyle's model for Sherlock Holmes), and the Crown presented what was believed to be a formidable case at the trial, satisfied that the means by which the murder was committed and the motive for

Thomas White. Midshipman at the Bar
of the high Court of Justiciary. for
the Murder of William Jones · Seaman
on the Shore of Leith. on the 15ᵗʰ of June. 1814. —

1 Midshipman Thomas White at his trial in 1814. (Author's collection)

2 The cottage at Haddington where Catherine Franks and her daughter Magdalene were murdered by Robert Emond in 1829. (Author's collection)

3 Robert Emond at his trial. (Author's collection)

4 Calton Gaol, where many condemned prisoners spent their final hours, including Robert Emond. It opened in 1817 and was demolished in 1930. (Author's collection)

David Dobie.   *Margaret Paterson.*   *John Thomson.*

5 A contemporary woodcut of the victim and perpetrators of the brutal murder at Gilmerton in April 1830. (Author's collection)

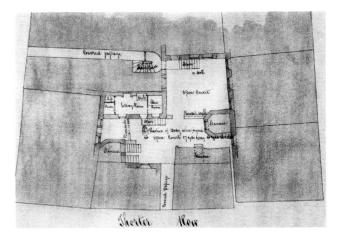

6 Dundee architect George Mathewson prepared a series of diagrams for the trial of Arthur Woods, who was accused of murdering his son in 1839. This one shows the square leading off Thorter Row.

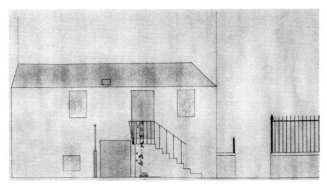

7 Mathewson's drawing of the exterior of the house in which the Woods lived.

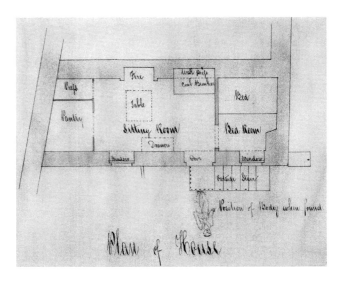

8 Mathewson's plan of the interior of the house, where the murder was alleged to have taken place. (All National Archives of Scotland)

9 Jessie McLachlan in the dock at her murder trial in 1862. (Author's collection)

10 Dr Edward Pritchard, who murdered his wife and mother-in-law in 1865. (Author's collection)

11 The murder of Thomasina Scott and attempted murder of
Jane Crichton in 1868. (*Illustrated Police News*)

12 Little Ann Swankie is beaten to death by William Cargill
in 1868. (*Illustrated Police News*)

13 The Murder at the Blackhill Toll Bar in 1869. (*Illustrated Police News*)

14 James Berry was the UK's leading executioner between 1884 and 1891. The first hangings of his career were those of poachers Innes and Vickers at Edinburgh in 1884. Others he hanged in Scotland included Jessie King and William Bury. (Author's collection)

James Berry

15 Jessie King, Scotland's most infamous baby farmer. (*Illustrated Police News*)

16 Eliza Clafton is accused of stealing, setting off a tragic chain of events in 1871. (*Illustrated Police News*)

17 William Bury's crime of 1889 led many to believe he was Jack the Ripper. (*Illustrated Police News*)

18 The hanging of William Bury at Dundee Gaol. (*Illustrated Police News*)

DECLARATION

THAT THE

SENTENCE OF DEATH

PASSED ON

WILLIAM HENRY BURY

By the Right Honourable LORD YOUNG, one of the LORDS COMMISSIONERS of JUSTICIARY, at DUNDEE, on the 28th day of March 1889,

Was carried into effect within the Walls of the Prison of Dundee, between the Hours of Eight and Nine o'clock a.m., on the 24th day of April 1889.

We, the undersigned, hereby declare that SENTENCE OF DEATH was this day executed on WILLIAM HENRY BURY, in the Prison of Dundee, in our presence. Dated this Twenty-fourth day of April, Eighteen hundred and eighty-nine years.

JNO. CRAIG, Magistrate.
WM. STEPHENSON, Magistrate.
WILLIAM GEDDES, Governor.
DAVID R. ROBERTSON, Chaplain.
C. TEMPLEMAN, M.B., Police Surgeon.
D. DEWAR, Chief Constable.
JNO. CROLL, Assistant Town Clerk.

CERTIFICATE

OF THE SURGEON OF THE PRISON OF DUNDEE.

I, JAMES WILLIAM MILLER, Surgeon of the Prison of Dundee, hereby certify that I this Day examined the Body of WILLIAM HENRY BURY, on whom SENTENCE OF DEATH was this day executed in the Prison of Dundee, and that, on that examination, I found that the said WILLIAM HENRY BURY was dead.

Dated this twenty-fourth Day of April, Eighteen hundred and eighty-nine years.

J. W. MILLER, M.D.,

MED. OFFICER, H.M. PRISON, DUNDEE

19 The official notification of William Bury's execution. (Dundee City Archives)

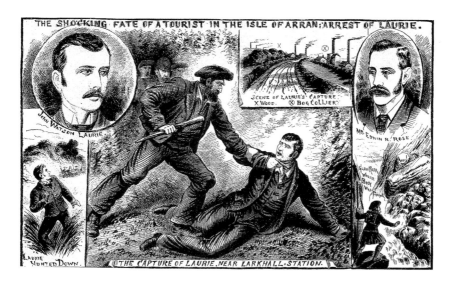

20 John Lawrie, suspected of murdering Edwin Rose on Arran in 1889, is apprehended. (*Illustrated Police News*)

21 The residents of Arran constructed a cairn in memory of Edwin Rose on Goat Fell. (*The Graphic*)

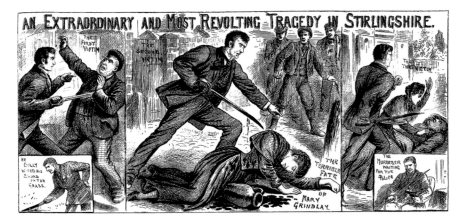

22 Mary Grindley met a tragic end at the hands of James Frazer at Polmont in 1892. (*Illustrated Police News*)

23 The villa at 56 Maxwell Drive, Pollockshields, where the dismembered corpse of an unknown woman was discovered in 1892. (*Illustrated Police News*)

24 William McEwan, the prime suspect in the Pollockshields murder case, attempted to take his own life when arrested. (*Illustrated Police News*)

25 McEwan's victim was identified as prostitute Elizabeth O'Connor, who made the fatal error in agreeing to spend the night with her murderer. (*Illustrated Police News*)

26 The body of Cecil Hambrough was discovered on the Ardlamont Estate in 1893. At first it was thought he had died accidentally. (*Illustrated Police News*)

27 Suspicion later fell on young Hambrough's companion, Alfred Monson, who was arrested and charged with his murder. (*Illustrated Police News*)

28 The mysterious Edward Sweeney, alias Scott. (*The Graphic*)

29 Cecil Hambrough. (*The Graphic*)

30 Alfred Monson. (*The Graphic*)

31 Major Hambrough gave evidence at the trial of his son's alleged killer. (*The Graphic*)

32 A police photograph of Oscar Slater, who was wrongly convicted of murdering Marion Gilchrist. (Author's collection)

33 Detective Lieutenant John Trench, who played a significant role in establishing the innocence of Oscar Slater. (Author's collection)

34 Marion Gilchrist, whose murder in 1908 resulted in one of Scotland's most notorious miscarriages of justice. (Author's collection)

35 The dining room in which Marion Gilchrist's body was found. (National Archives of Scotland)

the crime had been uncovered. Although it was Monson who stood to gain most by the death of the victim, it was claimed that Scott would have received a percentage of the insurance money for his help.

The defence called witnesses, including estate staff, who spoke of the excellent and close relationship enjoyed by Monson and Hambrough, and several described being impressed at how genuinely distraught Monson seemed when he thought the young man had drowned and also immediately after the fatal shooting.

As for the attempts to insure Hambrough's life, the jury was reminded that no proof had been provided by the Crown to show the explanation given by their client to the companies' agents was false. It was emphasised that all that could be proven by the evidence of the prosecution witnesses was that Hambrough was present at all the interviews and was fully aware that his life was being insured and that on each occasion, Mrs Monson was named as the beneficiary should he die. The Crown might suggest an underhand motive but it could not prove it. The defence urged the jury members to use their commonsense and ask themselves if it possible for an attempt to be made on someone's life by opening a plughole in the bottom of a small boat without the intended victim realising what was happening? The very idea was described as absurd and surely the intended victim would have notified the police. What the victim of the conspiracy would not have done was go out shooting the very next day with Monson and Scott if he suspected an attempt had been made on his life.

Witnesses were called who described the unsafe manner in which the deceased had sometimes handled guns. Philip Day, Monson's brother-in-law, told of going out shooting with Hambrough in the autumn of 1891. As the day progressed he became increasingly aware of just how careless the young man could be. He carried his loaded rifle at full cock even in rough terrain and in one unfortunate incident he accidentally shot the witness's fox terrier. Another witness, John Waters, a student at Guy's Hospital, testified that he was a member of the shooting party described by the previous witness and could confirm everything Philip Day had described and, in particular, the witness recalled the harsh words spoken to Hambrough after the dog was shot.

William Donald, an engineer from Paisley, did not know Monson but after reading newspaper reports of the case had come forward to describe a chance meeting he had with Hambrough on a steamer in the Kyles of Bute. They fell into conversation, in the course of which the young man told the witness how, on the day before, he was carrying a rifle that had gone off accidentally at the side of his head leaving him temporarily deaf.

On entering the witness box, Colonel George Tillard explained that he knew none of those involved in the case but had been urged by friends to contact the authorities and provide details of his own experience. Part of the colonel's ear was missing and he told the jury that although he was now living in Harrow, he had served in India for twenty-eight years. It was there, while out shooting snipe in March 1871, that he had stumbled and the double-barrelled shotgun he was carrying went off. It took away part of his ear from a backwards direction and the defence claimed that this gave weight to their argument that such an accident was possible, even when a weapon was in the hands of the most experienced shooters.

Summing up, the defence claimed that the Crown had failed to prove beyond reasonable doubt that a murder had taken place or that their client was guilty of any crime. Credence, it was said, must be given to Monson's claim that the shooting was accidental and that he had not previously attempted to murder Hambrough. The jury was absent for forty-five minutes before returning to their seats. When asked for their verdict, the foreman replied, 'My Lord, the verdict of the jury on both counts is Not Proven.' This was greeted by loud cheering in the courtroom and Monson was allowed to walk out of the dock a free man, although he was never to be accepted as an innocent man by the public at large.

Monson's subsequent career was followed with keen interest and details of his exploits were often to be found in the newspapers of the time. In March 1894, John Lear, a London cabman, took him to Westminster County Court to recover £3 he insisted he was owed in unpaid fares. Monson had given him a cheque for that amount but the bank refused to cash it when presented. Monson did not attend the hearing but was ordered to pay the full amount within seven days. Later the same year, Monson sued Madame Tussaud's in London, where his waxwork figure had been placed and used to point visitors in the direction of the room in which the models of notorious killers were housed. He claimed this implied that he was guilty of murder when a court had decided he was not. He won the case but the jury awarded him the derisory sum of one farthing in damages.

In January 1895, at the Court of Appeal, it was determined that Monson could not claim on the insurance policy on Hambrough's life with the New York Mutual Company as it was considered he obtained the policy based on a series of untrue statements. In February 1896, he deserted his wife and six children, claiming she had committed adultery with Hambrough shortly before his death. In November of the following year, Mrs Monson was forced to take him to court in Leeds, where he was then living, for maintenance which he had not been paying and he was ordered to pay £2 a week towards the upkeep of his family. In 1898, Monson was sentenced to five years penal servitude for his part in an attempt to defraud the National Union Life Insurance Company. He had conspired with others for a healthy man to pose as another, who was really close to death, at a medical so that a fraudulent claim could be made later when the sick man died. Monson afterwards fell out of public view.

As for the outlawed Scott, he surrendered to the court in April 1894. His real name was Edward Sweeney and he was a London bookmaker. Monson had become one of his clients and the two men became friends. He was invited to Ardlamont, which Monson said he was in the process of purchasing, and at this stage Sweeney did not know Hambrough existed. When he arrived in Scotland, Monson told him it might be embarrassing if people knew he was his bookmaker, which led him to agree to be called by a different name and to be described as an engineer. His version of events was accepted and it was believed that he genuinely knew nothing of Monson's plans and was not present when the fatal shot was fired. As a result, he was formally cleared of any involvement in the Ardlamont affair.

THE BODY IN THE GLADSTONE BAG

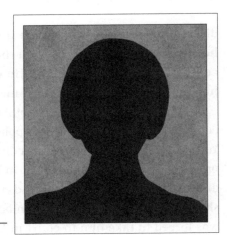

Suspect:	Laura Richards
Age:	21
Crime:	Murder

In early February 1900, twenty-one-year-old Laura Richards was working as a domestic servant in England, when she received a letter telling her that her mother was dangerously ill and she was needed at home. She returned to Motherwell immediately but, unfortunately, her mother's health deteriorated and she died towards the end of the month. Her late mother was a widow and Laura, the eldest child of the family, was left responsible for her four siblings. These were fifteen-year-old William, thirteen-year-old Thomas, Lizzie who was six and four-year-old Ada. The neighbours considered Laura to be a mature, capable and loving replacement for the children's mother, who was providing them with exceptional care at this difficult time.

For the first few weeks, Laura and the children remained in the family home in Abbotsford Place off Thorn Street but in late May they moved to new lodgings in Carlin, a mile and a half away, at the home of Mrs Underwood on Barrack Walk. She had been a friend of the children's mother and Laura arrived with the two boys and Lizzie. When asked about Ada's whereabouts, she explained that the little girl was staying with relatives in Glasgow.

In early August, Laura decided to move back to Motherwell, by which time William was working in a local pit and was lodging with a miner and his family. Thomas, who remained with Laura, was working as a messenger boy. Foolishly, Laura seems not to have finalised a rental agreement and decided to move into an empty house in Park Street. She did so without the knowledge of the owner and misled the person looking after the key to the premises to get hold of it, which enabled her to gain entry. If she thought the owner would simply accept the arrangement as a *fait accompli* she was wrong as he had agreed to rent the house to a newly married couple and demanded Laura and the children vacate the property forthwith and that she take all her furniture and other belongings with her.

Laura was able to rent rooms at 45 Dalziel Street but there was not enough room for all her furniture. However, a family friend, Mrs Cannon, who lived at 6 Russell Place on Park Street, agreed that Laura could leave some items in her home on a temporary basis. Among the possessions which she left was a locked chest. As Laura was leaving, Mrs Cannon asked about Ada and was also told that she was with relatives in Glasgow.

Several weeks passed and by late August there was a dreadful stench coming from the chest. Mrs Cannon was suspicious and decided to notify the police. Two officers called at her home, took possession of the offending chest and carried it to Motherwell police station, where Superintendent Alexander Moir opened it to reveal a Gladstone bag. This too was opened and the superintendent and his colleagues were presented with a terrible sight, for inside was the rotting corpse of a child, naked except for a chemise and its face so badly decomposed that it was impossible to discern

'the rotting corpse of a child'

any features. The head was resting on its breast and the feet had been drawn up so that it could be crushed into the very small space in which it was contained.

A post-mortem was performed on Saturday 25 August by Professor John Glaister of Glasgow University and Dr R.P. Jack of Motherwell. They described the body as almost skeletonised and wrapped around the neck and lower part of the face was a cotton cloth, which covered the mouth and nostrils. There were no bone fractures and no definite cause of death could be given. However, the doctors were able to state that it was the body of a girl, probably about four years old, and that she had been in the bag for approximately six months. Convinced it was the body of Ada, the police arrested Laura and, after being questioned for some time, she was charged with having committed her murder on a date between 1 March – when she assumed sole responsibility for the children – and 28 May, the date she left the chest with Mrs Cannon.

It was believed that poverty had driven Laura to murder Ada, who was half-sister to the other children. Following the death of the father of the four eldest, their mother began a relationship with her late husband's brother, John Richards. The couple married and Ada was born and she was followed by another child, a son called Andrew. The marriage was not a success and the couple separated and despite John always denying that he was Ada's father, he nevertheless agreed to pay weekly maintenance of two shillings and sixpence for each child. However, Andrew died and the weekly maintenance of five shillings was halved.

Following the death of her mother, John refused to help Laura with the cost of the funeral and she was left almost destitute. She applied for relief to Alexander Bryden, Assistant Inspector of the Poor in the district. It was agreed that she would be paid five shillings weekly for Thomas and Lizzie, despite Thomas having a little income from a job as a messenger boy. Nothing was paid by the parish for Ada as John continued to pay half a crown towards her upkeep. This meant that Laura received a total of twelve shillings and sixpence to keep her and the three children. It was claimed that she murdered Ada to lessen the financial burden.

When first arrested, Laura denied all knowledge of the dead child, claiming not to know its identity or how it came to be in her chest. When questioned about Ada's whereabouts, she replied that she was with a Mrs Hamilton in Larkhall but later changed her story, saying she was staying with a Mrs Rogers in Glasgow. Enquiries revealed both accounts to be untrue and when challenged by Superintendent Moir, she said simply, 'Oh well, I will take the blame, I did it myself.' Throughout her first night in custody in police cells, an officer sat with her and one of those on the rota was Constable John Stewart. He told of a conversation in which the prisoner told him that Ada died of natural causes and feeling ashamed of being unable to pay for a decent funeral, she decided to conceal her death.

Laura pleaded not guilty when her murder trial opened at the High Court of Judiciary in Glasgow before Lord Young, on Wednesday 7 November. The Crown acknowledged that its case was based largely on circumstantial evidence, which was the reason for relying to a great extent on the spoken admissions Laura was said to have made while in police custody. It was not possible to provide forensic evidence that the body was that of Ada due to the advanced state of decomposition. The police had asked Mrs Underwood, who knew Ada well, to look at the body but she was unable to identify it. The prosecution called Angus McDonald to give evidence to support the theory that Ada had been murdered. He was the headmaster of Murray Street Public School, who employed Laura as a servant in his home before she moved to England. She visited him a few weeks after her mother's death and he was told by Laura that all the children were well except for Ada, who had died.

It was also conceded by the Crown that the post-mortem had been inconclusive regarding the cause of death but the piece of cloth around the neck of the dead child pointed to her having met her end by strangulation. If Ada had died due to natural causes the jury was asked to consider why the accused woman's subsequent behaviour was inconsistent with this? Firstly, she hid the body, secondly, she continued to accept the half-crown weekly maintenance off John Richards and, finally, she gave conflicting accounts about where the little girl was. If Ada was still living, why did Laura not simply reveal her whereabouts to the court now?

The most important defence witnesses were Laura's remaining brothers and sister. William, Thomas and Lizzie all testified that Ada became ill a few days after their mother died and was put to bed by Laura. She remained bedridden for the next two to three weeks and during that time, all the children remembered Laura being very kind to their youngest sister. Nevertheless, they all recalled how the little girl seemed to grow paler and thinner as the days passed. Under questioning by the Crown's barrister, none could recall Laura administering medicine to Ada and admitted that the bedding was never changed and, as she frequently soiled it, she became dirty and began to smell terribly. When she disappeared from the house, Laura told them that Ada was being looked after by a family friend.

The defence did not attempt to deny the body was that of Ada, but emphasised to the jury that there was no medical evidence to support the Crown's case that the young girl in the Gladstone bag had been strangled or suffocated, as it was impossible to say that the material around the face and neck had been tied so tightly to have been used in that way. Also, the defence's reliance on Laura's verbal confessions in the police cells was questionable. It was pointed out that she was not accompanied by a solicitor at the time; was not warned of the possible consequences of making statements in such circumstances and, anyway, there was no corroborative testimony. There was no explicit suggestion that the Motherwell police officers were lying, but it was argued that Laura's statement that she was prepared to take the blame for what happened was not necessarily an admission to murder, but reflected her feeling of guilt that she could have done more to prevent Ada's death.

Her barrister urged the jury to find that Ada had died of natural causes, but even if they believed she died as a result of neglect, Laura should not be convicted of murder. The jury retired for fifteen minutes and found the charge of murder Not Proven. Accordingly, Laura Richards was released.

CASE THIRTY-ONE   1903

THE HOUSE OF DEATH

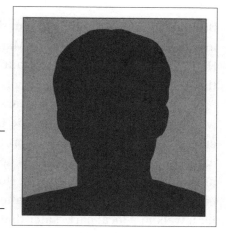

Suspect:	John Newbigging
Age:	32
Crime:	Murder

Lanark Lodge was a fine villa situated to the east of Duns in Berwickshire and was the home of the wealthy Mrs McKie, who had been living there for two years in early April 1903. She was visiting England for the purposes of improving her health and had left her two full-time employees, Peter Paterson the gardener and the coachman, thirty-two-year-old John Newbigging, to look after the property during her absence. The coachman and his family lived in a one-storey cottage, which also served as the gatehouse to the grounds.

Newbigging and his wife Margaret, the daughter of William White, the School Board Officer in Eyemouth, had married seven years earlier when she was eighteen years old. They now had four daughters: Maggie, who was five years of age; Mary, who was a year younger; two-year-old Jane and eight-month-old Helen, also known as Lily. Newbigging had worked for Mrs McKie for several years and was held in great regard by his employer. Maggie was a pupil at Duns Public School and although her sister Mary was not old enough to attend lessons, she was allowed to accompany her to some of them.

The first inkling his wife had that all was not as it should be was on Sunday 11 April. She and the children had spent the previous week at the home of her father in Eyemouth and her husband had driven there to bring them home. On seeing her, he complained he had been experiencing difficulty sleeping for several nights, which was most unusual for him. The next day, Margaret asked Dr McKenzie to visit John and he prescribed

Bromide of Potassium to help him sleep. The doctor called again twenty-four hours later to be greeted by Margaret, who told him, 'John is all right. He has had a sleep and is now out exercising his horse. I do not think there is any need for you to call again.'

Nevertheless, the doctor appears to have recognised worrying signs, which suggested to him that the insomnia was perhaps a sign of an emerging and far more serious problem. He warned Margaret to keep a careful watch on her husband as he could be liable to what he described as 'sudden mental derangement'. However, John's apparent improvement continued and on the Tuesday afternoon the couple took the children for a walk in a local park. Later that same evening, John's father, Robert, visited them to find his son in good spirits, singing to baby Lily as he bounced her on his knee. At his father's suggestion, John took another dose of Bromide of Potassium and when Robert left there was nothing to indicate the horror that would unfold over the next few hours.

There were several cottages quite close to the lodge but during the night none of the neighbours were disturbed in any way. One resident would later tell of seeing smoke coming from the gatehouse's chimney at one o'clock but nothing else of note was seen or heard. As eleven o'clock approached on Wednesday morning, Peter Paterson was troubled as he had not seen his colleague, nor had their neighbours heard the children playing outside the cottage as they normally did. A few of them gathered outside the front door as Peter banged on it, but there was no response. He next tried knocking on the windows but there was still no sign of the family. Someone ran to inform John's father, who lived on Currie Street, and he sent his other son Thomas to investigate. He broke the kitchen window and climbed inside. Within a matter of moments he cried out in horror and despair, 'They're all dead.'

'They're all dead'

The alarm was raised and John's father was soon at the cottage. He was quickly followed by Mr W.B. Macqueen, the Procurator Fiscal, and Dr McKenzie who, together with Sergeant Young of the local police, climbed in through the smashed window.

There were two beds in the kitchen, in one of which were the bodies of Jane and Lily. In the other was the body of Mary and lying on the floor next to it was Maggie, who in her final moments seems to have woken up and fallen out of the bed. The body of their mother was also in the room, but unlike her daughters, she had not been attacked as she slept. Much of the furniture in the room was upturned and Margaret had put up a desperate struggle before being overpowered. Her husband's corpse was lying at the door which led out of the kitchen and into the lobby and at his side was the bloodied razor he had used to slash the throats of his wife and children before killing himself in a similar manner. The killings were carried out several hours earlier as the bodies were cold and rigid.

Margaret was partially dressed and her husband was wearing his stockings and breeches. It was believed that his wife had lit the fire in the early hours, the smoke of which was seen by the neighbour, possibly with the intention of drying some washing. Her husband is thought to have started to dress, perhaps initially intending to help her, but had been overcome by feelings of depression and helplessness and in this state of 'homicidal mania' carried out the slaughter of his family. Why he should feel such despair was unknown as the marriage seemed happy, there were no financial difficulties and all the family members enjoyed good health.

What actually happened and the reasons leading up to the bloody conclusion will never be known. However, the phenomenon which modern-day psychologists and criminologists refer to as 'familicide' is not uncommon. It involves a spouse, usually a male, killing the couple's children and perhaps the other adult partner. These crimes tend to fall into two distinct categories. In the first type, only the children are murdered, after which the killer commits suicide; this usually follows an acrimonious separation. The killer, facing the loss of the children, reasons, 'If I cannot have them nobody can,' and the aim is to punish the remaining partner who is meant to suffer feelings of loss and guilt.

John Newbigging's crime appears to have fallen into the second category, in that he perhaps became convinced for some reason known only to himself that he would no longer be able to provide and protect the family he loved dearly from harm. It was thought by his surviving family members that he may have believed, wrongly, that he faced the loss of his employment and home. Fearing he would then be unable to support Margaret and the children, it was in this state of mind that he took the only way out that he could see.

The task of preparing the bodies for burial fell to the much-respected Nurse Bardsley, who was the daughter of the Bishop of Carlisle and who had cared for the sick of the district for some years. As was customary, she received many offers of help with the task from the women of the area, but chose not to accept them. She realised that no matter how experienced in such matters they may have been, it was probable that many of the women would find it too much of an ordeal and she feared they might not be able to cope. John Leslie, the district's Sanitary Officer, and Sergeant Young of the local police were on hand to offer any assistance she might require. It was later reported in the press that the children looked peaceful but their mother's face still bore an expression of terror and that of the father one of wild determination.

The 'chesting', or placing of the bodies in the coffins, took place in the local undertaker's parlour. Robert Newbigging was present and Margaret's father had planned to be there. However, he decided he could not face the ordeal although he did find the strength to attend the funeral two days later. There were three coffins, in one of which were placed the bodies of Jane and her father, in another those of Lily and her mother, and the third contained Maggie and Mary.

The grieving relatives wished to have a private funeral so the time it was to take place was not announced and at six o'clock on the following Saturday morning, family members and close friends met at the gatehouse. Two hearses and a wagonette were hired, each of which carried a single coffin. A single wreath of spring flowers was placed on top of that containing Maggie and Mary and the sad procession made its way through the silent village to the nearby cemetery. The coffins were put in a common grave as a service was read by Reverend D. Herald. Throughout the remainder of the day, as news of the burial spread, many hundreds of people visited the gravesides to pay their respects to this tragic family.

THE CASE OF THE POISONED SHORTBREAD

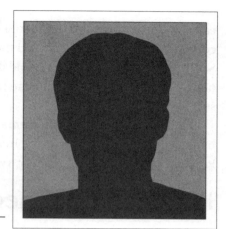

Suspect:	Thomas Matheson Brown
Age:	49
Crime:	Murder

On the evening of Monday, 19 November 1906, fourteen-year-old Elizabeth Thornton, a domestic servant at Woodside Cottage, Old Cumnock opened the door to the postman. He handed her a parcel, the postmark on which showed it was posted earlier that same day in Kilmarnock and was addressed to her employer, the elderly and now retired farmer William Lennox. Elizabeth informed the housekeeper, Grace McKerrow, who removed the brown wrapping paper to discover a small tin box, inside which was a single piece of shortbread covered with icing. There was also a short note which read, 'With happy greetings from a friend,' but nothing to indicate the identity of the sender. Grace put it on the kitchen table, where it remained untouched for several days.

On the following Thursday evening, Grace asked Elizabeth if she would like a slice of shortbread but the youngster declined as she was suffering from a toothache. She was not to know at the time that her decision not to eat a piece may well have saved her life. The next day, Mrs Bains, a neighbour, visited her good friend William Lennox and accepted his invitation to stay for supper. Grace cut the shortbread into portions for William, his guest and for herself. Each commented on how bitter it tasted before beginning to feel ill, Grace more so than the others. Dr Robertson was called to the cottage and Grace said to him, 'I've been poisoned.' She was correct, for the doctor recognised the symptoms of strychnine poisoning. Sadly, there was nothing he could do for her and Grace died within the hour. The others, who had not eaten as much of the shortbread as Grace, survived the ordeal.

The dead woman was the unmarried niece of William Lennox and had been living in comfortable circumstances in a house she owned on Prestwick Road in Ayr. However, two years earlier, her aunt, William's

'I've been poisoned'

wife, fell seriously ill and Grace came to Old Cumnock to help care for her. The old woman died, but not before making Grace promise to stay on and care for William. She did so, but it was always her intention to return to her own home in Ayr. Sadly, she would never do so and she was buried in Auchinleck cemetery on the Tuesday after she died. The service for this popular young woman was attended by several hundred mourners while the shops in the town were closed as a mark of respect and the curtains of the front rooms of many of the houses were drawn shut.

That she died due to foul play was recognised immediately and the police were helped in their investigation by the fact that neither Grace nor Elizabeth had thrown away the paper in which the shortbread was wrapped when it arrived. This would prove to be invaluable in the investigation of the crime as the name of the addressee and the brief greeting were written in the same hand. When shown to the surviving victims and others, many recognised the handwriting as that of Thomas Matheson Brown, who lived at Ardnith House in New Cumnock and whose wife was a niece of William Lennox. The Browns had been the first to visit Woodside Cottage to wish her uncle well after details of the poisonings became known.

Forty-nine-year-old Brown was a well-known figure in the Ayrshire coal industry, having only recently retired as chairman of the Lanemark Coal Company. He was also a member of several local bodies and had a reputation of being an unassuming and kindly man. It was no surprise therefore that his arrest on a charge of murder was met with a great deal of astonishment in the district. When asked to provide details of his movements on 19 November, Brown told officers that he had travelled to Glasgow by a morning train to shop at Cooper's store on Howard Street. In Glasgow he first called at the Conservative Club on Bothwell Street, which hall porters Walter Steel and David Laidlaw were able to confirm. He paid one shilling for a bath and police found proof of this as there was an entry in the club's Dressing Room Register. Furthermore, Henry Dougall of the grocery department at Cooper's store remembered Brown ordering his provisions and arranging for them to be delivered to the station at a few minutes to eleven, when he was due to take the train home and which he was seen to board, although it did not stop at New Cumnock.

However, police learnt from Brown's sister-in-law that by chance she met him on the train, which he left at Kilmarnock, saying he would be catching a later train that stopped there and which would take him to New Cumnock. Enquiries at Kilmarnock station found that he would have arrived there on the first train at 11.35 a.m. and the train for New Cumnock left at 11.57 a.m. This meant that Brown had more than twenty minutes in Kilmarnock, which allowed sufficient time to post the parcel to William Lennox. Coincidentally, James Borland, the Secretary of the Ayrshire Coal Owners Association, arrived on another train at Kilmarnock at 11.43 a.m. As he was leaving the station he met Brown, his old friend, who was entering the station from the direction of the town centre.

At Kilmarnock Post Office, counter clerk Thomas Hart was shown the wrapping paper in which the shortbread was sent and was able to identify the franking. He had stamped the parcel at about 11.30 a.m. on the day in question. Hardy McHardy, the Chief Constable of Ayrshire, walked the route from the post office to the station platform on several occasions to time the journey on foot. It took a few minutes only and the police were satisfied that their suspect could have alighted from the Glasgow train at Kilmarnock, walked to the post office in the town centre, posted the parcel, returned to the station and caught the train to New Cumnock.

A piece of the shortbread was sent for analysis to Sir Henry Littlejohn, the renowned surgeon and forensic scientist. He found no trace of poison in the shortbread itself, but the icing contained enough strychnine to kill several people. George Skinner, managing director of Messrs William Skinner & Sons, bakers and confectioners, confirmed that the shortbread was purchased at the company's shop on Argyle Street in Glasgow and that the wrapping paper and ribbons with which the parcel was tied were similar to those sold at the shop. Mr Skinner also assured the police that the company would never cover their shortbread with icing, which he believed had been added later in a very amateurish fashion. A search of Brown's house revealed a quantity of icing sugar, which it was believed he had laced with poison before spreading it on his purchase in the days before posting it to Woodside Cottage.

Investigators were aware that for the previous ten years, Brown had been a regular customer of Glasgow chemists, Frazer and Green, from whom he obtained the medicines he need for his health problems. An inspection of the shop's Register of Poisons revealed that on 2 May, he had bought 437 grains of strychnine, one grain of which was sufficient to kill an adult. He had told the assistant who dealt with him that the poison was needed to kill rats. However, Violet Lambie, a servant in the Brown household, had told officers that Mrs Brown only used the product 'Rough on Rats' to kill the vermin.

It was believed that William Lennox and not Grace was the intended victim, as the parcel was addressed to him. Despite the strength of the evidence against him, there was no apparent motive for the crime. Brown might have expected his wife, who was William's relative, to have inherited a part of his wealth on his death, but Brown was a wealthy man and did not need the money. The Crown, on this occasion, agreed with the defence that the accused man was insane and hoped to avoid a trial. However, Brown would not agree to this course of action and demanded a trial, insisting he was innocent.

A preliminary hearing took place to hear arguments from both sides, at the conclusion of which it was directed there should be a trial. This was held on Monday, 18 March 1907, at which the Crown presented its evidence linking the accused to the purchase of the poison, the shortbread, wrapping paper and the icing sugar. His handwriting was shown to be similar to that on the wrapping and card and he was shown to have been in Kilmarnock at the time the parcel was posted. A number of witnesses were also called, who gave details of his long history of epilepsy, which in the Edwardian era was still synonymous with insanity. The attacks were said to have occurred on a regular basis at home and at work. He was also said to have behaved very oddly on many occasions.

None of these witnesses were medically qualified and the Crown arranged for the accused to be examined by Dr John Carwell of Anderson's College in Glasgow, who specialised in this area of medicine, and Dr Donald Frazer, consulting physician, who also had extensive experience of working with mentally ill patients. Both experts highlighted Brown's morbid fears and suspicions, his delusional character and his frequent bizarre behaviour. They agreed that he was suffering from what they described as chronic epileptic insanity.

Brown was not called to the witness stand and his lawyers simply told the jury that the evidence against him was circumstantial. However, there was little surprise in the courtroom when the jury found that the accused was insane and not fit to plead. He was ordered to be detained indefinitely in an asylum for the criminally insane.

CASE THIRTY-THREE   1907

THE
DESERTER

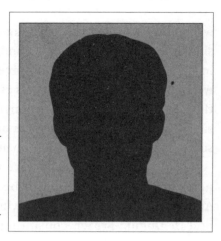

Suspect:	Joseph Hume
Age:	25
Crime:	Murder

The tranquillity of Lhanbryde, a village situated three miles to the east of Elgin, was shattered on the afternoon of Sunday, 29 September 1907. Mrs McGillivray was tending to the garden at the front of the two-storey cottage in which she and her family lived on the top floor when she became aware of a terrible smell, apparently coming from the rooms on the ground floor, which were occupied by fifty-one-year-old John Barclay Smith.

She became extremely concerned and contacted the police, who forced an entry. The source of the smell was immediately obvious, for it was the body of the tenant. He was lying partially dressed on his bed having suffered a significant head injury, which had been inflicted with a hammer, found on the floor close to the bed. A large pool of blood had accumulated under the bed, having seeped through the sheets and mattress to the floor. This, together with the advanced state of decomposition of the body, indicated to Dr Alexander, who made a preliminary examination at the scene, that the man had been dead for several days. There were no signs of a struggle and it was concluded he must have been attacked as he slept.

The doctor would normally have conducted a post-mortem examination at the cottage but the stench was causing problems for those living nearby and the corpse was therefore taken to the mortuary at Elgin. The doctor found the deceased to have been a healthy and muscular man, whose death had been neither the result of an accident nor had he committed suicide. The single and fatal blow caused a fracture to the left side of the skull and the destruction of the eyesocket, which would have resulted in his instantaneous death.

The deceased always kept very much to himself, but he was known to have been a heavy drinker. He arrived in Lhanbryde at the beginning of the year and started work as a labourer for a company with a contract to repair the district's roads. The son of a crofter, he was a native of Banchory, where his widowed mother was still living. He was separated from his wife, who remained in Aberdeen. The police could discover no motive for the murder at this early stage of the investigation, but they did learn that in the final days of his life, John was seen regularly in the company of a man, who was a shabbily dressed stranger in the village. The last sighting of the deceased was on Tuesday 24 September; thirteen-year-old Charles Duncan had travelled on the train to Elgin in the same carriage as John and the stranger and he saw them return together later that day. John was not seen alive again.

It also became evident that the stranger had been staying with John in his rooms. Grocer John Milne remembered the man visiting his shop and asking for a pennyworth of sugar and tea. He recalled this vividly because it was unusual for items to be purchased in such small quantities and the packets, into which those provisions were put, were found in John's kitchen. Further confirmation that the stranger stayed with John for a few days was provided by Margaret, the McGillivrays daughter. She saw him in the house a number of times and on one occasion he was looking out of the window, but when he saw her he drew back hastily, as though attempting to avoid being seen. At seven o'clock one morning, within a short time of when the murder was thought to have taken place, a group of farm labourers saw the man rushing away from John's door and out of the village, since when he had not been seen in the area.

The description of the unknown man was circulated throughout Scotland and was recognised by police officers in Edinburgh, to whom he was well known. He was identified as twenty-five-year-old Joseph Hume, who had enlisted in the Highland Light Infantry under the assumed name of Joseph Rutherford. He was based at Fort George but deserted a short time before the Lhanbryde murder. His former comrades told the police that when he deserted he could have had no more than one shilling in his possession and would have needed money urgently. Police believed that Hume met and befriended John, perhaps initially with a view to simply spending a few days with him and stealing what he could, but had chosen instead to rob and murder him.

Hume was eventually traced to his lodgings on St John Street in Stirling, where he was arrested on Wednesday 23 October. He was working as a labourer for a building company under the false name of Joseph Middleton. On being detained, he acknowledged his true identity and that he was a deserter. However, he denied any knowledge of the murder in Lhanbryde, saying simply, 'I know nothing about it. I never saw Smith.' In the account he gave of his movements following his desertion, he claimed to have walked from Nairn to Inverness and from there taken a train to Perth. When challenged about his lack of money, he insisted that he hid under a seat to avoid paying the fare. He took another train to Edinburgh, again not paying for a ticket, on 25 September. He finally reached Stirling where he was able to find employment. Nevertheless, when his photograph was shown to residents in Lhanbryde, who had seen the stranger with the murder victim, all recognised Hume and he was charged with John's murder.

In the period following his desertion and the murder, Hume met a young woman named Mary Armstrong, who, when questioned, said he seemed to have plenty of money to spend. He told her that he won it gambling in the barracks, before being honourably discharged from the army. It was also learnt that he visited his brother Robert and his family, arriving there on 25 September. Robert was a stonemason and at Hume's request had asked his employers, Turners & Sons, if he could start work for them, but under an assumed name. The company was highly suspicious and refused to hire him on those terms, which led Hume to decide to move on. His sister-in-law, Ann, said she was surprised at how much money he had with him, recalling on one occasion that he took as much as fifteen shillings from his pocket. He gave her son spending money and bought her husband a great deal of drink. He also had a silver watch, which would prove to be a crucial piece of evidence in establishing that robbery was the motive behind the murder.

Hume mentioned to Mary Armstrong that he had pawned a watch in Edinburgh, which led to visits being paid to the city's pawnbrokers by the police. The watch in question was finally discovered at Quinn's on Candle Maker Row, where it had been pledged for twenty-five shillings by a man giving the name of John Middlemas and the address 12 Grassmarket. Not surprisingly, these details proved to be false but staff at the shop, when shown a photograph of Hume, confirmed he was the man they dealt with. The watch was shown to his sister-in-law, who was able to say it was the one she had seen when he was staying with the family. Further enquiries led to Elgin watchmaker Andrew Junner, whose records showed he had repaired it for the murdered man earlier in the year.

Hume's trial opened in Aberdeen on Thursday, 6 February 1908 and lasted for two days. The defence lawyers highlighted the number of similar and as yet unsolved crimes which had occurred recently in Bathgate, Whiteinch and Dundee, none of which their client could have committed. It was suggested, therefore, that the murder Hume was accused of had in fact been committed by the person responsible for those other crimes. They also produced witnesses who claimed they saw the accused in Edinburgh on the 24th and 25th of September, when the crime was thought to have taken place. Other witnesses testified that they saw the victim in the company of another man in Lhanbryde on 25 September, meaning someone other than Hume could have been the murderer. However, his witnesses crumbled under cross-examination and after retiring for an hour, the jury found Hume guilty of wilful murder.

The trial judge, Lord Kincaid Mackenzie, told the now convicted prisoner that he agreed fully with the jury's decision as there could be no doubt whatsoever that he was responsible for the dreadful crime. After hearing the death sentence passed on him, Hume blew a kiss to somebody sitting in the public gallery.

A petition seeking a reprieve gained considerable support and was signed by more than 7,000 people. Nevertheless, on 5 March 1908 Hume was hanged by Henry Pierrepoint, protesting his innocence to the end. He was the last person to be executed at Inverness Prison.

CASE THIRTY-FOUR 1908

THE OSCAR SLATER CASE

Suspect:	Oscar Slater
Age:	36
Crime:	Murder

Marion Gilchrist was a wealthy eighty-two-year-old spinster, whose estate was estimated to be worth between £60,000 and £80,000. She lived in a luxury apartment at 15 Queen's Terrace, Glasgow, which had been her home for more than thirty years and was situated on the middle floor of the three-storey building. The rooms above her were unoccupied and living on the ground floor was flautist Arthur Adams. Marion employed a maid, twenty-one-year-old Nellie Lamb, and at a few minutes before seven o'clock on the evening of Monday, 21 December 1908, Marion sent Nellie to buy a newspaper. This proved to be the first act in what would come to be recognised as one of Scotland's most serious miscarriages of justice.

Nellie was away from the apartment for less than ten minutes and on her return she found a worried Arthur Adams standing outside Marion's front door. He had heard a series of loud banging noises coming from above and had come to investigate, but there was no reply to his repeated knocking on the door. Marion feared being burgled and attacked in her apartment and had an understanding with Arthur that she would bang loudly on her floor to attract his attention if she ever felt at risk.

However, it was now quiet as Nellie unlocked the door but as she did so, she and Arthur were startled when a respectable looking man, unknown to the maid or neighbour, walked calmly out of the apartment and past them without saying a word. Arthur followed him down the stairs and out into the street but lost sight of him. Meanwhile, Nellie walked into the dining room and screamed loudly on discovering the body of her employer, sprawled on the floor close to the fireplace. Marion had been the victim of a vicious beating and although there was no sign of a struggle, there were bloodstains and pieces of brain on the floor and all the walls in the room. Dr John Adams examined the body and he confirmed that death must have been instantaneous and her injuries caused by a heavy blunt instrument. However, no murder weapon was discovered in the apartment or elsewhere in the building.

Entry had not been forced and it was presumed that the killer was keeping watch on the building from outside. Seeing Nellie leave the house on her errand presented him with the opportunity he was waiting for, as Marion was now alone. There was an intercom system and he was thought to have rung the bell at street level. When Marion answered it she may have recognised the caller's voice, or she may have been persuaded to let him into the building and, subsequently, into her apartment.

The only trace of the killer's presence at the scene was a box of matches, which he left behind, and one of which he used to turn on the gas lights. A box had been opened and the papers it contained were strewn across the room as though he may have been looking for a particular document. Marion was an avid collector of jewellery but the only piece missing was a valuable diamond brooch – several gold items including an expensive bracelet, a watch and a ring had been left by the intruder.

The first senior police officers to arrive at the apartment were Superintendents Douglas and Ord, who were quick to assume that robbery was the motive, despite some unusual features. For instance, the killer must have realised that Marion was in the apartment but a professional burglar would almost certainly attempt to avoid any confrontation and the need to resort to violence. In this case, however, the level of violence used against the victim was out of all proportion to what would have been required to subdue an elderly woman. Furthermore, it might be considered odd that a burglar would give priority to looking through the papers in the box, when he knew the time before Nellie returned would be limited.

Nellie and Arthur were able to provide a very good description of the man who walked past them and out of the apartment. He was between twenty-five and thirty-five years of age, five feet nine inches tall, had a broken nose and was clean-shaven. He was wearing a fawn-coloured overcoat and a cloth cap. Enquiries in the surrounding streets on the night of the murder led to a neighbour's daughter, fifteen-year-old Mary Borrowman, reporting that she saw a man fitting the description of the man given to her by the police outside 15 Queen's Terrace, and had done so on several nights prior to the crime. The police believed this added weight to their theory that this was a planned break-in by a professional burglar who was interested only in Marion's jewels.

The police thought they had made an early breakthrough with the arrests at 11.30 that same night of two known thieves at a house in Cowcaddens, one of whom fitted the description of the suspect. They were held overnight but next morning, Nellie and Arthur both confirmed that neither of them was the man they saw leaving the apartment.

Hoteliers and lodging house-keepers were asked if anyone acting suspiciously had stayed with them in the days leading up to the murder, but this avenue of enquiry proved fruitless. However, the description was published in the press and a cab driver came forward to say that a man wearing a fawn-coloured coat and in a highly agitated state asked to be taken to Perthshire shortly after the murder was committed, but he refused to take him. The man was traced and, following an interview, he too was eliminated from the enquiry.

It was not too long before the behaviour of a man named Oscar Slater was brought to the attention of the police. Although Slater had no criminal convictions, he was known to be a pimp and petty thief with connections to Glasgow's underworld. He was said to have attempted to sell a pawn ticket with which the purchaser would be able to redeem a brooch and his photograph was shown to Nellie, Arthur and Mary Borrowman. The two young women were more certain than Arthur that he was the killer, especially as the man in the photograph had a broken nose.

Slater was born Oscar Leschlinerin in Upper Silesia in Germany of Jewish parents in January 1872. He left home in 1893 to avoid military service and came to the United Kingdom. Initially, he lived in London and moved north six years later, eventually settling in Glasgow.

Five days after the murder, Slater travelled to New York on the liner *Lusitania* using the name Otto Sands, accompanied by his girlfriend. The New York authorities were contacted and the suspect was detained on his arrival in the United States. Two Glasgow detectives and their three key witnesses took the White Star Line's *Baltic* from Liverpool and arrived in New York some days later to begin extradition proceedings. Slater's girlfriend was not thought to have any knowledge of the crime and was not arrested. Before the extradition hearing proper began, Charles Fox, the lawyer representing the British Government, issued a press statement, in which it was said that the pawn ticket was no longer relevant to the case. It was now known that the ticket was issued many months before the murder and related to a different brooch. Nevertheless, it was claimed that it served to illustrate Slater's interest in jewellery and his extradition would still be sought. As far as Slater's lawyer, Hugh Miller, was concerned this left precious little else to support the application and led him to observe disparagingly that, 'The British Government case relies on my client's broken nose.'

The hearing took place in New York before Commissioner Shields in late January. In addition to the three witnesses who had sailed across the Atlantic, twelve written statements were provided by others, who remained in Glasgow. Robert Beverage wrote that he knew Slater and two weeks before the murder noticed him standing opposite the building in which the murder took place, as though studying it closely. Gordon Henderson was in a drinking club used by Slater and saw him at the bar late on the night of the murder, wearing clothes similar to those given in the description issued by the police. Louise Quedman swore that three days before the murder, she saw Slater with a large quantity of jewellery. It was acknowledged by Charles Fox that this could not have belonged to Marion Gilchrist, but once again the statement was being produced to further demonstrate that the defendant dealt in jewellery.

From the witness stand, Nellie was adamant that it was Slater who walked out of the apartment. She added that she was now even more convinced after having watched him enter the hearing that morning. She said he walked similarly to the man and described it as 'a springiness of gait and side-roll of the body, with a jerking of the head backward and forward'. When Slater's lawyer rose to his feet he caused something of a sensation by opening with a question about Nellie's relationship with Patrick Nugent, a Glasgow bookmaker whose links to the city's criminal fraternity were well known. It was suggested that she was involved in an intimate relationship with him but she insisted this was not true.

She admitted, however, that he had accompanied her to Marion Gilchrist's home and had met her former employer on several occasions. Nugent knew that Marion was wealthy and owned valuable jewellery, but Nellie denied the insinuation that it was Nugent she saw leaving the apartment after the murder and lied that it was Slater in order to protect her lover.

Daniel Jacobs, a New York jeweller, appeared next and produced a letter dated 29 November 1908, written to him by Slater and informing him of his trip to America on business. This, it was argued, supported Slater's claim that the journey had been planned for some time and he was not fleeing the country to escape arrest for the murder. It was not necessarily conclusive evidence, as Slater could have timed the burglary close to the already arranged trip so that he would be out of the country before any suspicion fell on him. It was nevertheless helpful to his case.

The case for extraditing Slater was looking weaker by the hour and it seemed that he would be permitted to stay in America. A theory would emerge some years later that a group of corrupt senior Glasgow police officers were hoping the application would fail. If that was the outcome, Slater would not be returned to Scotland to stand trial and he would be allowed to disappear into the vastness that was America, still officially the prime suspect. After a little while, the investigation could be quietly closed and the real murderer, the identity of whom was allegedly known to the officers, could remain at large. Surprisingly, Slater decided to agree to return to Glasgow voluntarily, confident that he would be cleared of any involvement in the crime if he stood trial. It was a decision that almost cost him his life.

His trial for the murder of Marion Gilchrist opened in Glasgow on 3 May 1909 and lasted four days. Professor John Glaister gave details of the post-mortem and the true brutality of the crime became evident. There was a deep wound just above the left eyebrow and the eyeball had been forced into the brain. Fragments of brain tissue and bone were lying close to the body and the professor told the jury that it was, 'One of the most brutally smashed heads I have ever seen in the whole of my experience.' In his opinion, the murderer had at one point knelt on the victim's chest as she was lying on the ground, to beat her about the head and, in so doing, broke several of her ribs. He had been shown a hammer which was found in the accused's luggage and he believed the injuries were consistent with having been caused by it.

The Crown presented the accused as a professional criminal who in the past had attempted to pass himself off as a legitimate businessman dealing in jewellery and, at one stage, as a dentist. The prosecution poured

'One of the most brutally smashed heads I have ever seen'

scorn on the defence's suggestion that Marion Gilchrist was a receiver of stolen jewellery and that the murder may have followed a dispute with a criminal, perhaps over payment for a stolen item. Not far in to the trial it became clear that there was no eyewitness to the crime and no forensic evidence that could link any individual to the murder. The one fact that was acknowledged by the Crown and defence was that whoever had walked out of the apartment minutes after the crime was committed must have been the killer. The issue of identity was therefore going to be of the utmost importance to prosecution and defence alike.

The prosecution called several witnesses who claimed to have had a single or fleeting view of a man apparently keeping watch on Marion's apartment, and all swore that man was Slater, who they recognised because of his 'distinctive foreign features'. Among these new witnesses were Margaret Haffie and her daughter, also named Margaret. However, under cross-examination, the younger Margaret wavered and admitted she could not be certain. All of these witnesses attended an identification parade which contained twelve men. However, of the other eleven, nine were police officers and two were railwaymen, none of whom, it was acknowledged, was 'foreign looking'.

The Crown's identification evidence was hardly overwhelming but the jury found Slater guilty of murder, albeit by a majority verdict. This unease at the conviction became widespread in the days that followed and many people signed petitions seeking a reprieve. On Tuesday 25 May, the Under Secretary for Scotland sent telegrams to the governor of Duke Street Prison and the Lord Provost to say that he would not hang, but would instead serve a life sentence in prison.

However, doubts about the conviction refused to go away. In April 1914, an enquiry was held behind closed doors to investigate the claims made by Detective Lieutenant John Trench, an officer who played a leading role in the original murder enquiry. He claimed that those in charge at the time knew that Slater was not the murderer. For instance, they knew the hammer found in his luggage was with other tools and was considered to have been too lightweight to have inflicted the terrible injuries suffered by the victim. Trench confirmed that an expert advised the police of this at the time and that he thought a chair at the scene had been used by the killer. However, this expert was not called to give evidence at the trial, nor was the defence advised of his theory.

The detective also cast doubt on the identification evidence that had been so crucial in securing the conviction. A friend of Nellie Lamb's had come forward claiming to have been told by Nellie that she knew the true identity of the man who walked out of the apartment and had given his name to the police. This man was not Slater. The implication was that under intense pressure Nellie was persuaded to change her account. Following Mary Borrowman's original statement, Trench interviewed her sister and employer and was confident she could not have been in the neighbourhood at the time, as she had claimed. He believed she feared being told off by her parents for being out late that night and used the murder as an excuse for not arriving home on time. Afterwards, she was unable to extricate herself from the position in which she had placed herself. All of the individuals concerned denied the claims made by Trench.

If the claims of the detective were accepted by those appointed to enquire into them, it meant that at best the Glasgow police had been inept and at worse had knowingly conspired to secure the conviction and possibly the execution of a man they knew to be innocent. This could only have been done to cover up their own failings or to protect the individual they knew to be guilty of the crime. The enquiry found no grounds to recommend an official review of the case and Slater continued to serve his life sentence.

Trench retired from the police force and enlisted at the outbreak of the First World War. In August 1915, he was a sergeant in the Royal Scots Fusiliers and should have been in the Dardanelles with his comrades. Instead, he was on trial accused of receiving stolen jewellery on 14 June the previous year. These were the proceeds of a burglary at the premises of Charles L. Reis & Co. six months earlier, when items valued at £1,775 were stolen.

Trench was a serving police officer at the time of the burglary in 1914 and was put in charge of the investigation. He interviewed John McArthur, a well-known receiver, who, despite denying all knowledge of the crime, offered to make enquiries of his underworld contacts. He later approached Trench offering to retrieve the stolen property and return it to the firm's insurance company for a fee of £400. This was agreed to and Trench acted as middleman. Trench had kept his Chief Constable informed of these negotiations and the transaction went ahead. Nevertheless, he was arrested almost immediately and accused of being a corrupt officer. However, the jury found him not guilty and it was widely believed that an attempt had been made to frame him by senior officers within the Glasgow police.

Within a short time of Slater's conviction, Scotland's leading true-crime writer, William Roughead, wrote of his reservations about the case. His work convinced many others, including Sir Arthur Conan Doyle, who also wrote about the case and gave his support for a full pardon. The trial of Detective Trench and the outrage felt by many who were convinced the former police officer had been framed merely served to keep the Slater case in the public consciousness. This widespread unease continued and in 1927, William Park published his influential *The Scandal of the Century, the Truth about Oscar Slater*. To ensure that it was not ignored by the authorities, the author sent a copy to the Secretary of State for Scotland. On 29 July, Colonel Harry Day MP asked the Lord Advocate to either confirm or deny press reports that Slater's life sentence was being reviewed. In reply, the Lord Advocate said, 'I should be very surprised if it were correct.' Nevertheless, on 14 November, Slater was released on licence from Peterhead Gaol, but, as Conan Doyle told a reporter, 'Although Slater has been released, this by no means eases the scandal as regards his wrongful conviction.'

The campaign for a full pardon continued and the following year his appeal against the original conviction was heard. On 20 July 1928, sitting in the same courtroom in which he was sentenced to death almost two decades earlier, Slater heard Lord Clyde announce that his conviction was quashed. Two weeks later he received the following letter, dated 4 August, from the Scottish Office in Whitehall:

Sir, I am directed by the Secretary of State to say that he has had under consideration the decision of the High Court of Judiciary on the 20th ult., quashing your conviction at Edinburgh on 6th May 1909 and relative sentence.

On the recommendation of the Secretary of State, the Lords Commissioners of His Majesty's Treasury have assented to an ex gratia payment to you of £6000 in consequence of your wrongful conviction in May 1909 and subsequent imprisonment.

The Secretary of State is accordingly prepared to arrange for an order on His Majesty's Paymaster-General for £6000 to be sent to you at any address which you may intimate to this office.

Alternatively, he is prepared to arrange for the sum of £6000 to be placed to the credit of your account at any bank you specify. He would be glad to be informed of your wishes in this connection. I am sir, your obedient servant,
JOHN LAMB

Conan Doyle was among many of Slater's sympathisers who believed this sum to be insufficient and argued that he should receive at least £10,000. Nevertheless, Slater accepted the offer.

The murder of Marion Gilchrist remains officially unsolved but several theories were put forward in the years following her death. One suggested that the killer was a relative, angry at the contents of her will. Another put forward the idea that Marion often bought her jewellery from members of the Glasgow underworld and it was one of these contacts who killed her. Yet another theory was that the murder was committed by a gang of four burglars who broke into her home. One issue that almost everyone agreed upon, however, was that the killer was not Oscar Slater, who died in 1948.

CASE THIRTY-FIVE 1913

FAILED BY THE PARISH

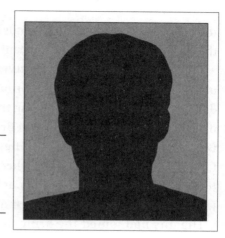

Suspect:	Patrick Higgins
Age:	38
Crime:	Murder

On the afternoon of Sunday, 8 June 1913, James Thompson and Tom Duncan, ploughmen on a farm near Winchburgh, were working in a field close to Hopetoun Quarry when they noticed a dark object floating in the water nearby. Initially, they thought it was a discarded scarecrow but soon realised their mistake for as the object came closer to the bank, the men were appalled to discover they were looking at the badly decomposed bodies of two young boys, who had been tied together with a cord. They attempted to pull the bodies to the bank but the rotting cord snapped and they floated away.

The bodies were later retrieved by Constables Galbraith and Adamson who made arrangements for them to be taken to the mortuary at Linlithgow, where post-mortems were carried out by Dr Robert Cross, who practiced locally, and Professor Harvey Littlejohn of Edinburgh University. They concluded that the boys were aged less than ten years but it was difficult to be more accurate given the length of time their bodies had been in the water, which may have been for as long as three years. However, they were certain the boys were murder victims.

A check through local records revealed no youngsters had been reported missing for several years. However, the police were aware of rumours that had been circulating throughout the district for some time regarding the children of a local man, thirty-eight-year-old Patrick Higgins. His two sons, William and John, who were of a similar age to the dead youngsters, had not been seen for at least two years. Several people reported their concerns to the police but there were no grounds to warrant an investigation. However, the discovery of the bodies now meant that one could proceed.

Patrick Higgins' itinerant lifestyle meant that he rarely stayed in one place for long and he often slept rough. However, he was traced without difficulty and on the day following the discovery of the bodies, four police officers visited a lodging house in Broxburn, in which they had learnt he was staying. When questioned, Higgins was unable to provide a satisfactory explanation regarding the whereabouts of his sons and he was taken to look at the bodies. He readily acknowledged they were William and John and he was charged with their murders.

Higgins had joined the army in his late teens and served with the Scottish Rifles in India. He was discharged after six years and returned home, since when he had worked as a labourer on a casual basis for a number of firms, but mainly in a local threshing mill and in the local brick fields. He met and married a local woman and they had two sons, before she sadly died in 1910, leaving him with sole responsibility for the boys. The widower struggled to provide adequately for his sons and in January 1911, they were admitted into Dysart Combination Poorhouse. However, Higgins failed to make the necessary financial contributions and on 24 June that year, he was sentenced to two months imprisonment for child neglect. Following his release the boys remained in the institution until August, when their father took them out, saying he had found suitable accommodation for them.

This was untrue; instead he had removed them from the poorhouse so that he would not have to pay towards their upkeep or be required to serve another prison sentence for not doing so. For most of the time, the boys simply wandered about the district with their father, dishevelled and hungry looking. The boys' grandmother told police that Higgins attempted to place them in two homes but he could not afford the nine shillings he would have to pay each week from his wage of twenty-four shillings. His sister Margaret had offered some help by giving him one of her rings to pawn, but the money raised did not last long.

For a little while they lived with his friend, Elizabeth Tarbax in Broxburn, but he failed to keep up with the agreed payments and she was forced to seek assistance from the parish. Higgins was traced to the brickworks, where he was working and where he was visited by William Brown, the district's Inspector of the Poor. He warned Higgins that the outdoor relief being paid towards their upkeep could not continue and that unless he started to contribute towards their wellbeing, he would again face a term of imprisonment. Within a few days, Higgins removed the boys from Elizabeth's care and the claim for parish funds ceased. The police found a number of people who saw William and John with their father in late October and early November, but sightings of the boys ceased therafter.

Higgins' mother and sister did not see William and John again after the last week of October and when they asked him what had become of the boys, he replied that he had handed them over to two respectable looking middle-aged women he met on a train. They had taken a liking to the boys and, having heard of his difficulties, offered to take them off his hands and raise them as their own. He had agreed and they paid him twenty-five shillings. However, when pressed, he could give no details concerning the identities or whereabouts of the women or his sons. The police learnt that he gave a similar account to his friends Archibald Farnie, Daniel Wilson and James Daly, all of whom had asked after the boys.

However, Higgins gave a different account to his workmate Hugh Shields, who, when interviewed by the police, recalled the boys visiting their father at the brickworks in early November. When he saw them approaching, Higgins said, 'Here are those kids of mine coming and I have nothing to give them today again.' Hugh watched as Higgins spoke to them briefly before sending them on their way without giving them money or food. Hugh met Higgins a few days later without the boys and when he asked about them, was told that they were well and arrangements were being made with a family to take them to Canada, where they could start a new life.

Higgins was a heavy drinker who, it was believed, preferred to spend what money he could raise on alcohol than on his family responsibilities, and had decided to rid himself once and for all of the burden of caring for his sons. When his trial opened on 10 September 1913, he put forward a special plea that at the time of their deaths he was insane. This was rejected out of hand by the Crown and the case was put before a jury to decide. The defence argued that Higgins was insane, proof of which was that he suffered from epilepsy. Work colleagues David Wilson, Charles Jones and Annie McWilliams testified they saw him suffering fits at the brickworks. His mother told the court that he was discharged from the army because of his epilepsy and during the first six months back at home he experienced a great many fits. She believed the cause to have been a head injury he sustained when three years old. His sister Mary told the court, 'He wasn't quite right in the head from an early age'. Dr Kelso of

'He wasn't quite right in the head from an early age'

Broxburn, the family doctor, confirmed under oath that he had examined the prisoner some years earlier at the request of his mother, who told him that her son often woke up in the night and threatened her with either a chair or a poker. At other times he had fallen out of bed and lay on the floor shaking violently.

As he was waiting for his trial to begin, Higgins' lawyers arranged for him to be seen by two experts. Dr Martin visited him on three occasions to make an assessment and reported finding scars covering his entire body, which he believed were sustained when Higgins fell during his epileptic fits and he too believed the childhood head injury was the cause of the condition. Dr G.M. Robertson, lecturer on mental diseases at Edinburgh University and Superintendent of the Royal Edinburgh Asylum, believed the murders of his sons stemmed directly from his epilepsy and, in his opinion, the accused was suffering from a serious mental weakness.

In his summing up, the judge took the opportunity to severely criticize the parish authorities. He emphasised that they exhibited a great deal of callousness towards the dead children. He felt it was scandalous that once they were no longer their financial responsibility, their welfare had simply been ignored. He continued by insisting that the authorities had a duty beyond avoiding expense or attempting to retrieve relatively small amounts of money and should maintain contact with such obviously vulnerable children. Nevertheless, the authorities were not on trial and the judge advised the jury they had a straightforward question to ask themselves, namely was Higgins sane at the time of the killings?

The jury was absent for a little under two hours and returned with a unanimous verdict of guilty of murder in relation to both killings, but added a strong recommendation for mercy. The judge undertook to pass the recommendation to the appropriate department before sentencing Higgins to death. In the condemned cell he was attended by a group of prison officers under the supervision of Chief Warder James Ross, and, prior to his execution, Higgins left the following note for the prison governor:

> I wish from my heart that you will accept this note from me thanking you for your great kindness to me during my incarceration in the prison. Hoping you will excuse my blunt way of putting it but believe me it is from my heart I say it. I also wish to thank Mr Ross for his kindness, hoping you will acquaint him of this note, I would also like you to thank all the officers that I have been under for their kindness and civility.
> Yours respectfully,
> PATRICK HIGGINS

There was no reprieve and Higgins was hanged at Edinburgh's Calton Prison on Thursday 2 October by John Ellis and his assistant, William Willis. Higgins made a full confession to the crimes and died bravely.

CASE THIRTY-SIX   1920
THE QUEEN'S PARK MURDER

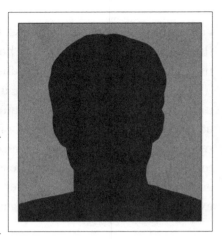

Suspects:	Albert James Frazer
	& James Rollins
Ages:	24 & 22
Crime:	Murder

Henry Senior, a thirty-five-year-old former soldier, was a single man who lived with his mother on Robson Street in Glasgow. On the evening of Tuesday, 3 February 1920, Henry was about to go out and took £10 from the tin in which he kept his savings. Mrs Senior thought this was far too much cash to carry and that he was inviting trouble should some ne'er do well see him with it and she persuaded him to take just £2. However, within hours Henry's badly beaten body was found in Queen's Park Recreation Ground, the victim of a violent robbery. His killers took all his cash, his overcoat, shoes, hat and a distinctive yellow pig-skin pocketbook.

A post-mortem was performed by Professor John Glaister, who reported the victim had suffered severe external and internal injuries as there were numerous cuts and abrasions to the whole of his body. Massive damage had been caused to the liver, which was no doubt the result of being kicked with great force as he lay on the ground. Death was due to shock and haemorrhage.

The stolen overcoat and shoes were traced to a Glasgow pawnshop and the owner was able to provide excellent descriptions of the two men who brought the items in. Further enquiries led the police to John McIntosh, a conductor on a tram which picked up two suspicious-looking characters close to where the body was found and at about the time the murder was committed. He remembered them clearly as one was carrying a shoe in each of his coat pockets, which he thought was a little unusual. The descriptions he gave tallied with those of the pawnshop owner and two suspects were very quickly identified. They were twenty-four-year-old Australian Albert James Frazer, and twenty-two-year-old Irishman James Rollins, who was also known as Slain. They could not be found in their usual haunts and the police received an anonymous tip-off that the pair had left the city and travelled to Belfast by ferry, accompanied by two young women. Chief Inspector Keith and Inspector Noble of the Glasgow force travelled to Ireland to begin the search for their chief suspects.

Their colleagues in Belfast were able to give important information as soon as the Glasgow officers arrived. The local police had received reports of two men who, for the past few days, were seen to be living rough in the city's Cave Hill Park. The men were soon identified as Frazer and Rollins, who had opted not to stay in a hotel or lodging house in order to avoid capture and, instead, to live in one of the caves in the park. Both were former soldiers and had put their army training to good use, as a subsequent search of the cave revealed they had lived quite comfortably and used a beef tin in which to cook their meals. The two women were staying in a city centre hotel and it was as the men were on their way to meet them there on the evening of Sunday 8 February that Frazer and Rollins were arrested. Their companions were detained one hour later in their hotel room.

The inhabitants of Glasgow were no strangers to violence but the savagery of Henry's murder shocked many. Therefore, when news leaked out that the prisoners were due to arrive back in Glasgow in the early hours of Tuesday, the detectives and their charges were greeted by a large and hostile crowd at Central Station, who booed and hissed the suspects as they were rushed to the police station. A few hours later, the four prisoners appeared in the Central Police Court and for the first time the identities of the two young women were revealed. They were Helen Keenan, also known as White, who was twenty-two years old, and nineteen-year-old Elizabeth Stewart. Both women were charged with being accomplices.

The four defendants made several appearances before the lower court and at each one the young men seemed quite unconcerned. From the dock they smiled and waved to friends and family in the public gallery. In contrast to these displays of bravado, their girlfriends appeared subdued and obviously distraught. It was a situation the Crown decided to take advantage of by offering to drop all charges against them if they agreed to become witnesses for the prosecution. It was an offer they readily agreed to and when the trial of Frazer and Rollins opened on Tuesday 4 May before the presiding judge, Lord Sands, Helen Keenan was the first and perhaps most important witness.

As soon as she entered the witness box, she broke down and sobbed uncontrollably before managing to regain her composure a few minutes later, beginning her testimony with details of her upbringing. She was born and raised in Aberdeen and when old enough, found work in Glasgow and later in Paisley. She returned to Glasgow two years before the murder, where she married a Canadian soldier by declaration in early 1918. He returned to active service in France and it was then she began her relationship with Frazer. At first they lived in Dundee before setting up home in Glasgow, where they met Rollins and Elizabeth Stewart.

On the night of the crime, she went into the city centre with Frazer, where they met up with Rollins, who was alone. After a short time, the men told her 'to get a man' and she was fully aware of what they expected her to do. She was to lure a man to a deserted spot with a promise of sexual intercourse for a small payment. The two men would follow her and before sex could take place, they would attack and rob him. Usually, the victim would be too embarrassed to report the matter to the police.

She met Henry Senior on Hope Street and after falling into conversation with him, she agreed to go to Queen's Park and have sex with him. They took a tram, on which Frazer and Rollins also travelled, which they stepped off at the park gates. Within a matter of a few minutes, at a remote spot, the two men approached the couple and told Helen to leave. As she hurried away she turned and saw Rollins put his arm around Henry's neck and place a knife in the small of his back. As he did so, Frazer punched him with great force in the face and then hit him with a fake revolver he often carried to frighten people. Helen returned to the city centre alone, where she met Elizabeth Stewart, with whom she visited a cinema to wait for the two men to join them. The four of them met up in the early hours of the morning and Helen noticed that an early edition of a newspaper was already reporting the discovery of Henry's battered corpse.

'Frazer punched him with great force in the face'

Elizabeth Stewart was next to stand in the witness box and began by stating that she could provide no details about the events in the park, but her evidence was nevertheless damning. When she and Rollins returned home a few hours after the murder, she had, for the first time, noticed blood on his hands. He was in an agitated state and was unable to settle. He then told her that he and Frazer attacked a man in the park and had probably killed him. He handed her the yellow pocketbook he said was taken off the victim and which in court was formally identified as the one Henry took with him on the night he died. The following day the four of them travelled to Belfast, where Rollins told her, 'It's awful to be the cause of the death of a man.' The Crown insisted this was tantamount to a confession to the crime.

The Crown's case was overwhelming and there was little the defence could dispute. In his summing up to the jury, the judge said he had never previously known a case in which so much evidence regarding the essential facts of a case had been laid before a jury. However, he instructed the jury members to put aside any sense of disgust they might feel about what he described as 'the deplorable and disgusting lifestyles' of the two accused and their girlfriends. He also reminded them that even if they believed only one of them had struck the fatal blow, both would be equally guilty as it would be a crime of joint enterprise.

After deliberating for just nineteen minutes, the jury came back with two guilty verdicts and Frazer and Rollins were sentenced to death. However, it was believed they would be reprieved as they had both served courageously in the Great War. This did not prove to be the case and they were hanged simultaneously in the city's Duke Street Prison on the morning of 26 May 1920 by John Ellis and William Willis. Among the officials invited to witness the executions was Major L.C. Parker, a representative of the Australian Imperial Force, in which Frazer had served in the war. Each of the two condemned men maintained a calm demeanour as the white caps were pulled over their heads on the scaffold. As the lever was about to be pulled, Frazer turned towards Rollins and uttered his last words to him, 'Cheer up'.

THE PRISON VAN RAID

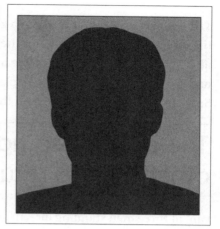

Suspects:	Daniel Patrick Walsh, Daniel Braniff, James McCarra, John McGarrigle, Vincent Campbell, John Carney, William Fullarton, James Fullarton, Michael O'Carroll, Sean O'Daire, James Kavanagh, Thomas Tracey, Francis O'Hagan
Ages:	Various
Crime:	Conspiracy & Murder

Frank Carty, a leading member of the Irish Republican Army, had escaped from prison in Ireland and afterwards made his way to Glasgow, where he was subsequently arrested on 28 April 1921. A few days later, on the morning of Wednesday 4 May, following an appearance at the Central Police Office, he was being returned to Duke Street Gaol to await transfer to the custody of the Irish authorities. It was feared there might be an attempt made to free him by IRA members with the help of local supporters and a number of precautions were taken to prevent such an occurrence. These included putting several armed police officers in the van. Sitting in the front of the vehicle alongside driver Detective Constable Macdonald were Detective Inspector Robert Johnstone and Detective Sergeant George Skirton. Another four officers were sitting in the rear of the van with Carty and another prisoner, who was in custody for unrelated matters.

As the van approached the prison gates, the officer's worst fears were realised when it came under attack by a large number of armed men, firing guns.

The attackers were split into three groups, one of which approached from the direction of Rotten Row, another from Cathedral Square and the third attacked from the rear. The police had no option other than to return fire and the main confrontation took place at the front of the vehicle. Detective Sergeant Skirton fired his weapon through the windscreen, from inside the

'The police had no option other than to return fire'

van, at three men standing directly in front of him. The three officers sitting in the front seats then jumped out of the vehicle and opened fire. Detective Inspector Johnstone fell to the ground, mortally wounded, a bullet having passed through his heart. Detective Sergeant Skirton stood over his fallen colleague, firing his revolver until he too was hit in the wrist, which forced him to stop shooting. Detective Constable Macdonald charged towards their attackers, shooting as he did so, and miraculously avoided being wounded. The incident lasted a matter of only a few minutes, scattering terrified passers-by, before the attackers dispersed, having failed to release Carty.

A passing car was requisitioned to take Skirton and Johnstone to the Royal Infirmary. However, nothing could be done for the fatally wounded forty-one-year-old Detective Inspector Johnstone, who left a widow and several children. He was a native of Castle Douglas and joined the Glasgow force in 1902. He was promoted to the rank of inspector in 1919, since when he had been responsible for the transfer of prisoners to Duke Street Prison. At a time when the Oscar Slater affair (see chapter 34) was casting a large shadow over the police officers of Glasgow, the death of this brave officer and the wounding of his colleague served as a reminder of the sacrifice some were prepared to make for their communities. Some may well have been reminded of the 1867 raid on a prison van by Fenians in Manchester, in an attempt to liberate one of their leaders who was being returned to the city's Belle Vue Gaol following a court appearance. This also failed, but a police sergeant was murdered and three of the Fenians who participated in the raid were publicly executed outside the walls of Salford's New Bailey Gaol.

It emerged later that the police had been keeping suspected Irish nationalists under surveillance for the previous five years and in the days that followed the attack, a number of arrests were made of men and women who were suspected of offences which included participating in the assault on the van, conspiracy, possession of firearms and ammunition, and murder. One of the first to be arrested was Francis O'Hagan, in whose house Carty was arrested. Several arrests were made at the Campbell family home on Abercrombie Street following a police raid and where a revolver and ammunition were discovered together with what were described as suspicious notes, which, it was claimed, incriminated many of the detainees in a conspiracy to release Carty. There was a sense of outrage when it was learnt that the police also raided a church in which the priest, Father Patrick McRory, was arrested.

More than thirty arrests were made but only thirteen would later stand trial, the others having been released without charge, including Father McRory. As news of the imminent releases spread throughout the Irish community, a large crowd of well-wishers gathered outside the prison gates to greet them. In Father McRory's parish, Sinn Fein flags and welcome home banners appeared in the windows of many houses in the district. There were said to be more than 1,200 supporters to welcome him home and Sinn Fein members acted as stewards to maintain good order.

The thirteen who stood in the dock when the trial opened on 8 August charged with conspiring to release Carty and with murdering Inspector Johnstone were Daniel Patrick Walsh, who was also known by the names Dunne and Mitchell; Daniel Braniff, who was also known as Charles Grier; James McCarra; John McGarrigle; Vincent Campbell; John Carney; William Fullarton; James Fullarton; Michael O'Carroll; Sean O'Daire; James Kavanagh; Thomas Tracey; and Francis O'Hagan.

Handwriting experts had examined the alleged incriminating notes found in the search of the Campbells' home but they failed to prove the existence of any plot involving the accused. Furthermore, none of those in the dock could be shown to have handled any of the weapons or ammunition that were found by the police. The identification evidence, most of which was provided by the police, was therefore crucial to the prosecution.

A number of officers were on foot patrol outside the prison gates when the attack took place and although most of the civilian witnesses rushed for cover when the shooting started, some were called to give evidence. George McCracken and Margaret Grant testified they saw James McCarra acting suspiciously outside the gates of the gaol and the police claimed he was acting as a lookout, ready to signal to others of the van's approach. Mary Sinclair described seeing Francis O'Hagan loitering at the scene and running away at the cessation of the shooting.

Earlier that morning, Constable Duncan McIntosh, who was on duty outside the prison, saw John McGarrigle with Thomas Tracey, Michael O'Carroll and James Fullarton. The latter was seen running from the scene with Daniel Patrick Walsh by Detective Constable Alexander Brown. Other police officers were able to place John Carney and James Kavanagh outside the prison gates. Constable Grant of the Marine Division was not on duty but when he heard the shooting start, he ran to assist and positively identified William Fullarton as one of those taking part. However, under cross-examination he conceded that he was about 70 yards away and the man he claimed was the defendant had his back to him. He was forced to admit that he did not see his face and was basing his identification on Fullarton's build alone.

No witness had so far been called who claimed to have seen any of the defendants firing a weapon but that would change when Detective Sergeant Skirton gave his dramatic evidence. He named nine of the accused as participating in the attack and shooting at him and his colleagues. These defendants were McGarrigle, O'Daire, Braniff, Kavanagh, Carney, Walsh, O'Carroll and William Fullarton. Finally, he also identified McCarra and added that he was on the point of firing his weapon at the defendant but was prevented from doing so when he was wounded in the wrist and could not pull the trigger.

When the detective sergeant was cross-examined by the defence, it was suggested to him that at the time he was under a great deal of stress as he would have been in fear of his life and therefore could not possibly be certain of what he saw. The detective sergeant, who had served in the army in the Great War and had been awarded the DSO, retorted, 'I don't think the Glasgow police are so frightened as to be overcome by fear.' Nevertheless, a further attempt to discredit the detective sergeant's evidence was made later when Alexander Drummond Drysdale, the governor of Duke Street Prison, appeared in the dock. Skirton had visited his institution, where he identified the nine prisoners, and the governor was forced to concede that he was very surprised, for in all of his experience he had never known a witness identify so many suspects from a crime scene at a single viewing.

Before the defence cases were formally opened, the lawyers representing O'Hagan addressed the judge, claiming their client's mental health had deteriorated to such an extent that he was now unfit to stand trial. He had been examined by James Harvey, the prison doctor, who believed he was genuinely insane and asked two colleagues from the Edinburgh Royal Asylum to assess his mental state. They did so and both agreed that O'Hagan was mentally unstable, which resulted in the Crown discontinuing its case against him. The judge directed the jury to return a verdict of not guilty and O'Hagan was released into the care of his family. O'Hagan's lawyers insisted that he would have called an alibi witness whose testimony would have demonstrated he could not have taken part in the attack.

The remaining defendants also relied on alibi evidence. However, most of their witnesses did not come forward in the immediate aftermath of the attack and the subsequent arrests. Their delay in doing so was highly suspicious according to the Crown, especially as some were members of Sinn Fein clubs, although this was not illegal. When asked under cross-examination why they did not approach the police earlier – implying they were committing perjury to save fellow nationalist sympathisers – all replied that they had been reluctant to become involved in such a serious case.

At the time of the failed rescue attempt, Daniel Patrick Walsh was lodging with Mary Lavin, who testified that on the day in question he was in the house all morning, until 12.15 p.m. Other evidence was presented claiming he ate lunch with a group of friends, all of whom worked for the Irish National Insurance Company and in whose company he remained until after one o'clock. If this alibi evidence was correct, Walsh could not have taken part in the attack.

Walsh's barrister also called Thomas Docherty to the witness stand. He too was initially suspected of involvement in the crime and spent several weeks on remand in Duke Street Prison before being released without charge. He was present in the exercise yard with the other prisoners when identification parades were being held. On one occasion he saw a prison officer looking up at the window when the parade was taking place, as though waiting for a signal of some kind. Suddenly, without any warning, he removed Walsh's hat and replaced it with a cap. This, his lawyer claimed, was to make him resemble someone who had been involved in the crime and was a deliberate attempt by the Crown to mislead eyewitnesses.

Daniel Braniff, a dealer in fountain pens, was lodging with Mrs McCulloch, who had known him for many years as he was a close friend of her late husband. She testified that on 4 May, he left the house at 11.45 a.m. and returned at 2.30 p.m., showing no signs of exhaustion or excitement. Others were called who could account for his movements during the time he was absent from the house. He visited the home of Mrs McCallum at 12.30 p.m. and left a bundle of dirty clothes for her to wash. Under cross-examination, she accepted that she and her husband were strong supporters of Sinn Fein, but insisted she was not lying to protect a friend. Shortly before one o'clock he bumped into Mr McCall, organising secretary of a local shop assistants union branch, who knew him well.

John Carney was a barber whose shop was on Govan Road and his two apprentices testified that he arrived late for work on the morning of the 4th and did not leave the premises until the shop was locked in the late afternoon. Shipwright Joseph Sims was having his haircut by the prisoner between 11.45 a.m. and 12.30 p.m., so he could not have taken part in the shootout. This witness also made it clear that in all the years he had known him, Carney had never shown any sympathy with the Irish nationalist cause.

Mrs McGovern conceded that her son, James McCarra, who was an active supporter of the nationalist movement, was serving a prison sentence for possessing detonators. She said that on the 4th, he was lodging with her and left the house at a few minutes after eleven. Two miners, Edward Docherty and Peter Gaytons, appeared on his behalf to say they were with him in a public house for two hours until 1.30 p.m. and he had not been out of their company the whole of that time.

Vincent Campbell, who was unemployed, denied having any links to Sinn Fein or strong republican sympathies. On the 4th, he left his lodgings at eleven o'clock and two shopkeepers appeared on his behalf to support his claim that he visited their premises to firstly purchase buttons he needed to sew on his trousers and later to buy a newspaper. Pottery turner John McDermid and the prisoner's cousin, Agnes Campbell, claimed to have met him over lunchtime, meaning he could not have been outside the gates of Duke Street Prison.

Brothers William and James Fullarton were not with each other on the 4th and provided different witnesses. William's mother and sister stated he was at home for most of the day, before going out at 4.30 in the afternoon. James called brother and sister Francis and Annie Mahon, who claimed to have spent more than an hour of the lunch period with him until he left, saying he needed some cigarettes. Francis agreed with the Crown lawyer that he was a supporter of Irish independence and was a member of the Springburn Sinn Fein Club, but insisted he would not lie in court.

James Kavanagh, a labourer on the Caledonian Railway, readily acknowledged that he was a social member of Sinn Fein but denied most vehemently any connections to the organisation's military wing. A friend, Mrs Smith, supported his claim to have visited her home at noon on the 4th and one of her neighbours confirmed she saw him leave thirty minutes later. This witness was certain of the time because she and Mrs Smith lived opposite a school and the children finished their lessons and came out into the street at 12.30 p.m. At one o'clock, Elizabeth Abercrombie, who knew Kavanagh, saw him sitting on a park bench reading a newspaper, and stopped to speak with him for some time.

Michael O'Carroll's mother opened her evidence by stating that she and her son were members of the local Tom Ash Sinn Fein Club but neither wished to see Ireland gain independence by military means. She continued by saying that since becoming unemployed her son had taken to staying in bed in the morning and on the 4th rose at noon, ate lunch and visited the Labour Exchange. These details were corroborated by the prisoner's father and sister, together with two family friends visiting at the time.

Sean O'Daire was an apprentice engineer in his third year with John Brown Shipbuilders. He lodged with Michael Connolly, who, with his wife, testified that on the 4th he left the house at noon. Several of O'Daire's friends told of being in his company during the time the attack took place. These included Louis Carroll, whose mother also testified that the prisoner arrived at her house at 12.15 p.m.

Undertaker Thomas Tracey was accused of taking part in the attack and also of allowing his company's vehicles to be used in the planning stages. His wife spoke on his behalf, saying he had no links to Sinn Fein and that on the morning in question he visited the parents of a young man recently killed in a road traffic accident. He returned home at 12.30 p.m. and left three hours later to attend a funeral. The accused man did leave the family home briefly at one o'clock but barber William Craig was able to confirm he had visited his shop for a haircut.

John McGarrigle was employed by turf commission agent Daniel Hargreaves, for whom he had worked for many years except when he was serving in the army. His employer and a customer, George Butchart, testified that he was at work at the time the attack on the van was taking place. William McCarrie was called as a character witness to speak on McGarrigle's behalf and he stated that he found it ludicrous that his friend should be accused of such serious crimes and spoke of the prisoner's distinguished service in the Great War. He had enlisted voluntarily and served in Egypt, Palestine, Gallipoli and Germany. He was wounded in the shoulder and when the bullet was removed by a surgeon it was handed to him as a souvenir. This bullet was found when his home was searched and prior to its true history being discovered, the Crown believed it would prove to be an important piece of incriminating evidence. The jury was told that he had been decorated for bravery and besides the bullet, it was revealed that McGarrigle's Military Medal was also found during the search.

The trial lasted for two weeks and when the jury retired to consider its verdicts, it was thought it would be many hours before they were reached. However, after just ninety minutes, the members returned to their seats and announced the following decisions; Not Proven in the cases of Walsh, Braniff, McCarra, Campbell, Carney and William Fullarton, and Not

Guilty in respect of James Fullarton, O'Carroll, O'Daire, Kavanagh, Tracey and McGarrigle.

Nobody was ever convicted of the murder of Detective Inspector Johnstone and the crime remains unsolved, the killer of a brave police officer never brought to justice.

CASE THIRTY-EIGHT 1921

THE WHITEINCH HORROR

Suspects:	William and Helen Harkness
Ages:	31 & 28
Crime:	Murder

It was Halloween 1921, so when Mrs Wardle heard a noise late that night at the rear of her home on George Street in the Whiteinch district of Glasgow, she assumed it was a group of revellers making their way home. However, at daybreak the body of a young girl was discovered and Mrs Wardle had in fact heard the killer or killers abandoning the body. The victim's hands were tied behind her back with a piece of rope and the belt of her coat was tied around her mouth. When this was removed, it was realised that a handkerchief had been forced into her mouth. There were no signs of a struggle at the scene and although there was blood on the rope used to tie her hands, there was no more to be seen. Given the information provided by Mrs Wardle, it was clear that the victim had been murdered elsewhere.

There was no difficulty in identifying the body as that of fourteen-year-old Elizabeth Benjamin, a popular youngster who was well known to many of the residents in the area. She lived with her parents on North Street, Clydebank and had left school the previous March to work for her father, who was a draper. Elizabeth acted as a canvasser, carrying samples of his work in the hope of encouraging people to buy his wares, and she also collected the weekly instalments of those paying for goods on credit.

A preliminary examination of the body at the scene by Dr Sutherland, surgeon to the Partick Police Division, led him to conclude that death occurred between six and twelve hours before she was discovered.

Professor John Glaister of Glasgow University performed a full post-mortem and confirmed that death was due to suffocation, the cause of which was the handkerchief being rammed tightly into the back of her throat. There were wounds and bruising to her head, caused by a blunt instrument, which would have rendered her unconscious. Other injuries found on her body were thought to have been caused as she struggled violently with her murderer. There were no signs of a sexual assault and robbery was the motive for the crime, as no cash was found on her. Elizabeth left the family home at eleven o'clock the previous morning, carrying a case with samples of women's and children's clothing and twenty shillings in change.

Her round for the day was known and following house-to-house enquiries it emerged that she called on a number of regular customers in Whiteinch, to whom she sold several items and from whom she collected a few shillings in payment. At 3.45 that afternoon, Elizabeth called on Elizabeth Graham in George Street, who asked her if she had yet called on Mrs Harkness, who lived a few doors down the street. She had not but said she was the next customer she was due to visit. The next day, after learning of Elizabeth's murder, Mrs Graham asked Mrs Harkness if the youngster had visited her. She was told she had done so but left after a brief chat. Twenty-eight-year-old Helen Harkness was the wife of thirty-one-year-old William Harkness, a shipyard worker, neither of whom had a criminal record. When visited by the police they confirmed Elizabeth called at their home on the afternoon of the previous day and that she had remained there only briefly.

After completing their house-to-house enquiries, the police were satisfied that the youngster visited no other customers that afternoon. A search of the Harkness's rooms revealed recent bloodstains on one of the walls and a rug thought to have belonged to the couple and bearing traces of blood was found in a nearby ash-pit. Spots of blood were also discovered on the walls of the communal washhouse, in which neighbours saw Harkness and his wife lock themselves on the evening of the 31st. Furthermore, a hammer with blood on it was discovered hidden in the apartment. This was the weapon police believed was used to beat Elizabeth unconscious.

Harkness was taken into custody for questioning and two days later, a Mrs Tolland came forward. Her daughter Katie was married to John Harkness, the suspect's older brother. John had confessed to his wife that he helped William and Helen move Elizabeth's corpse from their apartment a few hours after they told him they had murdered her. William and Helen Harkness were arrested and charged with Elizabeth's murder and robbing her of £2. John Harkness was charged with being an accessory.

The Crown had always accepted that John Harkness was not involved in planning and carrying out the robbery and murder, and his decision to assist in moving the body stemmed from a sense of family loyalty. Clearly, he did not inform the authorities of the murder, but this seemed to be due to the difficulty he had in being the individual directly responsible for betraying his brother. Nevertheless, he told his mother-in-law, a highly respectable woman, realising she would almost certainly report the matter and he did so as it was the only way he could find to deal with the problem. When it was learnt that he was willing to give evidence against his brother and sister-in-law, his offer was accepted and all charges against him were dropped. He was the main prosecution witness when the trial opened on 30 January 1922 and which lasted for two days. From the witness box, John Harkness described the events of the night of 31 October.

John had been estranged from his brother for some time, so was surprised when at eight o'clock that evening, Helen visited him saying William was in desperate need of his help. He agreed to return to their home with her, where, on arrival, she said to her husband, 'I told Johnnie everything and he is going to help us.' Turning to John, she pleaded, 'Surely you will help us? He is your own brother, your flesh and blood.'

John was appalled at what they had done but his brother told him, 'Johnnie, it is a thing you have never done and once you start you have to finish it.' William continued by saying he and his wife were short of money and hatched the plan to rob and murder Elizabeth. She put up a great struggle and Helen's legs were heavily bruised, where their victim kicked her, and the youngster also bit one of William's fingers, which was badly inflamed. John was taken to the washhouse, which was locked, and inside was Elizabeth's body. William attempted to clean the blood from the walls and floor and later threw the rug he used to do so in the ash-pit, where it was found the next day. John agreed, albeit reluctantly, to help carry the body to the spot at which it was abandoned. The brothers returned to the apartment, which Helen was attempting to clean, and she was burning several blood-stained articles in a bucket.

The Crown's case seemed overwhelming and there was no attempt by William's lawyer to deny that his client was responsible for Elizabeth's death. However, it was argued on his behalf that he put the handkerchief into her mouth simply to prevent her crying out and not to kill her. She had choked to death accidentally and therefore the jury should bring in a guilty verdict to culpable homicide and not murder. Helen's lawyers claimed that there was no evidence that she was involved in planning the robbery, hit the victim or had put the handkerchief into her mouth. She had admittedly helped her husband but this was after the event and stemmed from a sense of misplaced loyalty. Given these circumstances, she should not be convicted of murder.

After retiring for twenty-five minutes, the jury returned with guilty verdicts of murder in respect of both accused but there was a strong recommendation for mercy in the case of Helen. Nevertheless, both were sentenced to death and Helen was taken from the dock in a state of collapse. The rare event of a husband and wife being hanged simultaneously resulted in a huge amount of public interest in the case, but shortly before the executions were due to take place, Helen was reprieved and it was ordered she be detained during His Majesty's Pleasure. Her husband was hanged by John Ellis at Duke Street Prison on 21 February 1922.

CASE THIRTY-NINE   1923

ADDICTED TO METHS

Suspect: John Henry Savage
Age: 50
Crime: Murder

Forty-two-year-old Jemima Grierson had experienced many difficulties in her life, caused largely by her addiction to methylated sprits. In 1914, she left her husband Joseph Grierson, a miner, and their children in Flintshire and in the following decade saw her children on just one occasion. Shortly after leaving her family, she met engineman Richard Tillett, with whom she enjoyed a stable relationship, and the couple lived in Bridge Street, Leith with a five-year-old boy they had adopted. Nevertheless, she remained dependent on methylated spirits and other meths drinkers would visit her home regularly. Richard was an understanding man who tolerated the disruptions caused to their existence, but her lifestyle led her to a violent end in the early hours of Wednesday, 14 March 1923.

One of Jemima's regular visitors was fifty-year-old John Henry Savage, who in the past had worked as a marine fireman. However, as his addiction to meths worsened, it became increasingly difficult for him to find and keep employment and for several years he lived an extremely unsettled existence in the Edinburgh and Leith area. He asked Jemima to allow him to lodge with her and her family on a number of occasions, but Richard had always rejected the idea as he wanted to protect their little boy as much as possible from Jemima's addiction and her circle of acquaintants.

At ten o'clock on the night of Tuesday 13 March, Richard went to work, leaving his wife and son in the company of eighteen-year-old Michael Riley. The young man was not a drinker and was a good friend to both Richard and Jemima. Fifteen minutes later, Savage called at the house and after a short time, asked Michael to leave as he wished to discuss a private matter with Jemima. Michael was reluctant to do so but Jemima assured her young visitor that there would be no problem and he left them together in the house.

Later, at one o'clock in the morning, Jemima knocked on the door of her good friend and neighbour Mrs McLeod. She explained that she had asked Savage to leave her house but he was refusing to do so and she needed help to get rid of him. Mrs McLeod, a widow who lived with her daughter, put on a dressing gown and went out in search of a policeman. Failing to find one, she returned to Jemima's house and urged the unwanted guest to leave immediately. Sitting in a chair smoking a cigarette, Savage glared menacingly at Mrs McLeod and replied, 'If you don't hold your tongue I will cut your head off your body.'

Mrs McLeod decided to go home and dress, promising her friend that she would return in a few minutes, hopefully with a policeman. As she stepped outside into the street, the front door was slammed shut behind her. Seconds later she heard the distinct sounds of a violent struggle from inside, which were followed by a piercing scream. Her daughter was by now out of bed and had joined her mother in the street. They tried to

'blood pouring from a head injury and a gaping wound to her throat'

force open the door to Jemima's house but could not do so. Suddenly, however, it burst open and Savage emerged, threatening to harm anyone who might try and prevent him from leaving the area.

The two women were now able to enter the premises and were confronted with a horrible scene. Jemima was lying on the floor, blood pouring from a head injury and a gaping wound to her throat. Her little boy was cowering under his bedclothes but was unhurt. A police search unearthed no weapon at the scene but an empty razor case was discovered, which it was believed had contained the instrument used to inflict her terrible injuries. Jemima died in the ambulance on the journey to Leith Hospital.

Savage's description was circulated, low lodging houses were visited, a watch kept at railway stations and searches made of lorries leaving the area. He was eventually seen on Great Junction Street, just half a mile from where the crime was committed, and charged with the murder. However, before he was interrogated, arrangements were made for him to be examined by Professor Harvey Littlejohn of Edinburgh University so that an assessment of his mental state could be made. This was to pre-empt any defence claim that he was insane. The professor reported that he was satisfied that the prisoner had no mental health problems.

Savage's trial was held on Monday 21 May at the High Court of Judiciary in Edinburgh, before the Lord Justice-Clerk. The case was prosecuted by The Hon. William Watson KC, with Mr Fenton KC and Mr J.M. Hunter for the prosecution, and Mr Wilson KC defending. The accused man entered a special defence, that at the time of the killing – which he admitted – he was insane and thus not responsible for his actions.

Nobody had witnessed the murder, no murder weapon was found and there was no forensic evidence linking him to the crime, but there was a great deal of circumstantial evidence and the Crown rejected his plea in the knowledge that it had the support of Professor Littlejohn's assessment. Furthermore, a motive for the crime was revealed: it was believed Savage wished to begin a relationship with a friend of his victim. When Jemima refused to tell him of the woman's whereabouts, he lost all self-control, hit her on the head and used his razor to slit her throat.

As the Crown had anticipated, the main focus of the evidence was on Savage's state of mind when Jemima met her death. Called by the Crown, Professor Littlejohn gave full details of his meetings with the prisoner. He interviewed Savage on three occasions in March and described him as a man addicted to methylated spirits, which prevented him from functioning properly. Nevertheless, he exhibited no signs of mental abnormality and was sane.

The defence called Dr McAllister, Deputy Physician-Superintendent of Craig House Asylum, who examined Savage on one occasion in early May. He believed that at the time Jemima met her death, the accused was not responsible for his actions and his personal history gave sufficient proof of his long-standing mental health difficulties. To add credence to this claim,

John MacDonald was called to the witness box. He had known the accused for twenty-five years and told the court that his friend was prone to acting strangely at times. As an example, he spoke of an occasion on which Savage greeted him in a seemingly cheerful and friendly manner, but as they shook hands, he started to hit him violently across the head with a poker he was holding in his other hand.

The judge warned the jury that a history of eccentric behaviour by the prisoner did not necessarily mean he was insane. He pointed out the difficulty in deciding on an individual's sanity and said he would leave it to the commonsense of the jury members to decide on the issue. This the jury did in only thirty-five minutes, finding him guilty of wilful murder, after which he was sentenced to death.

Two days after the trial's conclusion, a meeting of the Edinburgh's magistrates was held to select those who would represent them at the execution and Bailees Sleigh and McMichael were chosen for the task. There was no support for a reprieve and on Friday 8 June, John Lamb, the Under-Secretary of State for Scotland, wrote to the Lord Provost sating that he could find no grounds to advise His Majesty to intervene and the execution would therefore go ahead as planned at eight o'clock in the morning of Monday the 11th.

A crowd of 800 gathered outside the gates of Calton Gaol and waited in silence for the official notice to be pinned on them to confirm the execution had been carried out. This was done and despite the practice having been discontinued in most other prisons, a black flag was also hoisted. The hangman was John Ellis, who was assisted by William Willis, and it was reported later that Savage displayed great courage on the scaffold.

Before the execution, the condemned man asked for a private meeting with the governor to thank him and his staff for the consideration he had been shown in his final days.

THE MURDER OF A COATBRIDGE NEWSBOY

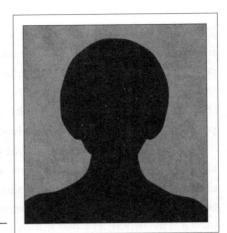

Suspect:	Susan Newell
Age:	28
Crime:	Murder

Thirteen-year-old John Johnston lived with his parents Robert and Margaret and older sister Mary on Buchanan Street, Coatbridge, and on the afternoon of Wednesday, 20 June 1923, at the close of the school day, he agreed to help a friend sell newspapers to earn a little extra pocket money. He had not returned home by 10.30 that night and his parents became concerned as it was not like him to stay out so late. His father went to look for him but after two or three hours there was no sign and, hoping he was spending the night with a friend, Robert returned home to catch a little sleep before he started work.

It was while he was at work, a few hours later, that Robert was visited by the police to be informed John had been murdered and the distraught father was taken to formally identify the body as that of his son. A suspect was already in custody; twenty-eight-year-old Susan Newell was arrested as she attempted to dispose of the body in a back courtyard on Duke Street, Glasgow several hours earlier. The corpse was wrapped in a blanket and had been put in a pram, which the suspect was pushing along the street, accompanied by her eight-year-old daughter, Janet. A lorry driver had pulled up to offer her a lift, which she accepted, but in retrospect this turned out to be a wrong decision on her part. She asked the driver to drop her off and as the pram was being lifted down to the pavement a woman noticed what seemed to be a human leg protruding from the bundle. The police were informed and Newell was detained by Constable McGennell only minutes after dumping the body.

When questioned, she claimed that on the previous evening, John knocked on the door of the rented rooms on Newlands Street, Coatbridge, in which she and her husband lived, to ask if she wished to buy a newspaper. At the time, she and her husband were arguing violently and he had struck her several blows. She ushered John into the room, hoping his presence would calm her husband down. However, John became frightened and when he cried out in fear, her husband grabbed him by the throat and began to throttle him. As he was doing so, Newell passed out and when she came round she found John's lifeless body.

'her husband grabbed him by the throat and began to throttle him'

Her husband was nowhere to be seen and, fearing she would be blamed, she wrapped the body in a blanket, put it in a pram and with young Janet at her side, she began to push it towards the centre of Glasgow, intending to abandon it there. This account was corroborated by Janet, who was questioned by policewoman Eleanor Blair. The little girl said her stepfather choked the boy and she saw blood flowing out of his nose. Her mother pleaded with him to stop, screaming that he would kill him if he did not do so. Eventually, the boy stopped struggling and fell silent, after which her stepfather left.

Nevertheless, the police were convinced that despite her claim of innocence, Susan Newell played an active role in the murder. She was charged and the search for John Newell began. There was no immediate success but on the following Sunday he walked into the Haddington police station of his own volition. He claimed to know nothing of the crime, saying the first he knew of being wanted for questioning was when he read a newspaper account of the boy's murder. He offered to provide an alibi to prove he could not have been involved, but he was arrested and charged with John's murder.

A post-mortem was carried out by Professor John Glaister and Dr John Anderson, Director of Pathology at the Victoria Infirmary. They found that death was due to throttling and dislocation of the spinal column at the neck. This could only have been caused by the use of great force, thereby making it difficult for the killer to claim it to have been unintentional. There were signs of a significant blow to the head, which might have been caused by a blunt instrument or if John had fallen against something solid as he fell to the floor. There were burn marks to the left side of the head and the blistering suggested he was still alive when they were inflicted. It was believed that a brief and futile attempt may have been made to destroy the body by burning.

Susan Newell was born into a family of travellers and as she grew up she began to drink heavily and was often violent. She had several convictions for public order offences and soliciting. For a number of years she lived with Janet's father but following his death she met and married John Newell. It was an unhappy union, marked by a great deal of violence, and Susan was more often the aggressor than the victim.

The trial of the accused couple opened in Glasgow on Tuesday 18 September before Lord Alness. John pleaded not guilty and Susan pleaded guilty, claiming, however, that she was insane at the time John was killed. The Crown's case was that they jointly murdered their victim after which they intended abandoning the corpse at some distance from their rooms. The Crown also said it would produce evidence that the couple desperately needed to find rent money or face being thrown out of their lodgings before they could find somewhere else to live. The motive was robbery, as the Newells believed John may have been carrying sufficient money from selling his newspapers to cover their immediate needs.

To convince the jury that the murder had taken place in the prisoners' home, the Crown called their landlady, Annie Young, into the witness box. She had ordered the prisoners to leave her premises because she was tired of their almost daily arguments. However, she agreed to Susan Newell's plea to let them stay until Monday 25 June, which would allow them time to find alternative accommodation, but this was on condition the couple paid the weekly rent of eight shillings by the weekend.

On the day of the murder, Mrs Young had visitors, her good friends Elizabeth Brown and Christine Morgan, who testified that they saw the paperboy enter the Newells' rooms. A little later they heard loud banging noises coming from the rooms followed by silence. Susan later called on her landlady to ask for the loan of a box, but she could not help as she did not possess one. The women next heard Susan leaving the house and minutes later, Annie McKillop, a barmaid at the nearby Duffy's Bar, served her with a gill of Spanish wine and a pint of beer which cost tenpence, after which she left. Other witnesses later saw her pushing the pram towards Glasgow and some testified they saw little Janet sitting on the bundle.

As the witnesses continued to give their evidence it soon became clear that none of them had seen or heard John Newell in the rented rooms at the time the murder was said to have taken place, or afterwards pushing the pram into Glasgow centre. His insistence that he had not been involved in the crime in any way was gaining credence. He was paid his wage of thirty shillings on the day of the murder, with which he bought a new hat and tie as he was attending his brother's funeral that afternoon, and this was confirmed by a number of family members.

A barman at the Olympia Theatre recalled serving him with drinks on the night of the murder and an assistant at a tobacconist shop testified he purchased a newspaper and a clay pipe on the same night. Further support was given by a member of staff at the Parkhead Model Lodging House, where the accused man stayed that night. After hearing this evidence, the judge agreed with his lawyers there was no case to answer and directed the jury to return a not guilty verdict. This was done and John Newell left the dock without a glance back at his wife.

Susan Newell's claim to have been insane at the time of the killing was rejected by the prosecution lawyers, who called Dr Greenhill, the police surgeon who examined her shortly after her arrest. He saw no signs of mental problems and reported that she answered all his questions rationally and in a lucid manner. Dr Garvey, the Medical Officer at Duke Street Prison, had kept her under observation since her detention began and he also considered her to be sane.

Probably the most damning testimony came from the prisoner's daughter Janet, who initially supported her mother's account of events. However, she gave a wholly different version from the witness box. On the night of the murder, she was playing outside in the street and saw the paperboy enter their rooms. Later, her mother came out and said she was going to visit Duffy's Bar. Janet did not see the boy leave and when her mother returned they both went indoors, where Janet saw his body lying face down on the couch, his head covered with her stepfather's underpants. She watched as her mother attempted to loosen the floorboards, telling Janet she intended hiding the body underneath them. However, this plan was abandoned and she later walked with her mother to Glasgow with the body concealed in the pram. Janet admitted accusing her stepfather of the crime, 'Because mammy told me'.

At the conclusion of the evidence, Newell's lawyer asked the members of the jury to ask themselves whether this bizarre killing and her subsequent behaviour were the actions of a sane woman. The robbery motive was called into question, as John would only have had a few coppers in his pockets, and in all the circumstances the jury could rightly conclude that she was not in her right mind when John met his death.

The Crown pointed out that there was no history of insanity in her family and she was not insane when she killed the youngster. It was acknowledged that John would have had only a little cash on him but the accused was not to know that. She only needed a few shillings to delay having to leave her lodgings and find a deposit for somewhere else to live. It was likely that after murdering him, she had discovered he had only a few pennies in his pockets. Realising this, she decided to visit Duffy's Bar to treat herself to a glass of wine and a beer, as by then she knew the proceeds of the murder would provide her with nothing more. It was not necessary for the jury to agree or not with this theory as the Crown was under no obligation to provide a motive and they had more than enough evidence to convict her.

After retiring for thirty-five minutes, the jury returned with a majority verdict of guilty to wilful murder but with a strong recommendation for mercy. Before sentencing her to death, the judge said this would be passed on to the appropriate authorities. A petition seeking a reprieve, which rejected the robbery motive and suggested Newell had killed the youngster in an irrational violent rage, was well supported. However, this failed and on the afternoon of 9 October, Sir Thomas Paxton, the Lord Provost of Glasgow and the Town Clerk, Sir John Lindsay, visited her in the condemned cell to advise her of the decision. On being told she would hang the next day, she screamed for her daughter before collapsing.

A small group of people gathered outside Duke Street Prison and Susan Newell became the first woman to be executed in Scotland for seventy years. For the first time, the black flag was not raised to indicate an execution had taken place. On the gallows she had refused to allow the hangman, John Ellis, to place a hood over her head and she died without a struggle. Susan Newell was the last woman to be executed in Scotland and Ellis later said she was the bravest woman he had ever met.

CASE FORTY-ONE   1925

A RACIST MURDER

Suspect:	John Keen
Age:	22
Crime:	Murder

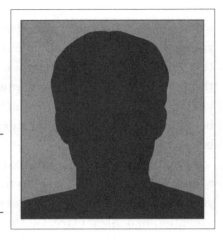

Shortly before eight o'clock on the morning of Thursday, 24 September 1925, the party of officials who were to attend the execution of twenty-two-year-old John Keen assembled in Duke Street Prison. They were the prison's governor Robert Walkinshaw, the institution's medical officer Dr Gilbert Garry, Chief Constable A.D. Smith and the Deputy Town Clerk, Thomas Picken. The group also included two magistrates, Dr James Dunlop and Mary Bell, who was due to become the first woman official to attend such an occasion in the modern era.

Her presence in the execution chamber generated a high level of public interest and when she left the prison afterwards, Mrs Bell was surrounded by journalists, eager to learn how she had coped with the morning's events. She described entering the condemned cell and coming face-to-face with the murderer. They spoke briefly and just as he was to be

'face-to-face with the murderer'

pinioned, he asked her if she would be willing to shake his hand. She told him she would be pleased to do so and she felt he gained some comfort from this simple humane act.

A few minutes later, she was standing close to the drop as the lever was pulled by the executioner, Thomas Pierrepoint. As he did so, another witness to the execution whispered to her that she should close her eyes, but she did not do so. She went on to explain that she was performing her elected public duty in acting as a witness on behalf of the citizens of Glasgow, adding, 'Many people urged me not to attend the execution, but I wanted to prove that a woman is fit to take her place on public bodies. When I took the oath as a magistrate I undertook to carry out the duties of a magistrate without having the option of picking and choosing. We women in the civic body of a city like Glasgow are pioneers of the women's movement and we have to show that we are fit to take the unpleasant with the pleasant.' As for the executed man, she commented, 'Keen was a very brave young man and one felt it a great sorrow that he should be in such a position. But I reflected that his doom had been brought upon himself and that the penalty he was called upon to pay was dictated by our social laws.' These words no doubt reflected the feelings of many Glaswegians, who believed that John Keen's crime had brought shame on their great city.

A number of Indian immigrants settled in the Port Dundas district in the years following the Great War and many became street traders, who specialised in selling items of clothing. Among them was Nathoo Mohammed, who had arrived in 1921 and was living with his wife Louie in Clyde Street. On the evening of Friday, 15 May 1925, Nathoo was visited at his home by two young Scotsmen, John Keen and Robert Fletcher, who said they wished to buy a scarf. Nathoo showed them a selection of his wares, one of which the visitors picked. It was not unknown for customers to call at his house at night, and such visits were usually tolerated to avoid trouble. However, Nathoo was surprised and worried when they offered either a gun or a knife in payment. In retrospect, it would appear the weapons were produced not as an offer of payment but simply to intimidate Nathoo. Anyway, he refused their offer and Fletcher handed him some cash, after which he and Keen left.

At 10.30 p.m. the following night there was another knock on Nathoo's door, which he answered to find Keen and two other men, William Dayer and John McCormick, who said they wished to buy some clothes. They would not leave when Nathoo suggested they return the next day. Instead, they pushed their way into his home, sat down and lit cigarettes, before demanding to see a selection of jumpers. They produced a knife and pistol and, pulling his thumb across his throat as he glared at Nathoo, Keen threatened, 'Give me a jumper or I'll kill you.'

Fearing for their safety, Nathoo and his wife ran to the house of a neighbour, Sundi Din, on Water Street. There were five men there and as Nathoo was explaining what had occurred a few minutes earlier at his house, there was a loud banging on the door. Noorh Mohammed opened it to find Keen and Robert Fletcher standing there. Furthermore, a 200-strong mob had assembled in the street, which seemed intent on attacking the area's Indian residents. Noorh was grabbed by Keen and dragged outside. Unable to offer any meaningful resistance, he was thrown down several steps into the street. As he lay helpless on the pavement, he was repeatedly kicked by a number of men. Eventually, his friends were able to carry him back inside the house and were shocked to discover that he had been stabbed. He was put on his bed but before his injuries could be treated, the front door was smashed open. Several members of the mob rushed in and Nathoo heard Keen scream that he wanted to kill all of the Indians who were there.

Louie witnessed Noorh being dragged out into the street again and saw Keen, knife in hand, urging the mob on and shouting, 'Rush them boys! Get ready for action!'

Brother and sister, John and Jeanie Stirling lived near to where the disturbance was taking place and recognised the voice of Keen, who they knew, encouraging the mob to commit further violence against the Indians. On going out into the street, John and Jeanie watched as one of the mob took a knife from Keen's pocket and hand it to him. Keen had then stabbed Noorh once in the chest. It was John who ran to the police station to report what was happening. Constable Mulvey was the first officer to reach the scene, by which time the mob had dispersed. He entered Sundi's house through the front door, which had been torn from its hinges, and attempted to reassure him and his friends, all of whom were cowering in terror behind the furniture. Noorh was lying in a large pool of blood on the floor and although still breathing, he died a short time later. A post-mortem revealed that death was due to internal bleeding resulting from a three-inch deep knife wound to the chest. Following their enquiries in the surrounding streets, the police were satisfied that none of the Indians provoked the violence and had not wanted a confrontation with their white neighbours; it was now recognised that the city had witnessed its first racist murder.

The next morning, Joseph McCall and James Purdon contacted the police and handed in the knife used to murder Noorh. They had done so with the agreement of two other men, Richard Stephen and Robert Purdon, brother of James, who also gave statements. This enabled the police to link the weapon directly to Keen, who was already emerging as their chief suspect, his name having been given by several witnesses. The previous night, Richard was on his way home from a local dance hall and saw the mob on Water Street. He saw his friend Keen, who was bleeding profusely from an injury to his thumb. Richard stopped the flow of blood by wrapping his handkerchief around it and, as he was doing so, he noticed Keen handing the knife to Robert Purdon.

Robert admitted he took the knife, explaining that he and Keen had been friends since childhood and he foolishly decided to help him, promising to dispose of it. However, unsure what to do with it, he passed it on to another friend, Joseph McCall, and the two discussed throwing it into the canal. However, Joseph decided to hide it in the chimney of a derelict building. By now, news of the murder had spread and Robert Purdon called on Joseph to ask what had become of the knife. Clearly, the men realised that they could find themselves accused of being accomplices to a murder and decided therefore to report what they knew.

A number of arrests were made but only four men were committed to stand trial, which opened on Monday 31 August. They were John Keen, Robert Fletcher, John McCormick and William Dayer, who were charged with threatening to kill Nathoo Mohammed. Keen, Fletcher and McCormick were also to be tried for the murder of Noorh Mohammed and with assaulting Sundi Din and Mohammed Bucksh. The men were also accused of stealing twenty-four jumpers, thirty-six scarves and two dresses. All four defendants denied the charges and part way through the proceedings the charges against Dayer were withdrawn by the Crown for lack of evidence and, on the direction of the judge, he was discharged and allowed to leave the dock.

It was acknowledged by all concerned that this had been a racist murder and the Crown portrayed Keen very much as the ringleader. He was said to have been responsible for taking his friends to Nathoo's house and organising the mob to gather on Water Street, with the intention of threatening and harming the Indian families. His co-defendants were described as willing accomplices and although Keen had inflicted the fatal stab wound, they were equally guilty of murder, describing it as a crime of common purpose.

The prosecution called a number of witnesses who identified the defendants as having been present on the night in question and others who had seen Keen stab the murdered man. The murder weapon was also linked directly to Keen. A great deal of significance was put on the fact that he had cut his thumb at the scene, as this was additional proof that he handled a knife. Keen had approached Dr Gilbert Garry in Duke Street Prison, where he was being held on remand, seeking treatment. He claimed to have sustained the injury a few days earlier after falling off his bicycle but the Crown argued that this was a desperate attempt by the accused to provide an alternative explanation for the cut, which was hugely incriminating.

The defence lawyers attempted to discredit the evidence given by the Crown's witnesses, including that of Nathoo. He was accused of being a drug dealer and a conviction for being in possession of opium three years earlier was raised. However, he explained that the drug had been sent to him by his brother in India – where it was used widely as a medicine – to relieve pain he was suffering at the time and he did not realise that it was illegal in the United Kingdom. It was also suggested that his wife had lied to the court from the witness box as she was terrified of Nathoo who had beaten and starved her in the past, accusations which she vehemently denied. The defence also claimed that those who were at the scene were not part of a violent racist mob intent on harming their Indian neighbours; instead, they had simply hoped to rescue Louie from a violent relationship. It was the Indians who initiated the violence and that none of the defendants had been directly involved.

When it later became known that Louie, a white woman, had assisted the police by identifying some of those who took part, she received a number of threats. However, she refused to be intimidated and insisted on appearing as a Crown witness at the subsequent trial.

After deliberating for thirty-five minutes, the jury members returned to their seats. Keen was convicted of murder, to which was added a recommendation for mercy, and Fletcher of culpable homicide. Keen and McCormick were found guilty of intimidation. It was decided that the theft charges were not proven. Keen was sentenced to death; Fletcher was sentenced to seven years' penal servitude, and McCormick to nine months' imprisonment.

A petition seeking a reprieve containing 90,000 signatures was submitted to the authorities but the Secretary of State for Scotland could find no reason to advise the King to intervene.

A CASE OF MATRICIDE

Suspect:	James McKay
Age:	40
Crime:	Murder

On the morning of Saturday, 15 October 1927, George Geddes and George Bisset noticed a parcel floating close to the King's Bridge in Glasgow and decided to investigate. Inside was the head of an elderly woman, two legs which had been severed below the knee, a thigh and a left arm from which the ring finger had been sliced off the hand. A preliminary examination of the body parts suggested the woman had been dead for three or four days but the body had not been in the water for that length of time. Also wrapped in the parcel were several other items, which included a woman's apron and underwear, a man's shirt and a newspaper, but there was nothing to indicate the woman's identity. It was hoped that publication of the little that was known would lead to members of the public coming forward with information.

The public response was immediate, for the police soon learnt that on the night before the parcel was discovered, a man was seen carrying one matching its description close to the spot at which it was retrieved. It was thought, therefore, that the parcel had not drifted very far after being put in the water and a search was made of the surrounding area. A man's footprints were found in the mud, casts of which were taken by Detective Sergeant Baron.

Among those reading the press reports of the mystery were friends Mrs Meiklejohn and Mrs McKay. When Mrs McKay said she believed the dead woman might be her mother-in-law, Agnes Arbuckle, her friend at first thought that she was joking, but soon realised she was deadly serious. Her husband, James McKay, had told her that his mother had moved from her home in the Gorbals to Blantyre, where she would be living permanently, and for the past two weeks James had been selling the contents of her home.

Mrs McKay reported her suspicions and was taken to the mortuary, where she identified the head as that of Agnes Arbuckle. Detective Lieutenant Stirton visited forty-year-old James McKay at his home in Thistle Street, where he was questioned about the disappearance of his mother. His answers were far from convincing and on being arrested on suspicion of having caused her death on a date between 27 September and 15 October, he was advised to say nothing until he had consulted a solicitor. Nevertheless, McKay said, 'She is dead. She died about two days ago. I put part of her in the Clyde, the rest is in the coal bunker.'

He was taken under escort to his mother's house, where he pointed to the bunker, saying that was where they would find the rest of her body parts and the saw he used to dismember the corpse. As he had indicated, hidden under the coal were the lower part of her body, her chest, the right arm and right thigh. The saw was also retrieved and on its blade were found traces of human tissue and blood.

Agnes had been married and divorced twice and James was the son of her first husband. He was one of her three sons, two of whom were killed in the Great War. James also fought in the war before being taken

'traces of human tissue and blood'

prisoner by the Germans, who put him to work in a salt mine. At the end of hostilities in Europe, he re-enlisted and served in India for two years before returning to his native Glasgow, where he found employment as a labourer. However, he had been unemployed for some time and his wife took a job as a cook in Rothesay while he remained at home to care for their children, an eight-year-old son and a fourteen-year-old daughter.

The police were satisfied that their suspect was guilty of a premeditated murder and amassed a great deal of evidence. Detective Baron compared the footprint impressions taken close to the spot at which the parcel containing the body parts was discovered to the shoes worn by the suspect when he was arrested; they were a perfect match. Other evidence gathered by the police pointed to financial gain being the motive for the crime. McKay was short of money, was heavily in debt, and he was soon to be evicted from his home because of rent arrears. He was drinking heavily and all of these difficulties were placing an intolerable strain on the marriage and he feared losing his family. He was apparently too embarrassed to approach his mother for help himself and arranged for his friend, Owen Watters, to do so on his behalf. Owen did as he was asked and Agnes gave him two guineas to pass to her son. She began to weep and told Owen she knew that James would spend the money on alcohol rather than use it to ease his money worries.

It also emerged that McKay had insured his mother's life for £100, naming himself as the sole beneficiary. Furthermore, furniture dealer Francis McKay had been approached by the arrested man who gave the name James Arbuckle and sold him the contents of his mother's home, claiming it was his to sell and he was doing so as he was moving into a smaller house. When McKay's home was searched, his mother's bank book was found together with several slips of paper on which he had clearly been practicing her signature. This, it was claimed by the police, was to enable him to withdraw cash from her account, which totalled £83. Also, a will was discovered which named him as the sole beneficiary. John Brown, a handwriting expert, was satisfied that the pen pressure and movements proved conclusively that all the suspicious samples had been forged by the accused.

McKay's trial took place on 12 December, at which it was alleged that he murdered his mother by slashing her face and neck with a razor, which led her to bleed to death. He was further charged with robbing her of a bank book and items of furniture, which included a sideboard, table, sewing machine and doormat, all of which he had sold. All of the evidence pointed to a carefully planned and premeditated crime. McKay entered a not guilty plea, claiming he was insane and not responsible for his actions.

The Crown ridiculed the suggestion that he was insane at the time the offences were committed and the defence called no witnesses to support that view. Indeed, his plea notwithstanding, the defence proposed another scenario to the jury. It was claimed Agnes had not been murdered, but instead a drunken McKay had visited her to find her already dead. In his drunken state he panicked, fearing he would be blamed, and in this confused state of mind he decided to dismember the body as he thought it would be easier to dispose of. It was argued that the facial and neck injuries had been caused when he cut the head away from the torso. As there was an element of doubt, the verdict should be not guilty or not proven.

The jury took twenty-five minutes to convict him of murder, after which he was sentenced to death by Lord Ormidale. An appeal failed and James McKay was executed by Robert Baxter in Duke Street Prison on Tuesday, 24 January 1928.

DUKE STREET'S LAST EXECUTION

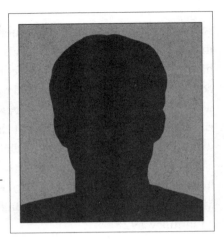

Suspect: George Reynolds
Age: 41
Crime: Murder

It was the end of the nightshift at Lang's Bread Company in Wesleyan Street, Glasgow on the morning of Thursday, 22 March 1928. Thomas Lee was responsible for tending to the boiler throughout the night and as his workmates entered the boiler room, they found him apparently asleep, lying on a bench with a coat covering his face. When the garment was pulled away, however, they could see that he had been beaten about the head. He was taken to the Royal Infirmary but did not regain consciousness and

'he had been beaten about the head'

died the following night. A post-mortem was performed by Professor John Glaister Jnr, which revealed several head injuries, which included two skull fractures, either one of which could have proved fatal. A branding iron found close to the corpse was identified as the murder weapon.

James Gray, the foreman baker, told police that when he reported for work the previous evening, the dead man, who was known to be a heavy drinker, was unsteady on his feet. The foreman, realising he was drunk, therefore asked the bakery's electrician, Joseph Martin, to keep an eye on him to ensure he was able to fulfil his responsibilities. Joseph looked in on him in the boiler room twice during the night and each time he did so, found him lying on the bench, asleep and snoring loudly. On both occasions, another man who was unknown to the electrician was also present, who told Joseph he had been drinking earlier with Thomas and was carrying out his friend's duties while he slept and sobered up. Satisfied the stranger knew what he was doing and not wishing to get Thomas into trouble or to disrupt production, Joseph allowed him to carry on.

The police did not know the stranger's name but had an excellent description of their main suspect and his identity was provided by the murdered man's wife. She had never met the man until the previous evening, when her husband brought him home after their afternoon drinking session. Thomas told her he was an old friend called George Reynolds, who would be accompanying him to work to help during his shift at the bakery. Reynolds was arrested not long afterwards when he was recognised by an alert police officer. He was charged with the murder of Thomas Lee and robbing him of a scarf, a pair of overalls and approximately six shillings in loose change. His trial began on Monday 25 June and lasted for three days before the trial judge, Lord Hunter. He entered a not guilty plea, claiming to have acted in self-defence.

Several bakery employees were called who saw Reynolds in the boiler room on the night in question but crucial evidence came from William Gordon, who lived with his wife on Tennant Street in Townhead. The accused was a friend and called at their house unexpectedly at 1.30 in the early hours of the morning of the 22nd in a distressed state. He paced up and down the room, unable to settle as he told William of the events of the previous few hours. He described visiting Lang's Bakery with Thomas, intending to help his pal, who was incapable of doing his job properly as he was so drunk. Reynolds pointed to the overalls and scarf he was wearing, which were later shown to have come from the bakery, and began to sob, saying, 'I have done a very despicable thing.'

According to their visitor, Thomas fell asleep and Reynolds decided to take the opportunity of breaking into an office which overlooked the boiler room to steal whatever he could find of any value and leave the building before Thomas woke up. However, his friend began to stir and, fearing he would raise the alarm, Reynolds hit him over the head with an iron bar that was lying nearby. Seeing he was unconscious, Reynolds went through his pockets and took the silver and copper coins he found together with the items of clothing. After finishing his account, Reynolds walked out of the Gordons' house at 5.30 a.m., leaving the overalls and scarf behind and promising to surrender to the police if Thomas died. William did not believe Reynolds story, as he presumed he was still under the influence of drink. However, he changed his mind after reading newspaper reports of the murder at Lang's Bakery and immediately made contact with the police.

At his trial, Reynolds opted to testify on his own behalf and began by giving some background information about himself and his relationship with the dead man. He was forty-one years old and a rigger by trade but he had often sailed as a ship's fireman. He first met Thomas Lee in Glasgow's Barnhill Poorhouse in 1926, since when they had remained friends. On 20 March Reynolds left Barnhill, having received a grant of seven shillings and sixpence from the Parish Council. The next day he met Thomas and the two of them spent the next three hours in a public house. They left at nine o'clock as Thomas was due to start work, but first walked to his home so that he could change into his work clothes.

He accompanied Thomas, who was very drunk and singing loudly, to the bakery and his friend told the boiler man going off duty that Reynolds was experienced in their line of work and would be covering for him until Thomas sobered up. Reynolds found a pair of overalls and was left to get on with it. As the night progressed, the engineer came into the boiler room and he agreed that Reynolds could continue to perform his drunken friend's work. He fell into conversation with the engineer, who, like himself, was an Englishman. When the engineer left the room, Thomas was said to have stood up and angrily accused Reynolds of attempting to take his job off him, shouting, 'I have fired this boiler for fourteen months and I will do so for another fourteen months. I heard you and the engineer. He is an Englishman and you are. Is that how you work it?'

Reynolds told the court that his friend refused to be reassured that he had no wish to take his job but Thomas picked up a shovel with which he threatened to strike him. He managed to take the shovel from his hand and to push him down onto the bench, hoping he would once again fall asleep. However, Thomas rose to his feet, grabbing an iron bar as he did so. He waved it menacingly so Reynolds hit Thomas twice on the head with the shovel. He explained his next actions to the jury, saying, 'I got the wind up, lifted my coat and still wearing the overalls walked out of the works.

I would never have struck him, only I was perfectly certain he meant to strike me. I would like you to understand we were the best of friends.'

He concluded his evidence by acknowledging he did visit William Gordon but denied telling him he had taken money from Thomas's pockets. He also insisted he did not say he considered stealing property from the bakery's office. When asked why he did not immediately report the alleged attack on him and the subsequent events, Reynolds replied he was worried that he would not be believed and acted in a panic.

The only other witness called by the defence was Professor Sydney Smith of Edinburgh University. In his opinion, 'The victim's skull would have been smashed to atoms' if he had been struck with the iron bar as the Crown claimed. The injuries were more probably caused by a shovel whilst the victim was standing up. This tended to give a great deal of credence to the claim by Reynolds that he acted in self-defence. It was therefore argued on his behalf that he should be found not guilty or, failing that, he should be convicted of culpable homicide. The jury chose not to accept this view and after an absence of twenty-five minutes decided unanimously that he was guilty of murder and robbery, which led to the death sentence being imposed moments later.

Two magistrates were required to attend an execution carried out in Glasgow and on this occasion the responsibility should have fallen on Bailies William Reid and Matthew Armstrong. However, Bailie Reid had attended the last execution in the city, that of James McKay the previous January (see chapter 42). The experience had left him a fierce and vocal opponent of capital punishment and he asked to be excused. His request was granted and Bailie Robert McClellan attended in his place on Friday, 3 August 1928 at what was to be the last execution carried out at Duke Street Prison. The hangman was Robert Baxter.

CASE FORTY-FOUR 1928

THE GANG FIGHT

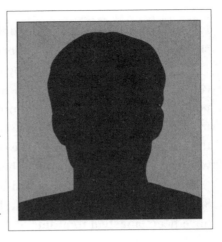

Suspect:	James McCluskey
Age:	16
Crime:	Murder

Glasgow was for some time noted for its often quite large, fiercely territorial and violent gangs. Clashes between rival gangs were frequent and the use of weapons led to serious injuries being commonplace and deaths were not unknown. In late April 1928, fifteen-year-old Abraham Zemmil, a member of the South Side Stickers, approached three girls he knew to be friendly with members of the rival Calton Entry gang. He asked them to pass on a challenge to a fight to Frank Kearney, the sixteen-year-old leader of the Calton Entry's junior faction. When told of the challenge, Kearney realised he was no match for Zemmil and would be beaten quite easily. Nevertheless, he could not refuse to meet Zemmil without losing face and agreed to do so, adding the proviso that each of them should be accompanied by three supporters on the night of Sunday 6 May near the city's Albert Bridge.

However, once word got out, there was little prospect of the fight being restricted to such a limited number. At the appointed time, therefore, many youths gathered at the spot and a massive and serious confrontation followed, in which seventeen-year-old James Tait suffered a stab wound to his back, which was later found to have pierced his lung. When it was learnt how serious the injury was, the fighting stopped and the gang members dispersed. Tait was taken to the Royal Infirmary, where he died two days later in the early hours of Tuesday morning.

Tait was a member of the Calton Entry gang, who lived with his mother in Charlotte Street. In common with many of the city's gang members, he had experienced an unsettled childhood, having been sent away from home when he was six years old to attend an industrial school. He returned to the family home only a short time before his death and found comradeship among youths with similarly difficult backgrounds and shared values in the gang.

On the night of the confrontation, Tait left home at 7.30 p.m. and met a friend, James Cunningham, who later acknowledged that he too was a member of the Calton Entry gang. Nevertheless, he was adamant they did not know a fight had been arranged with the South Side Stickers until they were close to the Albert Bridge. That the pair had come across the fight by accident and their claim that they did not participate was viewed with a great deal of scepticism by the police officers investigating the crime. However, whatever the truth of the matter, the deceased suffered a fatal wound to the back and wilful murder was believed to be the appropriate charge to be faced by whoever was responsible.

Within a short time of his arrival in hospital it was realised by the medical staff that James Tait would not survive his injuries. A deathbed statement was therefore taken from him at two o'clock in the early hours of Monday morning at which Sheriff MacDiarmid attended as a witness. The dying youth stated that he had been stabbed by a member of the Stickers he knew only as 'Tuskey'. He claimed it was an unprovoked attack as he was walking away from the fight and he had not threatened his assailant in any way beforehand.

It was established that 'Tuskey' was in fact sixteen-year-old James McCluskey, who, following his arrest, was brought to Tait's bedside, who identified him as the person who had stabbed him. Witnesses came forward who gave the names of several other members of the Stickers who were close to the scene of the stabbing. This led to the following being brought to trial together with McCluskey: Abraham Zemmil, James Walker, Alexander McCaughey, Archibald Gaughan and George Stokes, all of whom were sixteen years old.

The Crown viewed the murder as a crime of common purpose, which was reflected in the charge put to all of the defendants when their trial opened on Thursday 28 June, before Lord Hunter. The indictment read that:

They acted in concert on 6 May at or near the Albert Bridge, being members of a gang known as the South Side Stickers, formed part of a riotous mob of evil-disposed persons, did conduct themselves in a violent, riotous and tumultuous manner to the great terror and alarm of the lieges and did attack and fight with members of another gang known as the Calton Entry and threw stones, bottles and other missiles and brandished swords, knives and other lethal instruments to the danger of the lieges. And did assault James Tait, stab him in the back with a knife or other sharp instrument whereby he was severely injured that he died on 8th May and did thus murder him.

Not guilty pleas were entered by all of the accused except for McCluskey, who entered a special plea of self-defence, claiming that at the time he was being attacked by rival gang members, including the deceased, and he was forced to act as he did.

The Crown attempted to demonstrate to the jury that on the night he met his death, the victim was an innocent bystander who arrived at the scene with his friend James Cunningham by chance and they took no part in the fighting. However, Lord Hunter intervened when Cunningham was in the witness box as it was obvious he was finding this proposition difficult to accept. After a number of searching questions posed by the judge, the witness acknowledged that in the short time he was a member of the Calton Entry he took part in three gang fights. When the judge told him he found it difficult to understand how the two gang members could not have known beforehand of the arrangements made for the confrontation, James fell silent, unable to answer the question.

Joseph Adams, a fifteen-year-old messenger boy, was not a member of any of the city's gangs but was a witness to the fight and claimed to have seen McCluskey, who was standing with McCaughey and Zemmil, holding a knife. He did not see the actual stabbing but saw James Tait fall to the ground.

Members of both gangs had agreed to give evidence on behalf of the Crown in return for not being charged with any offences. Nineteen-year-old coal carrier Hugh Martin, a member of the Calton Entry, swore he heard McCluskey shout triumphantly, 'Thank God, I've got my revenge,' as his victim stumbled to the ground. This was supported by seventeen-year-old

James Burns, also of the Calton Entry, who testified he saw McCluskey actually stab Tait, even though he was posing no threat to him at the time. Seventeen-year-old Andrew McCartney of the South Side Stickers told of handing out several weapons to fellow gang members before the fight started, which included giving a knife to McCluskey. Later, McCluskey returned the bloodstained weapon to the witness, boasting, 'I've put that in one of them.' The murder weapon was disposed of and proved impossible to retrieve.

However, the turning point of the trial came when Frank Kearney of the Calton Entry stepped into the witness box. He acknowledged that he had asked James Tait to help at the fight and before it started he handed him a razor to use against the Stickers. After the stabbing, Kearney picked up the razor and threw it into the Clyde. This new information demonstrated that Tait was not the innocent bystander the Crown was attempting to portray him as. It was decided therefore, although only part way through the trial, to accept McCluskey's plea of culpable homicide. The prosecution lawyers also agreed to reduce the charges against the other defendants, which their representatives accepted, and those faced by Walker were dropped altogether.

The defence lawyers pleaded for leniency and in mitigation suggested their crimes stemmed from misdirected energy and not realising the grave consequences that using weapons could lead to. The defendants had all been set poor examples by their families and neighbourhoods. Their squalid living conditions were described and these were all said to be factors which had contributed to the youths finding refuge and kudos in the gangs. It was also added that they had been badly influenced by frequenting the picture houses in the city's East End.

McCluskey received a sentence of five years' penal servitude and the rest were convicted of mobbing and rioting. McCaughey was sentenced to eighteen months' imprisonment and Gaughan and Stokes, who the Crown accepted played less significant roles, received twelve months. Zemmil was dealt with under the provisions of the Children's Act and was ordered to be detained for twelve months.

CASE FORTY-FIVE 1944

A NAZI ATROCITY

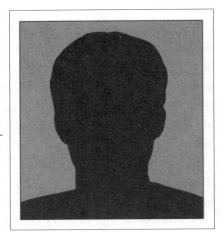

Suspects: Kurt Zuhlsdorff,
Rolf Herzig,
Josef Mertens,
Joachim Goltz,
Herbart Wunderlich,
Heinz Bruling,
Erich Pallmer Konig,
Hans Klein

Ages: 20s

Crime: Murder

During the Second World War and in its immediate aftermath, 6-8 Kensington Palace Gardens, London W8 was under the control of the military intelligence services. Behind its walls, many German prisoners of war faced interrogation and for ten days, beginning on 2 July 1945, it was also the scene of a murder trial, despite the alleged crime having been committed in Scotland. The eight accused were German prisoners of war, all non-commissioned officers aged in their twenties. They were said to have murdered their compatriot and fellow prisoner, thirty-five-year-old Wolfgang Rosterg at POW Camp 21 in Comrie, Perthshire on 23 December 1944. The men standing in the dock were Kurt Zuhlsdorff, Rolf Herzig, Josef Mertens, Joachim Goltz, Herbart Wunderlich, Heinz Bruling, Erich Pallmer Konig, and Hans Klein.

It was initially treated as a civil matter which was to be dealt with in Scotland. However, the Scottish legal authorities felt they did not have the necessary expertise to deal with the case, hence the decision to hold a Military Tribunal in London. The President of the Court was Colonel R.H.A. Kellie and there were five other senior military officers sitting in judgement.

The prosecution was led by Major R.A.L. Hillard of the Judge Advocate General Office. Major R. Evans, a solicitor in civilian life, represented Herzig, Mertens, Goltz and Bruling and Captain R. Willis, a barrister, acted on behalf of Zuhlsdorff, Wunderlich, Konig and Klein. Two British officers also acted as interpreters throughout the proceedings. All of the accused pleaded not guilty and called no witnesses to speak for them.

Many of the witnesses called to testify for the prosecution were German prisoners of war and their identities were not revealed in the court or given in the trial transcript. Each was allocated a number and anonymity was guaranteed in perpetuity as they feared reprisals against themselves and their families, not only in the immediate future but in the years ahead. Before any evidence was heard, however, the prosecution provided important background information in its initial address to members of the tribunal.

Following the allied landings on mainland Europe in June 1944, Rosterg was one of a large number of enemy prisoners captured in Normandy. All were taken initially to Kempton Park, where they faced a preliminary interrogation and an attempt was made to assess where their political sympathies lay. Once this process had been completed they were placed into one of three categories, which would determine to which camp they were allocated. 'Blacks' were those believed to be fanatical Nazis, 'Greys' were thought to have some sympathy with the regime, and' Whites' were considered to be strongly opposed to the principles of National Socialism.

Rosterg was placed in the White category and transferred to Camp 23 at Devizes in Wiltshire, where more than 7,000 prisoners were being held. He spoke excellent English and was asked to act as an interpreter by the camp authorities, which he agreed to do. He made no secret of his strong anti-Nazi feelings, which did not escape the notice of the prisoners who remained loyal to Hitler and who remained confident of a German victory.

In late 1944, British Intelligence became concerned that the German prisoners at Devizes were planning a mass escape and that contact had been established with other camps at which similar escape plans were being hatched. It was believed that following these break outs, the escapees intended to arm themselves by raiding British and American military bases before marching on London. It was feared that German paratroopers might be dropped into the countryside to link up with the escaped prisoners and a new front would be opened on the British mainland, spreading panic among the civilian population. The plan was doomed to failure but men, women and other valuable resources would have to be diverted to deal with it, which were still required in Europe to secure victory. It was decided therefore to transfer those considered to be ring-leaders from the camp at Devizes to Camp 21 at Comrie, in which many prisoners categorised as 'Black' were already being detained.

Included among the thirty or so prisoners taken north was Rosterg, who knew immediately that he had been placed in a dangerous situation. On arrival at the new camp, Rosterg contacted the British officers and explained the position. He was assured there had been an administrative error and he would very soon be returned to Devizes. However, it is believed by some that the British had transferred him deliberately as they hoped they would be able to use him as an informant. Whatever the truth of the matter, those sent to Scotland with him believed he had betrayed them and was responsible for the plan to open a new front being discovered by the enemy.

The contingent from Devizes arrived at Comrie on 22 December and later that same evening a group of the most fiercely loyal Nazis met to discuss what should be done with the supposedly treacherous Rosterg, as they believed he would continue to spy on behalf of their British captors. Without any proof and despite his record of valiant service in Russia and France, he was denounced as a deserter and was said to have collaborated with partisans in the east and with the French Resistance, providing intelligence on secret arms dumps and food stores. He was also accused of passing information on bombing targets to enemies of the Reich.

Early the next morning Rosterg paid the price for these allegations. He was subjected to a mock trial, and was beaten in a most savage manner before facing summary execution. It was accepted that as many as eighty men took part, many of whom also bore some responsibility for what happened. However, the eight prisoners were said to have played leading roles and as the hearing progressed, the evidence given by those who had witnessed some or all of the events and who were given numbers from one to six, combined to provide a vivid and disturbing picture of what occurred.

At a few minutes after six o'clock in the morning, all of the prisoners who had arrived on the previous day from Devizes were woken up and ordered to report to Hut 4. There, Rosterg was already being subjected to a beating and was barely recognisable. His face was badly swollen and blood was pouring from his mouth, eyes, nose and ears. A noose had been put around his neck and the end of the rope was being held by Konig. Each allegation was put to Rosterg as he was being punched continuously

'blood was pouring from his mouth, eyes, nose and ears'

by Wunderlich. He was also struck with iron bars by Klein and Goltz. Konig was heard to scream at Rosterg that if he had any honour he would hang himself. At this point, one of the prisoners proposed going to the hut used by the Germans for administration purposes where a decision could be made about what to do with him. Perhaps the prisoner who suggested this was hoping that the break of a few minutes would allow tempers to cool and Rosterg's life to be spared. If so, it proved to be a forlorn hope for it was there that it was subsequently agreed that he should be hanged.

As the group left the administration office, Goltz and Konig seized the end of the rope, forcing Rosterg to the floor. Goltz knelt down and, putting his hands around Rosterg's neck, began to throttle him. As this was happening Rosterg was being kicked repeatedly by several men and in particular by Bruling, Herzig and Zuhlsdorff, who were also helping to drag him towards the lavatory, where Goltz and Zuhlsdorff threw one end of the rope over a pipe. Mertens, assisted by Herzig, grabbed it and pulled, lifting Rosterg's feet off the floor.

It was by now roll-call and the prisoners assembled on the parade ground, at which Rosterg's absence was noticed by the British. At first it was thought he might have escaped but eventually his body was discovered hanging in the lavatory. A post-mortem was performed by members of the Royal Army Medical Corps. There were extensive facial and head injuries consistent with the dead man having suffered a terrible beating and the injuries to the rest of his body confirmed that he had been dragged along the ground. Death was said to have been due to strangulation, which probably occurred as he was being dragged and the rope tightened around his neck, which meant he was already dead by the time he reached the lavatory. Despite the eyewitness accounts given at the tribunal, Wunderlich and Klein were found not guilty part way through and allocated to other prison camps. Five of the remaining six accused made statements from the witness box, only Herzig declined to do so.

Zuhlsdorff made a voluntary written statement when first questioned about the hanging in which he stated:

I went along to the latrine and saw somebody pulling him into it. I helped in the hanging in so far that I held him under the arms and lifted him up. As I lifted him up I could not see Rosterg's face but I heard a groaning from him from which I must assume that Rosterg at this time was still alive. But it is also possible that the groaning might have been called forth by the exertions of a comrade.

In the witness box, when questioned by the prosecutor, Zuhlsdorff agreed that even if Rosterg had still been alive in the lavatory, he would have assisted in hanging him. As far as the accused was concerned, Rosterg was a traitor who deserved to die.

Konig claimed that initially he attempted to protect Rosterg from the other prisoners but was persuaded that he was a traitor who should be executed for his crimes against the Fatherland. He believed he and his comrades were entitled to take the action they did and he felt no shame or remorse.

Goltz opened his testimony by informing the tribunal members of his war service in Russia and France, insisting that he was a good soldier and his involvement in the hanging of Rosterg was a justifiable military response to the dead man's treacherous behaviour. He first saw Rosterg when the rope was already around his neck and he was crying out for help and begging for mercy. Nevertheless, he admitted he then took a leading role by pulling Rosterg to the floor, kneeling on his chest and tightening the noose. He offered to demonstrate what he had done in the courtroom and Mertens jumped to his feet saying he would be happy to play the part of Rosterg, but the offer was declined. Goltz said he knew Rosterg was dead by the time they reached the lavatory and when asked why he had helped hang a dead body, he replied, 'A traitor must be hanged.'

Despite a willingness to participate in a re-enactment of the incident, Mertens denied taking any part in the death of Rosterg, claiming he was already dead by the time he was dragged into the lavatory. Similarly, Bruling insisted he took no part and told the tribunal that he had been coerced by a British captain and sergeant into signing a written statement admitting culpability as they had threatened to kill him if he refused to do so.

At the conclusion of the prosecution's summary of the evidence it was the turn of Captain Willis and Major Evans to address the tribunal on behalf of their clients and they both made similar arguments. It was claimed that as far as the accused were concerned, Rosterg was a traitor and if he had not been killed they were convinced he would have continued to feed information to the British. His killing was not vengeful murder by Nazi thugs but a military execution that was fully justified.

Captain Willis said he had been told by one of his clients of an escape bid made by British prisoners of war being held in a camp near Breslau, which was prevented by their German captors only because the prisoners were betrayed by one of their own officers. This became known to the British prisoners who tried the traitor, who was subsequently hanged. The German authorities took no action against those responsible, believing it was a matter for the British themselves to deal with. The current case was no different and the accused should be acquitted.

The defence arguments did not find favour with the tribunal members, who convicted all of the accused and Herzig was sentenced to penal servitude for life. However, Zuhlsdorff and Goltz, both of whom were twenty years old, together with Mertens and Konig, who were twenty-one years of age, were hanged alongside twenty-two-year-old Bruling at London's Pentonville Prison by Albert Pierrepoint on Saturday, 6 October 1945. By this time, these young men were aware that their dreams of a great victory for National Socialism were, like their homeland, in ruins.

THE BOLFRACKS TRAGEDY

Suspect:	Stanislaw Myszka
Age:	23
Crime:	Murder

Peter McIntyre was a shepherd at Bolfracks, Kenmore in Perthshire, where he lived in Tower Cottage with his wife Catherine and their children. Their twenty-three-year-old son Archibald, a constable with the Edinburgh City Police, was staying with them and he left the cottage at eight o'clock on the morning of Friday, 26 September 1947, leaving his mother alone inside the cottage. He returned home at 5.15 p.m. to find the family's cairn terrier barking outside the front door. The morning newspapers were on the doorstep and a delivery of coal had not been put away. The front and back doors were locked and as he had no key, Archibald, who presumed his mother must be visiting a friend, selected one of the newspapers to read and sat down on the doorstep to await her return.

Some time had passed before a family friend walked by and Archibald shouted to him to ask if he had seen his mother. The man had not seen her in the garden or elsewhere in the vicinity at any time during the day and Archibald became rather worried. He feared she may have suffered some kind of accident and was lying injured inside the cottage, unable to call out for help. He gained entry by breaking a kitchen window and became immediately more worried when he saw the breakfast dishes still on the table unwashed and noticed several unopened letters on the table. He rushed upstairs but found nothing unusual in two of the bedrooms, the doors of which were open. However, the door to the third bedroom was locked and the key was nowhere to be seen. As there was no response when he knocked and shouted to his mother, he found an axe and smashed the door down.

Archibald was totally unprepared for the scene that greeted him in the bedroom. His mother's body was lying on the bed, a scarf and two aprons tied around her neck. Her hands had been tied at the wrists and

'there were horrific injuries to her head and face'

there were horrific injuries to her head and face. A post-mortem was performed the following day, which revealed she had been struck repeatedly with a rifle butt, but no such weapon was found at the scene. There were no signs of a sexual assault and the motive was clearly robbery, as clothing, which included one of Archibald's suits, was missing, along with £85 in cash.

A major breakthrough in the case came two days later, when a bundle of old clothes was discovered hidden in the bracken between 400 and 500 yards from the cottage. The police were convinced they had been discarded by the murderer, who then changed into the stolen clothing. When examined, the shabby clothes indicated that the wearer had been about five feet six inches tall. Also of great significance to the investigation was a sawn-off double-barrelled shotgun, found wrapped in the old clothes and bearing the number 64417-2, which had been used to inflict the terrible injuries suffered by Catherine.

This find led the police to William Chubb who worked on Tulloch Farm in Oldmeldrum. He had borrowed the gun from a neighbouring farmer and later reported it stolen. At the time, it was presumed the thief was a Pole named Stanislaw Myszka, who worked on Tulloch Farm on a casual basis between 1945 and early September 1947, when he disappeared with the gun.

The Pole's description was published in the Kenmore area and three witnesses came forward who had seen Myszka on the day the murder was committed. General merchant John Moir identified him as the man who had bought a pound of plums and who enquired about the times of buses to Aberfeldy. William Horn, a German prisoner of war who was being held at the Balhary camp as he awaited repatriation, identified him as a man he had spoken to. Bus conductress Janet Pringle recalled him boarding her bus and travelling to Aberfeldy.

Agnes Szewe came forward after reading an account of the murder in the press. She and her husband were good friends of the wanted man, who had recently been staying with them at their Peterhead home. On 22 September he left the house, saying he was going on the tramp to look for work, returning in a dishevelled state at 10.30 p.m. on the night on the 26th. Before going to bed, Myszka took a blue suit from his bag, which he gave to her husband as he said it would not fit him. When examined, the suit was identified as that stolen from Tower Cottage.

Agnes was very surprised when he handed her husband a £5 note so he could treat himself to a few drinks. She also noticed he had a great many silver coins. The next day, the Szewes went shopping with Myszka, who spent £6 on a suit and shirt for himself and he also treated Agnes to a frock. However, when he left the house a few days earlier, on the 22nd, he was complaining that he had no money. On the following Monday morning, Agnes returned home after shopping and had bought a newspaper. Myszka asked her to read out to him an article about the Bolfracks murder. As she did so, she noticed he became restless and paced up and down the room with a worried expression on his face. When she finished reading the piece, she asked who could harm a defenceless woman. Myszka replied, 'I did what was done at the farm, but I did not kill the woman.' He left the house within a few minutes and did not return.

A manhunt was launched across Scotland for the twenty-three-year-old suspect. On the morning of 2 October, Constables Ronald Duncan and Ian McLaren were searching a disused RAF camp near Peterhead when they saw a man running across a nearby field. They shouted to him to stop but he did not do so and the police officers gave chase. After about three quarters of a mile, the man attempted to hide behind a bush but the officers saw him and he was detained. He was asked if he spoke English and he nodded his head. When asked for his name he replied, 'Myszka'.

Later, before being charged with Catherine's murder, he was asked to explain how he came to be in possession of the several pound notes and ten shillings and ninepence in coins found in his pockets, but could not provide a satisfactory answer. The police believed this money was what remained of the cash stolen when Catherine was murdered.

Myszka's trial opened at the High Court in Perth on Tuesday, 6 January 1948, before Lord Sorn. This would prove to be another case where the outcome would be determined by the jury's views on the prisoner's mental state, for he acknowledged responsibility for the killing but claimed he was insane at the time. The Crown rejected this plea and produced two expert witnesses, Dr Jan Laiberg, a senior assistant medical officer at the Argyle and Bute District Mental Hospital, and Dr Charles Bruce, Medical Superintendent at the Perth Criminal Lunatic Asylum. Both had examined the prisoner and found no signs of mental disorder, although he was described as being of low intelligence. They agreed that Myszka was able to tell right from wrong and was responsible for his actions when he killed his victim.

The defence called Dr Angus McNiven, Superintendent at the Glasgow Royal Mental Hospital, who was forced to concede that, 'I could not contradict the assumption that the accused was sane on 26 September,' but added that Myszka was a man who might lose control temporarily, especially if he was under stress.

When Mr H.R. Leslie addressed the jury on behalf of the Crown, he urged its members to discount the possibility of the prisoner being temporarily insane at the time of the crime. This was the stance adopted by the three experts who had appeared and one of those had been a defence witness. The killer needed money, which was the motive for the crime; the Crown had been able to link him to the shotgun used to beat Catherine to death; he was in possession of Archibald McIntyre's suit and other items which had been stolen from the cottage; he was seen to have a large amount of money in the days following the crime, and he confessed to having beaten the victim to a friend. These factors did not simply implicate him in the killing of Catherine McIntyre, they also demonstrated he was thinking rationally at the time and was in full control of his emotions and actions.

In his defence, Mr F.C. Wall KC reminded the jury that for three days before the crime his client was living rough, without money, food or shelter. On 26 September he was in a depressed state of mind and the crime was an act of desperation. It was possible, therefore, that even though not insane, Myszka might act in an uncharacteristic and irrational manner. Mr Wall urged the jury to take this into account in their deliberations.

In his summary of the evidence, Lord Sorn placed some emphasis on the issue of temporary insanity and diminished responsibility but said he would leave it to the jury to decide whether or not he was in a state bordering on insanity when the crime was committed. The jury retired for twenty minutes and found Myszka guilty of wilful murder, after which Lord Sorn sentenced him to death.

There was no reprieve and Stanislaw Myszka was hanged at Perth Prison on Friday, 6 February 1948 by Albert Pierrepoint. It was the first execution at the gaol since 1909 and it proved to be the last.

MURDERED BY A MOTORCAR

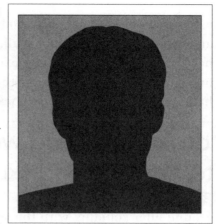

Suspect: James Ronald Robertson

Age: 33

Crime: Murder

It is rare that a serving police officer is charged with committing a pre-meditated murder. It was therefore inevitable that when James Ronald Robertson stepped into the dock of the High Court in Glasgow, before Lord Justice Keith on 6 November 1950, accused of such a crime, that the courtroom should be full of press and public, as it would be every day until the conclusion of the trial one week later.

The thirty-three-year-old constable, who was serving in Glasgow's Southern Division at the time of his alleged crime, was charged with the murder of forty-year-old Catherine McCluskey in the early morning of 28 July. He was accused of inflicting fatal injuries by driving a motorcar over her on Prospecthill Road, having previously knocked her unconscious by striking her with a rubber truncheon. He was also charged with stealing the car he used in the crime on 31 May from the premises of Maine Motors. He pleaded not guilty to all matters. The accused was a married man with two children who joined the police in 1945. His alleged victim, with whom he was said to have been involved in an intimate relationship which began in 1949, was a single mother of two sons aged three months and five years.

Catherine's body was discovered in the early hours of 28 July and the first police officers on the scene believed instinctively that this was not an accidental death. This proved to be correct when the results of the post-mortem became known. It was performed by Professor Andrew Allison of Glasgow University, who confirmed the deceased suffered extensive injuries to her upper body, including a number of broken ribs and wounds to her face and skull. However, there were no injuries to her legs, which he would have expected to find if she had been standing when hit by a motorcar. Furthermore, there were no marks on her hands, which should have been present if she had fallen heavily to the

'broken ribs and wounds to her face and skull'

ground after colliding with the vehicle that killed her. The professor concluded that the dead woman was not standing upright when hit by the car but was lying in the road. Injuries to her right temple led him to believe that she had been knocked unconscious before she was run over. The relatively high number of injuries she suffered and the distribution of the blood on the road led him to conclude that she was run over twice, the car having first reversed over her before moments later being driven forward and over the body a second time.

The body was identified by Catherine's neighbour and friend Grace Johnson, who told the police that to her knowledge the deceased had no enemies. However, Catherine had told Grace that she was having an affair with a married police officer and had named Robertson. Catherine added that Robertson was the father of her younger child and that he had agreed to pay eight shillings weekly maintenance towards his upkeep. Grace never met Robertson, but Catherine's sister Elizabeth and friend Rose O'Donal had done so and they picked him out at an identity parade.

Robertson was on duty at the time the murder is thought to have been committed but his colleague, Constable Moffatt, recalled that at eleven o'clock on the night of the 27th, Robertson left him for some time, saying he had a private matter to deal with. He therefore had no alibi and, when his truncheon was examined, traces of blood were found on it. When it was discovered that he was in possession of a stolen car, which showed signs of having been involved in a recent collision, Robertson became the prime suspect.

The car, on which it was claimed Robertson had put false number plates and drove for several weeks, was examined by Sergeant McCallum, an experienced investigator of vehicles involved in serious crimes. Damage was restricted to the exhaust system and other parts of the underside, on which he also found human bloodstains. However, there was no damage to the bumpers or upper bodywork. These findings led the sergeant to conclude that it had not hit a person who was standing upright but had been driven over someone lying on the ground.

As for motive, it was believed that Robertson wanted to rid himself of the financial commitment of maintaining Catherine's baby and prevent her from possibly informing his wife of their affair. When she registered the baby's birth, Catherine had not given the name of the father, but this was thought to have been Robertson. It was believed that on the night of the crime, he met her on some pretext or other, knocked her unconscious, and drove the car over her before leaving the scene.

In his cross-examination of Professor Allison, the prisoner's barrister suggested that he was wrong to suggest there were no injuries which could have been caused when Catherine was standing. He highlighted a number of abrasions to her left knee, which, given her height, could have been caused by coming into contact with the bumper but on which there would be no indentations. The professor, however, insisted that his conclusions were correct and the scenario proposed by the defence counsel could not have happened.

Robertson entered the witness box to defend himself. He denied any sexual relationship with Catherine and was adamant that he was not the father of her baby, nor had he agreed to pay maintenance to her. Therefore, he had no motive to murder her. They met several months before she died but the relationship remained platonic. He agreed to meet her on the night in question after she contacted him to say she was being forced out of her home and had to find new accommodation within the next few days. He promised to help her move to another part of the city and they met to discuss the arrangements. He acknowledged finding the car abandoned on waste ground some weeks earlier and that he put false number plates on it to use as a run-about.

Catherine sat in the passenger seat as they drove around trying to decide what she should do. However, when she realised there was little he could do to help her, she became angry and demanded that he stop. She got out and he drove away, intending to re-join Constable Moffatt on their beat. However, he began to feel guilty about leaving her alone so late at night and decided to return to the spot where he left her. He pulled over but there was no street lighting and he could see no sign of her. He put the car in reverse gear, unaware she was standing behind. He felt a bump and realised he had hit her but he could not help her as she was stuck under the vehicle. As an experienced police officer he knew she was dead and began to panic, because he had caused her death in a stolen car, albeit accidentally. He drove off and in so doing ran over the body a second time.

Robertson's version of events was supported by defence expert witnesses. Engineer Charles Wicks examined the car and found minor damage to the rear of the vehicle consistent with the prisoner colliding with Catherine when reversing, as he claimed. Dr Frederick Fiddes, a lecturer in forensic medicine at Edinburgh University, had studied the post-mortem report, had been provided with photographs of the body and had inspected the vehicle. He too insisted that there was nothing to contradict Robertson's claims.

Despite this strong support for his account, the jury of eight men and seven women took just sixty-five minutes to find him guilty of murder and, interestingly, there was no recommendation for mercy. His appeal against conviction failed and James Robertson was hanged by Albert Pierrepoint at Barlinnie Prison on 16 December 1950.